A MIRASI CHILD.

(MIRASI CHILDREN ARE TAUGHT TO DANCE AND SING FOR THE AMUSEMENT OF ZENANA LADIES.)

VILLAGE, TOWN AND JUNGLE LIFE IN INDIA

VILLAGE, TOWN AND JUNGLE LIFE IN INDIA

by

A. C. NEWCOMBE

WITH ILLUSTRATIONS

GYAN

Published by

Gyan Publishing House
5, Ansari Road
Daryaganj, New Delhi-110002
Phone: 011-47034999, 9811692060
E-mail: books@gyanbooks.com

Distribution Network
gyanbooks.com
India, USA, Canada, UK, Australia, France

ISBN : 978-81-212-6131-9 (PB)
First Published, 1905

2nd Impression 2022

Printed at: Gyan Press, Delhi.

Village, Town and Jungle Life in India
Author: A. C. Newcombe

VILLAGE, TOWN, AND JUNGLE LIFE IN INDIA

BY

A. C. NEWCOMBE

WITH ILLUSTRATIONS

PREFACE.

In an article in 'The Calcutta Review' of January 1893 on "Cold Weather Visitors in India," after commenting on the mistakes made by one of them, the writer remarks that such crude and undigested impressions of India are useless and mischievous, and that, as they pass muster at home for real facts, perhaps more might be done to place a true picture of the state of things before our countrymen. He suggests that a few who have passed much of their lives in India might record the facts "before Indian impressions have had time to fade away, and while they are still surrounded by all the local colour."

My long experience of life in that country between 1874 and 1902 in many parts—town and jungle, hills and plains—has enabled me to collect much detailed information.

I have arranged these notes in the hope that they may be interesting to those about to proceed to India, and to many who stay at home.

CONTENTS.

LIST OF ILLUSTRATIONS.

LIFE IN INDIA.

I.

FROM ENGLAND TO BOMBAY.

THE VOYAGE TO INDIA—BOMBAY—ARRIVAL AT AMRITSAR—PREPARING FOR CAMP LIFE.

My first voyage to India was in the troopship *Malabar*, which left Southampton on October 7, 1874. The party to which I belonged consisted of eleven of the first batch of fifty young Civil Engineers just appointed from Coopers Hill College to the Public Works Department of India. The pleasant company of the naval and military officers and the luxury of a military band twice a-day were what civilian travellers rarely get; and, as none of us had travelled before, sights such as the rock of Gibraltar, Malta, the Suez Canal, and Red Sea were most interesting.

On arrival at Malta, where the troops on board, the 101st Regiment, were to land and be replaced by the 18th Royal Irish, we who were only civilians (and therefore entered in the ship's lists as "doctors") asked permission to go ashore. It was then found that all that was known of us by the authorities on board was that we had berths allotted to us, and that they were in possession of no orders concerning us. We were not specially under the authority either of the captain of the vessel or of the officer in command of the troops; and we found ourselves free to go ashore some time before any one else could get permission.

We visited the church of the Knights of St John, a museum in which were some well-preserved mummies, which we found more interesting than anything else, some vineyards, and those parts of Valetta which, to us who had never seen a foreign town, were quaint and amusing. Had we been older and more in earnest, we should probably have gone into the town well read in its history and in search of relics of the past, for Malta has been in turn held for long periods by Phœnicians, Greeks, Carthaginians, Saracens, Crusaders, Moors, Spaniards, and Turks.

There was plenty of fruit to be had, the Maltese pears and grapes being much appreciated. Some grapes, which would have cost perhaps half-a-crown in England, cost only three-halfpence; and we were afterwards told that the dealer had charged a halfpenny too much.

A squall shortly before reaching Port Said made most of us unhappy; but another run ashore at that place was especially interesting, as it was our first introduction to a real Eastern town and Eastern people. We were warned not to go far, as the town in those days had a bad name, being insanitary and full of lawless characters. It is much better now, though by no means a desirable place to visit for more than an hour or so, and that should be in the daytime.

Were it not for the passing of other vessels at every few miles where the waterway is broadened for the purpose, the Suez Canal would be wearisome before reaching the end of it. Only one of a line of vessels can pass along at a time, those going in the opposite direction having to stand aside at the broadened parts. On those vessels we saw the homeward-bound passengers within easy talking distance. Bundles of newspapers were exchanged for others from India and Australia; but some, when not thrown properly, fell short and dropped into the Canal.

An occasional mirage, a flight of flamingo or red ibis, a few camels or Arab children on the banks, afford variety; and on passing out into the Red Sea one has a view of Mount Sinai, which is genuine, and the place where Moses crossed, which is not.

Unfortunately, during the passage through the Suez Canal, the captain of the *Malabar*, having exposed himself too much one night on the bridge, died of pneumonia. The funeral at Ismailia was attended not only by the English soldiers, sailors, and civilians, but by Egyptian troops.

Another impressive funeral was that of a baby buried in the desert at night. In those days vessels had to stop in the Canal at night, there being no electric light then, as now, to enable them to proceed in safety.

One other incident was a surprise to us who had never been abroad, and were not aware of the courtesies customary among civilised nations. We passed a Russian transport crowded with troops. All the Russian soldiers, at a signal from their officers, raised their hats in salute of the British flag. No doubt a suitable salute was given in reply by the British commander.

The journey through the Red Sea and Indian Ocean was quiet and uneventful. An occasional dance, practice in the use of buckets in case of fire, various games, a shoal of porpoises, a sight of some well-known wrecks now long ago broken up, and such minor matters, served to interest us; and, though it was all very pleasant, probably most of us were not sorry when we came in sight of Bombay harbour. Gladly as we landed, no doubt, there were few who realised how much more gladly they would leave it again *en route* for England at some future day, perhaps years ahead. I have often remembered the remark made at breakfast on the morning of our arrival, by a Scotch doctor who, when some one said with pleasure, "Bombay at last," replied sadly, "Hey, I wish it was Glasgow."

The city of Bombay and its picturesque harbour have often been described. It was our first possession in India, having been part of the dowry of Catherine of Braganza when she married Charles II. in 1661. It is the first large city of the Far East that travellers have the opportunity of examining in comfort and in detail when they visit India. They disembark in the midst of 800,000 people, different in race, character, and customs from any they have seen before, and in an Oriental city of much beauty in its architecture and surroundings. The well-built and well-kept though narrow and crowded bazaars, the handsome public buildings, the quaint customs, the variety of costumes, the vegetation,—all are in striking contrast to anything in Europe. The traveller is made so comfortable, and is so free to wander and inquire, the people are so friendly and polite, the scenes and incidents are so varied and amusing, that his impressions are vivid, and he is filled with wonder and gratification.

Though a typical Eastern city, there is strong contrast between Bombay and its people and the cities and peoples of the interior. There are not a few parts of India from which, if a native were to visit Bombay, he would be as much surprised at the contrast with his own locality and his own people as the European. The language, customs, clothing, even the food, might all be, at least to a large extent, strange to him. The English visitor at Bombay is therefore only at the beginning of a long series of interesting and novel scenes; and, for one who comes to pass the greater part of his active life in India, it is his introduction to important duties which it is a privilege to undertake. Probably some of the more thoughtful and sympathetic of new arrivals feel enthusiastic at the prospect of a useful career, and remember that they have the example of such men as Clive, Hastings, Dalhousie, and Lawrence, and that there is a population of nearly 300 millions in whose interests they are to devote the energies of the best part of their lives.

Many people in England, otherwise well informed, are much astray in their ideas of India. For instance, how often it is said that "the natives of India are Buddhists." Of the whole population of India only eleven millions are Buddhist. Some are under the impression that the natives of Bombay are all, or nearly all, Parsees; the fact being that in Bombay city there is only one Parsee in every fifteen of the population, and in the whole of the Bombay Presidency only four or five in every thousand are Parsees. Of the rest, ten in each thousand are Buddhists and ten are Christians, the great majority being Hindu and Mahomedans in the proportion of 750 Hindus and 175 Mahomedans per thousand.

In Bombay city the cotton-mills, railways, docks, Government and merchants' offices, and the municipality, supply occupation for all classes. Rich Parsees, Armenians, Jews, Hindus, and Mahomedans, as well as English, are employers of labour on a large scale. The foreign trade consists of exports, chiefly of grain, raw cotton, and oil seeds, and of imports of Manchester goods, mineral oil, machinery, and hardware; and the local movement of grain, native-made cotton, and silk goods is considerable.

An early morning walk before the sun is strong enables the sight-seer to visit the large Crawford

COOLIES IN THE CRAWFORD MARKET (BOMBAY).

market when the fishermen and fruit-sellers bring their fresh fruit and the fish caught during the night. The medley of costumes and characters of the men and women who come to buy or sell and to act as coolies or carriers, and the profusion of strange fruits, vegetables, and fish, together with the importunate way in which the sellers invite visitors to buy,—all make up a scene which can hardly be satisfactorily described. And over all there is a peculiar quiet business-like style, with no shouting or rough pushing as would be the case in England.

Of the fish, the pomfret and very large prawns are peculiar to Bombay. The Bombay "duck," used for seasoning, is really a fish of the herring kind. It is, however, in the fruits that Bombay and tracts of country near it excel. The plantains and bananas are of unusual excellence. The large red-skinned plantain has a rich full flavour, and the very small yellow bananas are the best in India. The mango of this part is preferred "up country" to any produced there. Custard apples, guavas, papaias, pummelos, pomegranates, pine-apples, melons, and several fruits grown in hilly country and well known in Europe, such as grapes, apples, and pears, are available—some always, and a few only in their season.

The majority of the people one meets in the streets are Mahrattas, a Hindu race spread over the western half of India. The Mahratta may be said to be an average good Hindu, as, though he does well as a cultivator or trader, lawyer or journalist, there is no very prominent trait in his character, such as we find developed in the Sikh, the Rajput, or the Bengali. Mahrattas respect the Brahmin and the cow, and worship, for the sake of propitiating, among other deities, a goddess named Kali, whose vengeance they fear. Temples in honour of their various deities are seen in the bazaars; but their architecture, though curious and attractive to the traveller from Europe, is much inferior to that of many of the famous shrines, mosques, and tombs to be seen "up country." The handsomest buildings in Bombay are those erected during the past thirty years in the business quarter. No visitor can pass without admiring the Law Courts, Post Office, Telegraph Office, Secretariats, Hospitals, the School of Art, and the terminus station of the Great India Peninsula Railway. These, with the good hotels and clubs, tramways, public gardens, well-kept walks, rides, and drives on the sea face, electric lighting, the extensive native and European quarters and the docks, make Bombay as fine a city, with the exception perhaps of Calcutta, as can be found anywhere in Asia.

In the afternoon it is better for the English visitor to drive rather than walk, as, even in the cold season when tourists travel, the heat of Bombay is unpleasant except in the early morning and evening. Even the horses wear hats to protect them from sunstroke.

One of the best drives is over Malabar Hill, where many Europeans and Parsees live to enjoy the cooler nights there, the purer air, and the fine views of town and sea. Cocoanut, date, and

Palmyra palms add to the beauty of the scenery. Here also are the Towers of Silence where the Parsees leave their dead. The bodies are not buried, but are exposed on the top of two high towers for vultures and other birds to eat.

An evening walk on the esplanade when one of the military bands is playing is refreshing in the cool sea breeze and full of interest. Crowds of natives of the better sort come on foot or in well-equipped carriages, and dressed in great variety of colours. The very rich colours of the dresses of the Parsee ladies are especially pleasing. Though reds and greens, blues and yellows, and other combinations usually avoided, are frequent, the blending is so arranged as to be agreeable and attractive.

Though the Parsees are only about one in fifteen of the population of Bombay city, they soon attract the attention of a visitor from Europe. The ladies of all classes of Parsee society move about freely in public, just as English ladies do. There is no *purdah* system among them, as exists among Hindus and Mahomedans, requiring the ladies of the zenana and the harem to remain out of sight. Their handsome Jewish features and the taste they show in dress cause them and the Parsee gentlemen with their peculiar black hats to be more noticed than others. They worship fire as a symbol of the Deity, and the men may be seen in numbers every morning and evening on the beach repeating prayers and bowing to the sun. Their reverence for fire is probably one reason why they do not smoke.

Having had a pleasant and instructive halt at Bombay, we had to proceed to our destination and join our posts within the allotted period. Four of us had been posted to the Punjaub, and we were to report our arrival at Amritsar. The journey by train was, at that time, one of three days and three nights; and though many places of interest were passed, we could not stay to see them. After travelling through the Western Ghauts to the high lands of the interior, we found the climate cold, especially in the early morning, —for it was November, the beginning of the cold season. Travelling on the railways of India is comfortable; and, though there was plenty to occupy our attention when we stopped at the stations, there was little in the scenery to attract notice. This contrast between the climate and appearance of the interior and those of the tracts adjoining the sea is the same in South Africa.

After getting orders at the Public Works Secretariat at Amritsar, my friends and I found ourselves posted in different directions, and we had to part. I was then left alone in Amritsar to work under an "Executive" engineer who had been many years in India, and was now nearing the end of his service. Fortunately, he and his wife were most friendly and hospitable, and many a pleasant evening I had with them at their bungalow in Amritsar and in camp. A start like that, with every assistance in the many little difficulties which arose in adapting myself to the new conditions of life, was most helpful. I was left at Amritsar for several days to collect servants, to buy a horse, and to engage camels and carts for conveyance of my camp-equipage on a journey in the interior along a line of canal which my "Executive" was about to inspect. This by way of introduction to my new duties and to render me familiar with the ways of travelling and managing the natives.

II.

IN THE PUNJAUB.

AMRITSAR—THE SIKHS—THE NATIVE SERVANTS—PECULIARITIES OF HOUSEHOLD ARRANGEMENTS—TROUBLESOME DETAILS.

AMRITSAR is one of the most interesting of Indian cities. It is the capital of the Sikh community, and has 162,000 inhabitants, of whom about 18,000 are Sikhs. Though there is little either in or around it that is picturesque, its Golden Temple on the "Pool of Immortality," the curious customs regarding the bull, and the character and history of its people, make it unusually attractive to visitors. Outside the city a prominent feature is the strong high wall with a moat surrounding it. Its length is about eight miles. Entrance is gained through large gateways, each named after the largest town towards which it faces, though that town may be hundreds of miles away. This is similar to the plan on which some other large towns of the north of India are built—Delhi for instance. The same arrangement of wall and gates exists at Jerusalem. In the Punjaub it suggests what must have happened in the old days when frequent irruptions of conquerors like Ghenghiz Khan, Tamerlane, and Baber from the North, caused widespread misery and made it

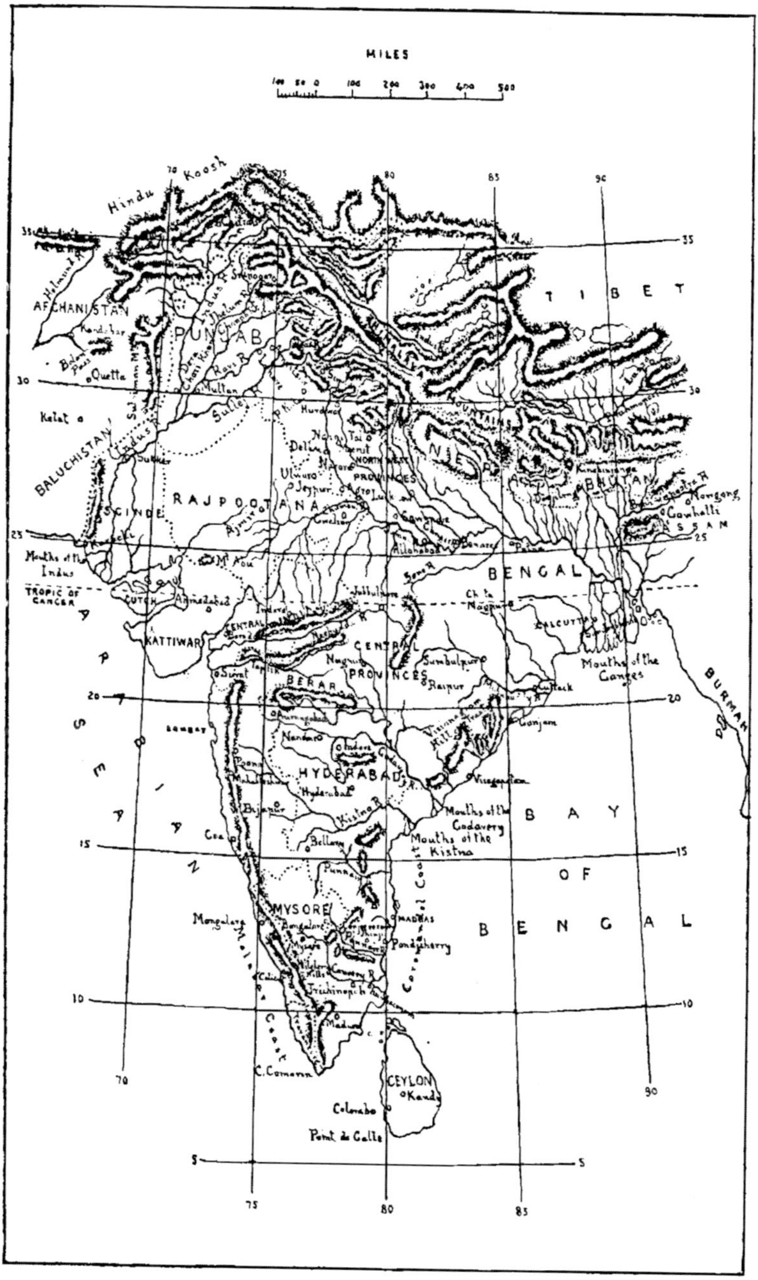

MAP OF INDIA, SHOWING PLACES REFERRED TO.

necessary for the inhabitants to exert all their energies to defend themselves. The zenana and the *purdah* system among Hindus originated in those times of necessity, having been copied by them from their Mahomedan conquerors; and women, chiefly of the better classes, go about wearing a cloth covering the whole face. Very inconvenient and insanitary no doubt it is; and to a new arrival it appears one of the quaintest of all the peculiarities of India. It is seen as much at Amritsar as anywhere; and here the animosity between Hindus and Mahomedans is still strong, and was even stronger when I first arrived. About half the people of the Punjaub are Mahomedans and half Hindu and Sikh—the total being nearly twenty-seven millions.

The Sikhs or "disciples"—Singhs or Lions of the Punjaub—first became prominent about the end of the fifteenth century, when their *guru* or prophet, Nanak of Lahore, attempted to combine Hindus and Mahomedans in one sect. Nine *gurus* took up the work after him with varying success, till the last one, Govind Singh, finally rejected Mahomedanism, and the sect became more markedly Hindu, though advocating the worship of only one god. Of the many gods worshipped by Hindus, the one retained by the Sikhs is a benevolent one, named Vishnu. Monotheism is taught in the Sikh Bible, the Grünth, which is read aloud continuously, day and night, in the Golden Temple, by the light of an oil lamp which is never allowed to be extinguished.

The change was caused about 1675 by the

aggressive action of the Mahomedan dynasty then reigning at Delhi. The Mogul emperor, Aurungzebe, persecuted the Sikhs and beheaded Guru Teg Bahadur. Govind Singh, whose two sons had been walled up alive at Sirhind by Aurungzebe, then organised the Sikhs as a military nation, and at the same time forbade the use of flesh meat among them.

On the decline of the Mogul power in the eighteenth century the Sikhs became independent; but after some severe wars with the Afghans, and serious internal dissensions, they quarrelled with the British, and were finally defeated by Lord Gough at Chillianwallah and Gujerat in 1849, and their country was annexed. The splendid way in which they contested the British supremacy, and their superiority and reliability as soldiers and civilians in the service of the British Indian Government, have brought forth warm expressions of admiration from Lord Gough, Sir Henry Lawrence, Lord Roberts, and other Indian administrators.

The founding of the Sikh nation was, therefore, a humanitarian movement in that it was an attempt to blend two opposing religions, the burning of widows was discountenanced, and the establishment of the sect on a military basis was accompanied with the adoption of a humane diet. Though not "Hindus" in the sectarian sense of the term, the Sikhs are at one with the Brahmins and other Hindu castes in their veneration for and kindly treatment of the bull. In the sacred city, Amritsar, the bulls may be met in the narrow streets wandering about ownerless, and as free to jostle their way through the crowd as any other pedestrian. Though ownerless, they are under the protection of the whole community. They are often seen with garlands of flowers round their necks, and are quite friendly towards strangers. I once saw, in a street of Amritsar, a bull walk in at the open door of a house. The whole family of Sikhs, sitting in a circle on the floor, rose and salaamed and made way for the animal to take what place he chose. If in want of food, the bull simply takes it from a stall where it is exposed for sale or from a family meal. Any inconvenience to the owners is obviated by their selecting and offering him what he wants before he makes unintentional mischief in appropriating it himself. About the year 1870, such was the indignation aroused in Amritsar at the slaughtering of bulls for food for Europeans and Mahomedans, that one night all the Mahomedan butchers were killed.

The Sikhs are, *as a rule*, of good physique, and are recognised as the finest race in India. Their food consists chiefly of wheat, millet, pulse, milk, butter, and sugar. Subsidiary foods are vegetables, fruit, and condiments. By the few who occasionally eat flesh, the goat, wild pig, and fowls are used. As I was several times stationed in the Sikh country and travelled through the towns and villages with the advantage of being able to talk with the people in their own language, I have had exceptional opportunities of ascertaining the facts. Careful inquiry among the headmen and others led me to conclude that 70 per cent of the Sikhs eat no flesh, and that the remaining 30 per cent consist of those who enter the army or a rich man's service, or are themselves successful in business in towns or are not too scrupulous to refuse a little meat on the occasion of a hunt or a feast.

The good physical qualities of the Sikhs appear, but not so markedly, among the Rajputs and the Purbeahs, who, as a rule, do not eat flesh, and among the best of the Mahomedans of the Punjaub and some others of the meat-eaters and "would-be" meat-eaters of the North. What meat-eating there is among them is, however, on a very small scale compared to that of Europe. There are millions of Mahomedans and of the lower classes of Hindus who would eat meat if they could get it, and who do eat it on rare occasions, but they are, *nolens volens*, a vegetarian peasantry.

Good physique is found chiefly in the north of India, where the food is largely of wheat and pulse; poor physique among the Bengalis and some of the races of the south of India, who live much upon rice, and where the climate is hot and damp, and they are liable to frequent fevers and enlargement of the spleen. To inferiority of food are added the effects of centuries of insanitary habits and the influence of certain injurious customs, such as the very early marriages. Rice, of course, is not satisfactory as a mainstay. The vigorous races of the North—Sikhs, Rajputs, Purbeahs, Mahomedans, and the men of the North-West Provinces—seldom eat it.

Some of the Sikhs in the Indian army were

SIKHS.

present in England on the occasion of the late Queen's Jubilee and the Çoronation of our present King. Their fine build was much admired, but it was not possible for all to note their broad and deep chests and their powerful voices. Those who had the opportunity of looking at them from above may have noted the bright steel quoits, called *chakras*, which they carry on the top of, and just inside, their *puggrees*. These are thin, flat, sharp-edged rings of steel which they fling ahead very dexterously at an enemy when charging. Like the Parsees, they object to the extinction of a flame by means of the breath and to the use of tobacco.

It was good fortune for me to start on my Indian experiences in such a city and amid a people so interesting. I was now to see them under various aspects in camp and in their villages, and to deal with them as workmen and contractors, and as some of my personal servants. My move was made from Amritsar in company with the Executive engineer to whom I had been posted as assistant. After a short journey by train we found our horses, which had been sent on by road, awaiting us; and we rode to our first halting-place, a camp bungalow on the banks of one of the large irrigation canals which have become so useful in the Punjaub and North-West Provinces. Each day my "Executive," accompanied by his wife and assistants, travelled along twelve or fifteen miles of the canal, inspecting the earth-work, bridges, and other works in progress; and each night we stayed at a different bungalow.

The mornings were occupied on the journey of inspection, the afternoons in office work; and a pleasant evening together closed the day at an early hour, as we had to start next morning at sunrise.

Of my many new experiences on this my first journey in the jungles, those which interested me most were the quaint details which are seen by a novice and are no longer noticed when one is accustomed to them. For instance, native servants in the North always take off their shoes before entering the rooms in which are Europeans. This is a mark of respect paid by them to their masters, European or native, except in Bengal and a few other parts, where European methods are creeping in. It looks strange and uncomfortable, and the idea of servants walking about one's rooms with bare feet is not altogether agreeable. One cannot at first help pitying them for the trouble they go to in slipping off their shoes (or slippers as they really are) each time they enter, and putting them on again on leaving the room. As they do it many times in the day they become quite expert, doing it quickly and apparently with no trouble at all.

The number of the servants was surprising. Each one of our party had his own set, for each one of us had to travel for months at a time alone and required a staff of his own. For every one a "bearer" or head servant was necessary to attend to his furniture, clothes, packing, and general arrangements, and to be always within call and the medium of communication with the other servants. A cook, a table servant, a man to get water (not from a tap but from a well often at a distance) and to distribute it to the house, the kitchen, the stables, servants, and gardens; a man to look after each horse, and one to be out the greater part of the day collecting grass; messengers to carry letters and distribute orders to the overseers, contractors, workmen, villagers, and others scattered over great distances,—these and various others are none too many. Each keeps to his special work, and in some cases will not touch work belonging to another servant, even in case of necessity, partly because caste observances and custom forbid. A Hindu bearer would be much to blame, from his own point of view as a Hindu, if he were to touch one of the dishes which it is the business of the Mahomedan *kitmutgar* (table servant) to handle. It is really a good arrangement in the end, though at first sight it appears the reverse. The new arrival is surprised at and half contemptuous of a system that requires one servant to go and search for another to do a simple piece of work like that. It is only in the north of India that this rule is so rigid, for in the South the servants are not so strict, and the different kinds of work are not so definitely parcelled out.

One naturally notices the servants in India at first more than other natives as one comes more in contact with them. Upon their doing their work well or ill depends one's personal comfort and the smooth working of the general arrangements, especially when absent from one's bungalow or tent on outdoor work. There are, of course, good and bad among them; but, certainly in the north of India, the good are the rule. In the same way they speak of their masters as good and bad sahibs. Strange to say, it is occasionally the bad sahib that is served best by them as a matter of precaution against punishment. Most of them are dilatory and unable to appreciate the value of time. It was just that want of punctuality and ordinary foresight and the neglect of simple precautions among the Mahrattas that enabled Lord Lake to win his victories. They have not only an inadequate idea of the need for cleanliness, but a belief that some of the precautions we take and try to drill them into are needless. The Hindus of caste bathe often, keep their cooking utensils and drinking-vessels clean, and select clean places in which to eat their meals; but these habits are counteracted by some uncleanly ones which, no doubt, they would abandon if only they could be induced to see how injurious they are. Their fathers and forefathers, however, followed the same course; and they reason that what was good enough for their forefathers is good enough for them. The worst refuse, for instance, is used to plaster the walls, inside and outside, and the floors of their houses, and sometimes as fuel for the cooking of their food. After a bath they may sit in what we consider dirty and insanitary places.

One's "bearer" is generally, in the North, a Hindu of caste, and the inconvenience to himself and others of the caste customs is occasionally noticeable; but it is on a small scale, and the frequent bathing is a good thing. In the case of Hindus of the higher castes, the wives and other female members of the family being kept in seclusion, caste requirements are troublesome and insanitary. The ventilation and drainage of a zenana or harem are bad, and the need for the women to remain always in the same set of rooms—sometimes one room—has results which may be imagined, but are not seen by Europeans. Our presence would be considered a defilement, as we were not born within the sacred pale; we are not of their caste, we wear leather boots, and are in other ways undesirables. Lady missionaries, especially those who are doctors, sometimes get permission to visit the native ladies. But the best way of helping them would be through the young educated natives who study at our universities, and who should be able on their return home to teach their caste brethren the lessons in sanitation they must have learnt during their stay in England.

Baboo Vaikuntrai Ambalal Desai of the Elphinstone College, Bombay, in a prize essay, wrote:—

> "Many young men, on their return to India, try to introduce wholesale Occidental reforms in their family; their illiterate wives, mothers, and sisters oppose them, and many disastrous and painful scenes follow."

Partly owing to the custom of the servants of moving about with bare feet, and partly to their quiet manner in the presence of their employers, the results of their habitual politeness and wish to please are not altogether pleasant to a new arrival. Our doors and windows are seldom shut, even at night,—there being curtains in front of them which are rolled up when ventilation is required or dropped to secure privacy. It is rather uncanny at first to wake up just before sunrise and find two or three silent men gliding about one's room. They come to arrange our clothes and to put early morning tea in the room before waking us and saluting us with a salaam. Or one may be writing or reading, and on casually looking up notice the flutter of the white dress or *puggree* of a native disappearing from the room, the only sign that one of the servants has just passed through. It gave me a peculiar sensation—of wonder more than anything else—on looking up from my book one Sunday afternoon to find a messenger standing close by presenting a letter for me to take as soon as I might happen to look his way.

The Englishman in India usually is, and ought always to be, a reformer. His business, when a Government official, requires him to be continually finding out what is wrong and devising means to set it right. We should be of little use there if we went about simply noting what is good in the native systems and character and praising the native for it. Much better that we help to bring to light and remedy the evils, of which there are many, causing suffering and perpetuating ignorance and superstition. On a small scale the individual has to do this in dealing with his household; and, as the fault-finding has to be rather frequent if things are to be kept in working order, it appears to some, who are perhaps only cold weather tourists, that this is too prominent a feature of the European's bearing towards the native servant. Severity is not needed, but strictness is; and a master who is strict and just is more respected and liked than one who is lax and indulgent.

There are certain propensities of the Asiatic servants for which they should not be unduly blamed, but which must be watched and checked. For instance, a cook will curry very bad meat which he gets cheap in the bazaar because it is too bad for ordinary use. When curried, of course its bad and perhaps even poisonous character is hidden by the strong pungent flavour of the curry powder, and it is a source of danger which the cook had no idea of causing. Bad meat in England, it may be remembered, is used up much in the same way for sale among the poor of the East End of London. One of my servants on pay-day used to bring a bad rupee with him and hand it back to me after receiving his pay, as if it were one of those I had given him. Very dirty dusters are occasionally used for cleaning plates and dishes for the table, and a black streak may be left across a plate from the much-used cloth passed over it in cleaning. The ends of the white flowing garment or *puggree* a man is wearing come in useful for him to wipe a plate clean when the usual dish-cloths are not at once forthcoming and the plate is wanted quickly for the table. Little things like these have to be stopped, as they are important to one's health and in other ways; but they frequently recur if supervision is relaxed. A man busy with his official duties cannot give enough time to such household details, and, if a married man, he leaves them wholly to his wife to deal with. She finds plenty to do in this way, and has to interfere so often, and to correct so many of these small but serious irregularities, that the servants prefer to serve with bachelors.

An illustration of the kind of detail and the real necessity of attending to it may be given in the filtering of the drinking-water. A good native servant, one would think, could well be trusted to look after such matters. One of my servants in the Punjaub had to see to the boiling and filtering of water for the table as one of his daily duties. I inspected the filter now and then to see that it was in order and clean. But one day the water was discoloured and tasted bad. On inquiry the servant assured me that it had been filtered, but it turned out that he had forgotten to put the water into the filter in time to get a good supply for dinner. Annoyed at the slowness of the filtering, he had taken out the "nasty black lump" (the carbon block) to make the water run through more quickly. It was done no doubt in my interests according to his own lights, and it was hardly an error I could foresee he was likely to fall into.

The same peculiar danger exists in the fact

that most of the cooking utensils are of copper. Of course, if no precautions were taken, the copper would at times corrode and poison the food. To prevent this an amalgam of tin is laid over the inside of the copper pots and pans. This has to be done once a-month to prevent exposure of any part of the copper through wearing away of the tinning. When properly done, and often enough, it is convenient and safe; but there is lurking in the system a danger not readily suspected. After some years of satisfactory working I found in the Madras Presidency that the men whose business it is to do the tinning were using a mixture in which lead was a component part. This was easier to lay on, and probably cheaper, but of course it was likely to injure and even poison the food. To obviate such risks I tried using block tin (and lately aluminium) instead of copper utensils, so that no tinning would be required. When, however, the cook's monthly accounts came to be paid, "tinning" was charged for as usual. It being the custom to tin the cooking-pots, the servants saw no reason why tin ones should not be tinned as well as copper ones, especially as a certain percentage on all charges for work done is pocketed by the cook in his department and by the bearer in his. My next experiment was to discard the pots and pans altogether and introduce instead a Warren's cooking apparatus made of block tin. In this there are several compartments through which steam passes, and we get what is called "conservative" cooking, by which, the food being steamed instead of boiled, the nutritious salts which Nature provides are not dissolved out into the cooking-water and lost. I explained to my cook, and with the customary native politeness he expressed his strong approval of the change. The meals were satisfactory for some weeks, until it was discovered that he was not using the Warren's cooking apparatus at all. He had borrowed some old copper utensils, for they were what he was used to, it was the custom to use them, and therefore they were, in his opinion, the proper things to use in spite of the cranky ideas of his master.

Troublesome as such details are for one whose time is generally fully occupied, and who comes from his outdoor work or his office tired and hoping that all the arrangements are in order, it is only right that credit be given to the servants for not causing inconvenience and danger intentionally. This is clear if it be remembered that there are many occasions on which they spare themselves no pains (at least in the North) in the interests and for the sake of the comfort of their master. On long journeys, which in the cold weather (the camping season) are made frequently, sometimes almost daily, for weeks at a time, the native servant of the Punjaub and North-West Provinces is seen at his best. It is rare that he becomes discontented however continuous the work required of him. The bearer, cook, table servant, messengers, and others are all at work before daylight, however cold the weather, even though freezing as it occasionally does in the North. After looking to their master's comfort in the way of *chhoti haziri* (early breakfast), they collect, pack, and load up on the camels and carts all the furniture, crockery, stores, tents, and various packages required on a tour. All the household arrangements are carried with us, and the servants travel on foot with them at the rate of two or three or four miles an hour, according to the capability of the bulls or camels. On arrival at the new halting-place they rearrange the things as usual in a bungalow, if there is one, or in tents which they have first to erect. They then prepare our lunch or dinner and serve it before making arrangements for themselves. If journeys are to occupy a whole day, a second set of tents, and extra furniture, crockery, &c., are necessary; and these are sent on during the night with some of the servants and arranged early next day. We then find all ready at the end of the morning's ride, and, after breakfasting, can attend to office work during the day while the bedroom furniture and the other servants are coming on behind.

On such journeys food can be had at almost any time of the day or night if the right servants are at hand. With three bricks, a frying-pan, and a kettle or saucepan, they prepare an intermediate meal good enough to serve till the regular meal is ready. A fireplace is made with the bricks set on edge at right angles to one another. Tea, boiled eggs, toast, and such things as pancakes and fritters, are quickly got ready.

In several other ways their real consideration

for their European employer is shown. Instead of breaking in on his privacy or interrupting what may be important work when they have something to speak about or a letter to deliver, they stand at a respectful distance and await his convenience or give a small cough to attract attention. I once noticed two of my servants sitting in the verandah outside my room holding a conversation, but, in order not to disturb me, their conversation was quite silent. The whole of their talk consisted of expressive movements of their eyes and lips. It was amusing to see the workings of their mouths in framing the words without sounds.

Though generally careful not to disturb us during the day, they are not always so careful at night. This is probably due to their power of sleeping soundly themselves in the midst of noise, and their not sufficiently keeping in mind our inability to do the same. After their masters have retired it is customary for them to sit together in twos and threes to chat and pass round the hookah. If in our verandahs or too near the tent or bungalow, their strong voices are annoying to those who are trying to sleep, and we find the odour of the tobacco of the hookah unbearable. It takes a good deal to disturb them. I have seen a man in the daytime lying sound asleep with loud singing going on to the accompaniment of a tom-tom not far from his head.

These men are neither intemperate nor dishonest, and in these and other characteristics they are superior to the servants of the south of India. Their honesty in regard to cash, jewellery, and other valuables is remarkable. We sleep with our doors and windows open, yet have no need to be anxious about our goods. I have at times in the Punjaub had occasion to send hundreds of rupees of Government cash in charge of a single *chuprassy* (messenger), whose pay was only five or six rupees per month, to distances occupying three or four days in traversing on foot. He would wrap them up in his waistband, and, taking a stout stick and his blanket and cooking utensils, would, after making a salaam at starting, trudge the whole distance there and back, sleeping on the money to guard it at night, deliver it to the proper person, and reappear perhaps a week afterwards, reporting with another salaam that he had delivered it safely, and ask if he might have leave to go and eat his food. It was not dangerous to trust him, as these men (Sikhs generally) are honest, and the people among whom they travel are also honest. Thieves there are of course, here and there, but they are known, and are rather pilferers than highway robbers.

The servants identify themselves so thoroughly with their masters' interests that they speak of the whole set of arrangements, property, &c., as their own. They talk of "our" horses, "our" goods, meaning those of their master. It is only in the case of pins, needles, thread, buttons, string, cloth, and other small items, that they go so far as to consider themselves as free to use them as their owner. It is annoying to find on a journey that all these very useful trifles have been monopolised. Occasionally one may recognise a lost handkerchief as part of the *puggree* round the head of one of the servants. The gunny bags, so useful for a journey, are at times, when wanted for use in packing, found to be useless, as they have holes in the sides caused by the twine with which they were sewn having been abstracted for use elsewhere. One of my hammocks gradually became useless through bits of it being appropriated when string was scarce.

These tiresome failings, however, do not make up a sum total of inconvenience anything near enough to be weighed against the solid work done for us. And if the intention be properly considered, it will be seen that some are not really faults at all. "Teach them better," say folks at home, when we relate these things. And so we do when we can, but they will not always learn because they have ingrained ideas opposing ours. Immemorial custom is much respected by them, and there are many changes that require experience and practical proof of their utility over and over again before innovation can gain the upper hand.

III.

CAMP LIFE—AND VILLAGERS.

KHLASSIES—SURVEYING—THE VILLAGERS—VILLAGE DOGS—THE RETURN TO CAMP—POSTAL RUNNERS—BAD GODS.

AT the end of the tour of inspection I was entrusted with a small set of surveys for the alignment of *rajbuhas—i.e.*, minor irrigation channels to be used for distributing the water from the main canal over the fields to be irrigated.

The first thing to do was to engage men to go with me to do survey work, erect tents, and to be generally useful. They are called *khlassies*, and were then paid fourpence a-day. With eight of these and a *tyndal* or headman, two *chuprassies* or messengers, eight servants for my private work, my horse, three or four camels, a set of tents, camp furniture and stores, I began the first of the many camp tours of my life in India.

The *khlassies* were rough country villagers with hardly any training. They were willing and anxious to do well, but hard to teach. When applying for employment, those who had them produced a bundle of *chits* or letters of character from former employers. These are eagerly sought for after a term of service, and are carefully kept. Unfortunately, there is a practice of lending them to one another to enable a friend to get work. If a man is successful in getting employment through the use of another man's *chits*, none of his fellow-servants either object or disapprove or allow any word or look to pass which may cause the employer to suspect a fraud. They sympathise with the man in his endeavours to obtain a livelihood, and, if by such means he is sharp enough to get work, they appear to respect him for it. If he fails and gets caught they express their disapproval of his want of honesty, meaning in reality his want of smartness. I have more than once engaged a servant under one name—the name on his set of *chits*—and found that the other servants were calling him by another name. After a time I was accustomed to surprises of all sorts, and when a man was working well I did not trouble myself in the matter, but let well alone.

The *khlassies* gave no trouble at all. They were always at hand to do any work required. With only a blanket and a drinking-vessel each or a few cooking utensils, the property of three or four of the same caste, they were able to move on a journey at a few minutes' notice. They slept on the ground in the open, or in small tents supplied for them, or under the outer flies of large tents used by myself and for the office and Government stores.

Of the curious ways which attracted my notice at this time, it was funny to see these men and others of the poorer classes, instead of stooping to pick up small things, take them up with their

KHLASSIES OF THE PUNJAUB.

toes and pass them on to their hands. When receiving their pay at the end of a month those who could not write got others to sign for them, they themselves touching the pen as a sign acknowledging that it was their own signature. They were as pleased as children at the smallest mark of unexpected consideration for their comfort. It was strange to find a tall bearded man crying like a child at some (to my mind then) trivial slight or loss. Caste feeling, however, is strong,—and the loss of a few pice (three pice were then equal to one penny) was no doubt to them a serious matter.

In loading the camels or pitching the tents the men showed their very clumsy ways and want of thought. Some camels were overloaded, while others had too little to carry; the loads were placed lop-sided or tied loosely or too tight, in either case chafing the camel's skin; and heavy weights might be placed above breakables. There was much shouting and waste of energy in doing a thing several times wrongly, even though the same thing had to be done just in the same way nearly every day. With some of these men no amount of showing enabled them to remember how to do things better. One must see this sort of thing to know how backward even such well-meaning men may be when brought up in parts in which for many generations there has been only one dull round of simple or sordid daily tasks, and where the quickening requirements of town life have had no influence in sharpening their wits.

It was still the cold season. The early morning ride and the day's outdoor work were bracing and healthy, and the climate at that season of the year was superior to that of England. My work was over an open plain partly covered with crops. In the distance were the high ranges and peaks of the Himalayas with their mantle of perpetual snow.

Of the work itself little need be said, as technical details would be of no interest. There were frequent delays, due to the peculiar ideas or want of ideas of the men. Among the villagers who used to come and look on at the strange proceedings there was a belief that the theodolite was an instrument which enabled the sahib to see through them. Occasionally, when taking a sight through the telescope, a villager could be seen running fast across the field of view to escape being seen through.

The villagers were interested, partly because they wanted the arrangements made for irrigating their crops, and some specially because they hoped that the alignment would not fall on their own plots of ground; for they do not like having to part with any of their land, even though good money compensation be given. They were respectful and willing to give information and assistance, and would bring presents of milk, that being all they had to offer in the way of hospitality. When help or information was wished for from a villager, the *khlassies* would give him an order in a most peremptory way, superior though he might be to them in the social scale.

This they did, as is done elsewhere in India, because they were acting on behalf of one in authority, and therefore the action and the tone in which they spoke they considered appropriate to the occasion. The tone and manner are used as well as the words to indicate more clearly the full meaning to be conveyed; and this is well understood by those who are spoken to.

The villages consist of very small houses with mud walls and floors, or built here and there of sun-dried bricks. When a new village is built it is sometimes called the "New village," and gets no other name, though others are built later on and are also called "New village."

The villagers lead quiet monotonous lives. Apart from their work in the fields during the ploughing, sowing, and reaping seasons, they occupy themselves in attending to their bulls, making earthen utensils, weaving coarse cloth, thatching, chopping wood, pressing sugar from the cane, preparing their meals, smoking hookahs, bathing, and other necessary matters. There may be a smithy or a carpenter's shop in the village; if not, there is in some neighbouring village, for carts often want repair and must be kept in good working order. A fair or feast day causes them to turn out in their brighter clothing and collect at a central village where there is a temple or other attraction. They are then more cheerful, especially if plenty of sweetmeats are to be had.

The floors of the mud huts are usually bare, and may have patches of damp or small pools of water round which the occupiers walk instead of clearing them up. Some of the more luxurious use an old gunny bag or a mat of reeds to sit on; for no chairs or tables are used, all meals being taken on the floor. The rest of the furniture consists of a very small movable iron stove, some brass drinking-vessels, a few cooking-pots, and, but not in all cases, one or two bedsteads of the simplest kind. When the weather is cold and cooking is done inside, as there is no chimney the smoke has to come out at the door or through a small hole in the wall which serves as a window.

A man living with his family in this style may possess savings which would enable him to live in what Europeans would call real comfort. But he does not want it. He has fresh air when he does not shut himself up, shelter from rain, his blanket, his own plot of land,—which in many cases may have been in his family for hundreds, or even, it is said, for thousands of years,—and he grows, when the seasons are propitious, enough food for himself and his family and some to spare for the market. His savings are in evidence in the silver bangles and other ornaments on his wife and children, and he probably knows of a secret hole in the ground where there is a pile of rupees which, though bearing no interest, are in his opinion safe. Under a strong Government he enjoys freedom to worship in his own way, and has no fear of being proselytised by force or plundered by conquering tyrants or thieving dacoits.

JAT VILLAGERS OF THE PUNJAUB.

Water for household use is got from wells if there is no stream near. The wells are the meeting-places of those who come to draw the water, chiefly women. They balance the earthen pots, when filled, on their heads when carrying them homewards,—a practice to which is attributed their graceful carriage in walking. A rich Hindu is considered a public benefactor if he sink a well, plant a tree, and beget a son.

In nearly every village is a collection of rough two-wheeled carts without springs, used for conveying the crops to market. Round the villages are heaps of cow refuse, collected daily by the low-caste or out-caste people, and spread out to dry for use as fuel. The bulls are never far away, and are indispensable for drawing the carts, for ploughing, for working the Persian wheels and other contrivances used for drawing water, and for irrigating the fields when no canal water is available. The cartman sits close behind the bull, with one hand holding a stick and the other ready for twisting the bull's tail to make him go faster. Though the Hindu has a great liking for the bull—and no wonder, seeing that he is so necessary for the agricultural work required for obtaining food crops—yet, when he wants his bull to go faster and euphoniously addresses him, "Go along, my brother," he will not hesitate to apply at the same time a good whack with the stick or a twist of the tail. At another time he may use strong language about the bull's ancestors and call him the "son of a pig"—an expression not uncommon when the men are quarrelling with one another. Besides the bull, and used for the same purposes, is the Indian buffalo, a black ugly animal very unlike the American buffalo. He is fond of wallowing in mud, and, as he is of about the same colour, it is not easy to distinguish them when a herd are enjoying themselves in a mud-bank or a very dirty pool.

Trees are few and seldom large in and round the Punjaub villages, and fruit and flowers scarce. Succulent vegetables are grown in the wet season, such as water-melons and cucumbers and some kinds not known in England. Here and there are small temples and shrines with ugly idols of mud or stone or wood named after the Hindu deities, and occasionally a small Mahomedan mosque or burial-ground.

The village dogs are smooth-haired, of a tawny colour and unattractive appearance, and have a harsh discordant bark. They are good watch-dogs, barking loudly at the least noise at night or in answer to one another. They live a good deal on garbage, and share with the jackal and the vulture the duty of scavenging the surroundings of the village,—one result being that they are often mangy and covered with sores.

In the country between the villages it is a fine sight to see, towards the close of the cold season, the enormous areas of wheat ripening. In many parts, as far as can be seen in all directions, there is corn, and one wonders wherever the reapers are to come from and the carts and bulls to carry it all away. The Punjaub now produces two and a half million tons a-year of wheat, much of which is exported.

The return to tent in the afternoon or evening was always enjoyable after a long day's work in the open air. Breakfast was sent out in the middle of the day, and, if not gone astray, eaten under a *keekar* (acacia) or other tree giving little shade. On arriving at the tent a bath and change were ready, and after a rest one's dinner about six or seven o'clock. But there was work to do also at the tent as well as in the field. Some of the arrangements had perhaps gone wrong and had to be put right, and the plans for the next day's work or moving of the camp ahead next morning had to be made. There might be waiting a few of the headmen of the villages, come to salaam and see if they could be of service, or there were sick villagers who wanted physic, as they believe in English medicines, and know that English people carry them about in camp. Complaints against my men for extortion or ill-treatment of the villagers had to be inquired into, and sometimes charges brought by my men against the villagers. The complaints, however, were never serious, and were easily disposed of.

After dinner it was comfortable to lounge outside in an arm-chair and thick rug, for the evenings were cold but clear. It was a strange experience to sit there after dark and listen to the chorus of a pack of jackals passing near. The cry of the jackal is very peculiar. It begins with a howl which gets louder and louder, and is supposed to resemble the words—"Here lies the body of a dead Hindoo-oo-oo." This is followed by two short barks which are like "Where? Where?" Then comes a long whine like the slow repetition of "Here, here, here," and the performance is closed with a series of snapping yelps. When there are many doing this at once, some at one part of the chorus and others at other parts, the effect is exceedingly curious and fantastic.

A prettier sound was heard if it happened to be the time of arrival of the *dâk* or post. Our letters were sent from the head post office at Amritsar, a hundred miles or more, in leather bags carried by men who each ran six miles and then delivered them to the next man, and so on till they reached my camp. The men carry a spear-headed pole, useful in jungly places to defend themselves from wild dogs, mad jackals, or bears (in Assam); and to this is attached a set of bells which jingle at every step the man takes. The bells could be heard faintly at first in the distance, and the regular musical jingle growing louder and louder as the runner approached. And then came the interesting work of opening the bag to find what news from civilised parts, all the more interesting if letters and papers had arrived from England. Letters rarely went astray.

At odd times I would talk to my bearer or *syce* (horse-keeper) to practise my Hindustani; but it was necessary to talk seriously, as they are sometimes unhappy if one jokes or ridicules things, being afraid that they themselves are being made fun of. They have humour among themselves, but it is not the same sort as ours. This was brought to my notice by the look of astonishment on my syce's face when I asked him if my horse was a Hindu or a Mussulman.

One evening when riding back to my tent I noticed a Hindu putting an oil-lamp into a small shrine of masonry, and as he did so he called out "Gunputti! Gunputti!" the name of the god of that shrine. I asked my bearer how many gods the Hindus have. He replied, "Only one god, sahib." I was surprised, and then asked what all the temples and images and shrines were for, bearing names of different gods—Durga, Seeva, Ganesh, and others. He explained that these are *shaitans* or bad gods, and that it is necessary to worship them or they would get angry and cause harm to come to themselves, their children, and their cattle. On my again asking about the one god he spoke of, and whether he also was bad, he said, "Oh no, sahib. He is very good. There is no need to worship him, for he will do us no harm."

This camping tour was one of the pleasantest experiences of my life in India. Everything was comfortable and interesting. The life in the open air and cold weather enabled me to sleep soundly all night, and the solitude had not become oppressive. Though with a vague knowledge that it would not always be so pleasant, I had not any adequate idea of the very trying times in store.

IV.

HORSES AND DOGS AS COMPANIONS IN INDIA.

HORSES AND PONIES—SYCES—POLO PONIES—FOX-TERRIERS—DOGS AND THEIR ENEMIES—VILLAGE DOGS.

IN India riding is so much required that most Englishmen there possess one or two horses, and they become much attached to them. Though it is at times rough and trying, the freedom to go in almost any direction adds much to the pleasure it gives.

Horses are often quiet and amenable with a strange rider. They are possibly taking notes of his character, just as the rider is trying to judge that of his horse. Especially if considerately treated, they are inclined to be obedient until a frosty morning or a rest of a day or two in the stable makes them anxious for exercise. It is best always to ride with the foot only about three inches in the stirrup, so that in case of a fall the horse may not drag his rider with him.

It is not always either the horse's or the rider's fault when a spill occurs. A hidden hole in the ground or the loosening of a girth may cause it, but it is sometimes the occasion for a good deal of chaff on the part of one's friends.

At the end of a ride it is customary to talk a little to one's horse, pat him on the neck, and give him sugar or bread before he goes off to his stable.

It is common for one who considers himself knowing as regards horses, when buying one, to ask, "What is his fault?" for the horse without a fault is perhaps not to be found. One of mine was satisfactory in every way, except that on a hot day, when crossing a river, he would, if not held tightly, lie down in perhaps two or three feet depth of water, making it necessary for me to jump off into the stream. I had to keep tapping him rather sharply with my whip; and as he could not kick up while in the water he found it best to make haste to get to the other side and leave his bathing till a more convenient time. Another had a trick of sidling up to a post or a wall and purposely squeezing my leg between it and himself. When two country ponies are driven in the same conveyance, each tries at the time of harnessing to push the other on to the whip-side; and the groom has a rough time in harnessing when they are both very determined.

The habit some riders have of jerking the bit or using the whip as soon as a horse shies is bad policy as well as bad treatment, for shying may be due to nervousness or defective sight. Cases occur in which any horse may be pardoned for becoming restive. For instance if, as once happened, a piece of thorny brushwood catches his tail and, at every motion of his canter, stings him sharply, he naturally wonders what is the matter and begins to bolt. One morning in Assam, while attending to some work, I left my horse grazing on the rich long grass which is plentiful in that country. After remounting I was surprised at his taking several leaps in his canter. Pulling him up and finding him snorting and restless, I dismounted and was much puzzled, as was also the syce, to find out what was the matter. At last the syce put his finger up the horse's nostril and drew out a leech. The jungles of Assam contain a great variety of creatures, and the leech had crawled on to the horse while grazing. Once on returning from a journey I found that my boots and feet were covered with blood, caused by leeches hanging on several parts of my legs.

The way to catch a loose horse is not, as is often done, to run after him with a rope. This results in many an absurd chase over a large area. The better way which good syces use is to go quietly towards him with the nose-bag or bucket in which he is accustomed to get his food. Empty as the bucket may be, the ruse, though used over and over again, is always successful.

On a river or sea voyage when nearing a port, even though not yet in sight, the horses know well and get excited, neighing frequently. Probably they recognise the preparations being made for landing them. It is a pretty sight to see a row of horses at evening when feeding-time comes and the buckets in which their food is given them are brought. They look handsomer than usual in their excitement.

The syces (horse-keepers) are hard-working men, and generally treat the horses well. Occasionally one is caught stealing the horse's food or using the horse's blanket on a cold night for extra warmth for himself, but such cases are rare. Syces are fast runners, and follow up quickly on foot, even on a journey of twenty or thirty miles.

The native ponies used for drawing the *eckas*, or small country cars for passengers, go well for long distances. They are used also as beasts of burden. Some of the owners and drivers are very kind to them, but cases of cruelty are common in parts and among some sorts of natives. It may be thoughtlessness or sometimes necessity caused by poverty that makes them overload the ponies and use very old harness or girths that gall the skin. Bits of string or rope may take the place of a broken or worn-out leather or girth, and a lame pony may be overworked. I have at times in the bazaar called attention to a badly overladen animal or to one quivering with pain from a cut or sore caused by a tight girth, and over which a girth was again being fastened. The man in charge would look ashamed of himself, and an indignant crowd would collect and express disapproval of his conduct; but they do not interfere, as far as I could tell, in such cases themselves. It seems they want a lead in such matters as well as in many others. At times, on the main roads where the *ecka* drivers compete for the passenger traffic, one may see a willing horse going fast and being beaten all the time. To prevent horses from straying it is usual to hobble them or tie one hind-leg to one foreleg so that they can only move slowly. When I pointed out that one pony near a village had his feet so drawn together by the rope that he could not move about and could barely keep from falling, the villagers, who had taken no notice before then, were most indignant with the owner. "Yih zulm hai," one man called out to him—*i.e.*, "This is tyrannical"—and the horse was at once made more comfortable. It is too bad to find, as I once did, a pony standing in the cold wind with his head tied high to a branch of a tree and in a perspiration caused by his having come a long journey in an *ecka.* The men who had driven him were sitting down to their evening meal, and would have attended to him perhaps an hour afterwards. In the meantime the pony had to stand in that uncomfortable position with the much-needed grass just under him. A rub down, his blanket thrown over him, and a long rope to enable him to graze, were all that were needed.

Some natives, if able, will pension their horses, keeping them in food for the rest of their lives when too old for work. There is also in India a Society for the Prevention of Cruelty to Animals.

The country horses and those from Burmah, Pegu, and Bhutan are, naturally, less troubled by the climate than are the imported ones. They are, in a way, more hardy, and will bear neglect and extra work which would soon incapacitate an Arab, an English, or an Australian horse. Arab horses are kept only by those who can afford to pay a high price and to keep them in comfort. They are handsome and docile; but, at times when their services are required, they must be kept for a week or two in the stable to ensure recovery from some trifling injury which would practically make no difference to the country pony. English horses are much admired, and a few are used as carriage horses by both Europeans and the richer natives. Australian horses are imported more for cavalry than for ordinary purposes.

The best ponies are in demand for polo playing; and they appear to take interest in the game. If, for instance, his rider misses the ball, a polo pony will, of his own accord, stop or slow down in anticipation of having to go in a different direction after it.

Excellent as a horse is as a chum, a dog is in many ways even more desirable. For one who lives much alone in India dogs are almost a necessity for companionship. They are not only companions but guardians. The smooth-haired varieties stand the climate best, and better than any other is the fox-terrier, a dog that seems to care little how hot or cold or damp the weather may be. Now and then one sees a valuable collie or St Bernard, but they require much care, and have to be sent to the hills for the hot season. Many a fine dog gradually droops and dies through exposure to the damp heat and insects of the plains.

Though at one time I had a bull mastiff and a bull pointer—and trusty companions they were—all my other dogs have been fox-terriers. These lively little dogs are always on the alert, apparently even when asleep. They move rapidly about the bungalow and compound and inspect every part many times a-day. No snake or other objectionable creature is likely to be long there without their knowing it, and barking till attention is drawn to the fact. No thief or stranger can approach without their disapproval. The natives admire European dogs, but rather fear them if the dogs do not recognise them as belonging to their master's circle of servants or friends. They know every hole in the ground round the bungalow, every tree and bush that may be a possible refuge for squirrels; and no squirrel that descends to pick up crumbs, no crow that tries to pick up a stray bit of food, is free from their onslaught. Squirrels and crows, however, are too quick as a rule to be caught, but this consideration never weighs with a fox-terrier. Mine would chase squirrels a hundred times a-day, and stand barking at the foot of a tree up which the squirrel had taken refuge; and yet the pursuit would be as keen as ever next time one appeared. Monkeys are viewed by them with special aversion. A fox-terrier would have no chance in a combat with a fair-sized monkey: yet I have seen a troop of several hundred large baboons all rush back to their clump of trees and take refuge in the branches when my terrier chased them. I was on a journey and had no time to stop for the dog's amusement, and it was with difficulty he could be induced to leave the trees under which he was running about barking and casting vindictive looks up at the monkeys. From a distance I could see one old baboon, the leader perhaps, descend and creep cautiously a little way from his tree towards the dog, possibly with the intention of getting in a blow and a bite from behind and then making himself safe again; but the dog soon discovered him and charged at him, sending him back up the tree in ignominious haste.

On that same journey, when I was surveying along a line of country full of brushwood and scrub jungle, the dog would remain out of sight for an hour or two at a time, but never far away. I used to get anxious about him and would whistle frequently; but he was too busy examining the ins and outs of the jungle to come to me, and apparently thought my whistle was merely intended to let him know that I was all right. Occasionally I would get a sight of him busy with his nose and paws and thoroughly enjoying himself. After eight or nine hours of this delightful work he would return with me to camp and proceed to investigate all round it. At night he slept near me with, if not one eye, at least one ear open, and ready to chivy any village dog or stray animal that might come near. The distant howls of the jackals would elicit only a low growl, as much as to suggest that it was lucky for them they were so far away.

Some of the villagers that came to sell milk or grain, and others who came as sight-seers or on business, the dogs would recognise as unobjectionable; but, whether from some special instinct enabling them to judge character or not, they sometimes, for no apparent reason, show much animosity to one or other of such visitors. One day my terrier was much alarmed and distressed when one of them who had just come to the camp was talking to me. He got between me and the man and threatened to bite his bare legs. The others were as much strangers as he was, and apparently there was no reason why the dog should have singled him out for special aversion. I knew nothing wrong about him, but perhaps the dog did, for nothing would pacify him till he had gone.

A peculiar instinct is that which causes a dog at night to warn his master before barking loudly when anything is wrong. One night in a part where the villagers had a bad name my two fox-terriers, sleeping close to me in tent, awoke me by growling very low, and as soon as I was awake barked excitedly. Immediately there was the rapid patter of feet as a man ran quickly away back to the village. He had, no doubt, thought to come stealthily in the darkness and pick up a few miscellaneous articles. On another occasion, when I was sleeping just inside the open door of my bungalow, with the bull mastiff chained to my bed, he awoke me by rubbing his nose on my hand. At first I told him to lie down, but he persisted in drawing my attention to the door. On getting up and looking out, I found a night thief crawling along on his hands and knees round the bungalow. The dog then screamed with excitement, and could hardly articulate owing to the tightening of his collar in his efforts to get at the man. Luckily he was chained, for the man was only a petty pilferer and was caught by the *chokidar* (watchman). Some of these night thieves oil themselves, so that, if caught hold of, they can the more easily slip away.

It was a more alarming case once when I was travelling in the Himalayas and the dogs acted differently. I had slung my hammock for the night between the pillars of the verandah of a small isolated rest-house in a jungly hill tract, with my bull mastiff and the bull pointer chained beneath. In the middle of the night from a sound sleep I became suddenly wide awake. I did not know why, but in the stillness I sat up in the hammock, feeling that there was something to listen to or something to do. Immediately there was the noise of a rush, evidently of some large animal making off into the darkness. I spoke to my dogs but got no reply; and, on putting my hand down to them, found them both crouching close to the ground, trembling and covered with cold perspiration. Possibly it was a leopard, an animal common in the hills and very fond of dogs for a meal; and, anyway, there was no danger to myself, as these creatures are easily frightened and my sudden movement was enough.

Though brought up in places free from wild animals, dogs know by instinct when danger of that kind is near. At Mussoorie, about two miles from the bungalow, the growl of some beast of prey in the jungle on the slope of the hill below caused my bull pointer to leave me at full speed in spite of my calling and whistling. On my return I found him — a most unusual thing— hiding under my bed.

The natives say that dogs can see *shaitans* (evil spirits) which are invisible to men. This they imagine when the barking is at apparently nothing at all; and if it happens about the time a *shaitan* scare is on, their fears suggest this explanation.

Dogs are not always friends with one another, but are firm allies against a common enemy. At evening at feeding-time I have seen a plate of food placed before each of two dogs about four yards apart. Each dog wanted to have some of the other's food as well as his own, and formed the idea of securing this by getting at the other's food first. They crossed over, each to the other's dish, and had a satisfactory meal, by the end of which neither wanted any more.

The dogs of the villages have already been described. They are often ill-fed and have difficulty in picking up a living, even as scavengers. When a bull or a buffalo dies in the neighbourhood of a village there may be seen a crowd of vultures feeding on the carcase, and the village dogs waiting at a distance for their turn. If only one or two vultures are there, it is a question with the dogs whether they can be driven off or not. "Pariahs," as these dogs are called, are not attractive to Europeans, and when they come foraging round a camp they occasionally get shot. At railway-stations they search about under the trains, and beg food from the passengers. A dog with one leg gone may sometimes be seen on a station platform begging his food and tolerated by the sympathetic native station-master.

At villages where the natives object to killing dogs they increase in an inconvenient way. I once found, at a village near the railway, that it was a custom for the villagers to get rid of their superfluous dogs by tying them at night inside a goods waggon when the guard and porters were not at hand. It was, perhaps, not till the train had gone a hundred miles or more, and daylight showed up the stowaway, that he was turned off the train to find his living at the nearest village. If the people of that village were Hindus they would feed the dog; but, perhaps, as an intruder, he would be killed by the dogs already in possession.

V.

LIFE IN A CANAL BUNGALOW, AND AMONG THE WORKMEN.

IN AND AROUND THE BUNGALOW—ARTICLES OF DIET—COOLIES—NATIVE CONTRACTORS—IRRIGATION WORKS AND ACCOUNTS—INVERSION OF IDEAS—SIKH HEADMEN.

By the end of my first survey it had become unpleasantly warm, the cold season in the Punjaub merging into the beginning of the hot season about the end of March. I was then given charge of a sub-division of the division of the Bari Doab Canal held by the Executive engineer. It was thirty-seven miles long, and the masonry and earthwork were already approaching completion. My headquarters were in an isolated part, the nearest Europeans being three or four stationed only about ten miles away—at Gurdaspur. My bungalow was a large comfortable one near the banks of the canal. Besides the office work, there were daily visits to be made to works in progress within seven miles on each side, and occasional longer journeys to the ends of the sub-division, with rests at night at smaller bungalows erected specially for use of canal officers travelling on duty.

Though not so much as on the survey, my work

was still largely out of doors, and there was more office work. The bungalow arrangements were very different, there being more room and better protection from the sun and weather. The servants were more at a distance, as they lived in a separate set of small houses—the whole, together with the garden and stables, forming what is called in India the "compound."

When examining the new arrangements, being curious to know how articles for our daily consumption were bought, I went with my cook on one of his marketing visits to the neighbouring village. There were no shops, no merchandise, and no dealers, as far as I could see. The servant stopped before a large bare recess in the wall of a mud house and informed me that it was a shop. He explained that all goods were inside the house or in the fields, and that the dealer was somewhere at the back. I did not venture on further investigation, but interested myself in the ugly village streets—irregular, untidy, and altogether unattractive, but having one redeeming feature in the many bright-eyed children to be seen in all Indian "bazaars," as the streets are called where anything is sold. In towns the shops are prominent, and a native bazaar is full of life and better kept, besides being picturesque; and in cities the best shops are more on the European plan.

There is a custom among the shopkeepers of having two or even three different prices of the same article, according to the status or means of the purchaser. An extreme case was when at three different shops in the same row in a town in Assam I was asked twelve rupees, seven and a half rupees, and three and three-quarter rupees for exactly the same thing, the difference representing the various estimates made by the shopkeepers of my ability and willingness to pay. At Amritsar, when one of my friends who had travelled with me from England had to buy a horse, this was done for him by the Executive engineer, a Major of Royal Engineers, under whose orders he had been posted. The price asked at first was too high, till the Major explained that it was not for himself but for a young engineer just beginning his career. On this assurance the dealer put the price at a reasonable figure, but said that he would never have heard the last of it from his fellow-traders if he had sold the horse at that rate to the Major himself, he being presumably quite able to pay a higher price.

My bearer was a "Purbeah"—*i.e.*, a man belonging to a tribe of Oudh, the members of which are good as head servants for light work or for carrying dhoolies, sedan chairs, or palanquins. He was quite satisfactory as a servant, and I have always since then tried to have one or two Purbeah servants; but they do not like going to the South. He had a habit of half-repeating many of his words, and would speak of a "kutta-utta" (*kutta* being the Hindustani for "dog") and "roti-oti" (*roti* being "bread"), just as some English children speak of Charley-Barley and coachee-poachee. When I had a small attack of fever, he and some of the other servants went one day without food to punish themselves, they said, as they must have been bad servants for their master to get ill like that. When the horse of one of my friends died, some of his servants cried demonstratively to show their sympathy for his loss.

Of the other servants, the *chokedars*, or men who watch and patrol round the bungalow at night, are, in some parts of India, themselves members of well-known thieving tribes. If one of them is employed as *chokedar*, it appears a point of honour among the fraternity to leave the bungalow he guards unmolested so that he may not get into trouble. In some parts the disorderly tribes are kept in order by subsidies from Government given them specially on the condition that they keep order in their own territories, and it is then safe to travel through those parts. They become police instead of marauders; and it is cheaper for Government to arrange in that way than to keep an expensive force to overawe them. In the case of a troublesome village in British territory a punitive police force is sent to keep order, the villagers being made to pay for the extra police till they can be trusted to behave better.

The *chuprassies* or *peons* are the messengers, and are usually quite reliable in charge of letters. On rare occasions there were amusing instances to the contrary. One letter-carrier in the North-West Provinces I saw from my window as he came sauntering leisurely some distance before he reached my bungalow. When close by he began to run and arrived at a great speed, delivered a letter to me, and sank down on the ground breathing hard, as if he had been running for a long time. Another had been sent by me with a letter requiring an answer. He returned and told me that my friend's reply was to a certain effect. This *chuprassy* was a peculiarly simple one, for he handed back to me, *unopened*, the letter I had written. How, then, could my friend have known what my request was, and what reply to send; and how had the *chuprassy* been able to frame a reply? He had probably heard from some of my other servants the nature of the news I wanted, which I might have talked of in their hearing. Such a thing would never happen in the north of India.

In the south of India it is common for the telegraph-office messengers, when bringing a telegram, to know what is in it and to communicate its contents to one's servants before the telegram itself has been opened and read by the person addressed. The telegraph clerks probably speak freely of the news it contains in the presence of their messengers. A few years ago, when a telegram reporting a small railway accident requiring my presence had been sent to me, the first intimation I had, before opening the telegram, was through my servants asking if they should pack up my things for the journey.

In the Punjaub in 1875 it was necessary to have one Hindu *chuprassy* and one Mussulman, as the feeling between Hindus and Mahomedans was so unfriendly that it was not advisable to send a Hindu messenger to a Mahomedan village, or a Mahomedan one to a Hindu village. There is nothing like this tension now.

One man came to me for employment and handed in *chits* of character from former employers. Among them was one simply stating that in reply to his application he was informed that "there is no vacancy." The idea seems to be that if a sahib's name is attached to a letter it is worth using in that way. Once when dismissing an unsatisfactory servant, on his asking me to write him a *chit*, I replied, "If I give you a *chit* it will have to be a bad one." It opened my eyes when he answered: "That does not matter, sahib, if only your name is signed on it." He would possibly have sold it to some luckless applicant who could not read, and who would have produced it as a testimonial of his own character.

The weekly accounts of expenditure were at times puzzling. Some were fairly good; but, in the case of those of the less intelligent servants, as they had written them or got them written by a clerk who knew English, they were either incomprehensible or manifest frauds. A certain amount of commission and charges based on imaginary purchases have to be passed to save time and trouble, but these are small and may be looked on as due to the custom of the country and part of the usual perquisites which servants look forward to when engaged. Things also were left out which ought to have been put in. Bachelors soon get rid of such matters by paying a fixed sum per month on agreement with the cook to supply all meals for that sum. One *syce*, after having his accounts for the horses' food, shoeing, &c., paid up regularly each week as he presented them, quietly asked me one day when his account was going to be settled. These men, especially when not able to read or write, are at times in the hands of others in the background who manipulate their accounts and do not treat them fairly.

We have to get accustomed to their habit of addressing us from behind our backs and of giving indirect answers. They appear at times to evade giving a direct reply, with the idea of gaining time to judge what we are driving at in asking for the information, and to decide whether it is advisable to let us know all we want. Magistrates have told me how difficult it is to get genuine reliable evidence in Court.

Except for their occasional irregularity the meals are well served. Many of the dishes were new to me, but tasty and good. In some the seasoning was too high, and such things as assafœtida, lime, turmeric, and chilis were used too freely. If the cook was fond of his hookah and smoked while preparing the dinner, his strong tobacco would flavour the food; and then it is best to go without. Now and then the table servant would not be particular in the cloths used to clean the plates, and, if he ran short, would borrow some from the bearer who uses his for cleaning the lamps. Then the flavour of kerosine oil would be over all. Kerosine from America and Russia is used for our lamps, and, when empty, the tins are sometimes useful as packing-cases for a journey; but when eggs, for instance, are carried in them, the odour of the kerosine gets through the shells and affects the eggs. This is a better explanation than one once put forward that the hens had been drinking the oil.

Eggs are much used, but it is puzzling when an English-speaking cook of the South asks if they are to be "har boiled." Whether "half" boiled or "hard" boiled is intended is generally a mystery. The best way is to answer "Yes," and take whichever comes. When first setting up housekeeping, I asked the man who made my bread if he knew how to make brown bread and muffins. He replied, "Certainly," and after inquiries from my clerks as to what was meant, made a brown loaf by putting treacle into the white flour used for making the ordinary loaf. His muffins, too, rather astonished me. I cannot describe them, but they were not muffins in my opinion.

The cat, for purposes of explaining disappearances of sugar, tea, &c., exists in India in the shape of the village dog and the numerous crows which are always on the look-out for morsels, especially bright ones, spoons and forks included. Our losses, however, in this way were never worth troubling about. In the south of India things were not so satisfactory.

When travelling in 1874 with my "Executive" and his wife on the first journey, we received a notice from the magistrate at Gurdaspur requesting all Europeans to put a stop to the practice of their native cooks of killing turkeys by pulling out their tongues and leaving them to bleed to death. This thoughtlessness is one of the blemishes of the Mahomedan and low-caste cooks. Fowls may be seen outside the cook's house shortly before dinner slowly dying, their throats having been only partly cut through, instead of their being killed outright. Sometimes the business is entrusted to boys, relations of the cook's, who are in training to become cooks themselves. I once heard a lady call out from the verandah of a hotel to one of these boys, "You have been quite twenty minutes killing that hen!" One feels inclined to remark that she need not have watched him so long.

The fowls roam about the compound during the day. At night their legs are tied together to prevent their straying, and they have to lie still or flutter about in an unnatural way till morning. Shortly before dinner, especially when it has to be got ready at short notice for a traveller just arrived at a Government wayside rest-house (called a "dâk bungalow"), there is a hurried chase round the house by one of the servants after the fowls. When one is caught it has to be hastily killed, plucked, and cooked or curried. When using one of these bungalows myself, I noticed an Englishman at dinner eating part of a fowl that had been running about the compound less than an hour before, and the white filaments of the nerves and tendons could be seen working backwards and forwards, and the ends curling up with the life apparently still in them.

At that time I myself was trying a diet excluding flesh food. My reason was that as the natives lived generally on cereals, fruit, milk, and eggs, these would probably be the foods most suitable to the climate. The Mahomedans and low-caste Hindus eat goats and fowls, but they get little of such food. Only a few high-caste Hindus go so far as to reject milk and eggs. Milk is one of the commonest articles of food. It and eggs when fresh are much more free from impurity than killed flesh, especially in hot climates, where anything dead quickly begins to putrefy. With the Hindus abstinence from flesh food is more a matter of religion and of custom than of health. Among them the bull and buffalo are sacred; and it would be disastrous for their agriculture if the three hundred millions of people were in the habit of eating beef. They would soon dispose of the whole of the live stock available, and then where would they be for means to plough and irrigate the fields and to cart to market the enormous crops of corn, pulse, rice, cotton, oil seeds, jute, opium, tea, and indigo now raised?

As for variety in my food there was plenty. An excellent dish is made of the *dâl* or Indian lentil, and there are some vegetables, such as the *brinjâl* (or egg plant) and the *bindi* (lady's finger), not known in England but much liked by Europeans. With porridge, milk, butter, and cheese, good whole-meal bread, the fruits and vegetables of the country, and the tinned, bottled, and dried foods imported from England, there was no need for flesh. The sustaining power of the food could not be doubted in the presence of the powerful native workers everywhere in evidence. The subject of food, however, had not been one of my studies; and as soon as fever in the hot weather, and a little dysentery in the rainy season caused me to take the advice of the local doctor at Gurdaspur, I was easily induced by him to abandon vegetarian diet.

At times the solitude became wearisome, especially as the hot weather and rainy season advanced. My horses were useful even in their stables; for, when there was a monotonous wet day and office work, reading, and writing had become tedious, I could vary the monotony by paying them a visit. Fortunately most of my time was spent out of doors, even in the hot and wet seasons, and the continual occupation or travelling helped to keep away low spirits.

Not only with my servants but with the coolies, the contractors, and the lower subordinate staff, my dealings were directed towards finding out what was wrong and arranging to get it put right and kept in the right groove. On the works frequent inspection was necessary. It was astonishing how often, in moving about, something new was discovered that could not be allowed,—things not likely to be suspected and which might easily pass undetected. Some were due to native ways not fitting in with European methods, and some to dishonest tricks played by the less reliable workers. They took peculiar and amusing shapes, and are good illustrations of the curious and puzzling details to be dealt with, and of the relations of the natives to one another.

There need be nothing but high appreciation of the coolies of the north of India as labourers, especially those who do the earthwork of the large irrigation and railway projects. They are willing, patient, hard-working, and respectful towards the officials of all grades under whom they serve. When any difficulty arose on my journeys—if, for instance, anything had been left behind, or a cart had broken down—they would run to help even at the cost of considerable extra labour, for which they looked for no reward. Broadly speaking they are honest, the peculiar ideas they have as to *meum* and *tuum* in small matters being specially Asiatic, and even telling against themselves in the case of *dasturi* or commission, which they pay as a normal due when extorted from them in accordance with the custom of the country. In cold or hot weather they work, women as well as men, ten or twelve hours a-day, and often with wet mud or lime streaming down them from the basket-loads they carry, or from the concrete they ram. On large works it is a sight worth seeing when, after their day's labour, having had a wash down, they collect in caste or family groups round fires and cook their evening meal. With most of them it is the one meal of the day, and consists chiefly of *chupatties* of whole-meal flour, *dâl* (the Indian lentil), butter, milk, and a little condiment. At odd times during the day they eat some parched peas, which they carry tied up in a corner of their *puggrees* or other clothing.

In some things, as is the case all over India, they are much averse to the adoption of new methods. A story is told of an English engineer endeavouring to introduce wheelbarrows for removal of earth. The native custom is for one coolie to dig and put the excavated earth in a basket. Another, after lifting the basket on to his or her head, carries it a hundred yards, more or less, to throw the earth on to the bank to be raised. This is, of course, a waste of energy, but it is what the coolie is used to and suits him best. The wheelbarrows were viewed with much disfavour; but it was thought that the coolies might in time learn to use them and find them so convenient that they would be glad of the change. Having left them wheeling them backwards and forwards, the engineer went to other work, no doubt satisfied at the advance he had made in Anglicising the native; but on his return he found the coolies were, in the absence of baskets, carrying the earth in the wheelbarrows on their heads just in the old sweet way.

Of the better class of workmen the carpenters and blacksmiths were the most satisfactory. Though when they were only villagers their work was rough and elementary, they were more intelligent than the coolies and readily learn new devices of their trade. Years before my arrival some engineers in jungly parts had found difficulty in explaining to the village carpenters the meaning of a cubic foot. At last they made a piece of wood of the size and shape of a cubic foot. This appeared quite satisfactory till it was discovered that the carpenters had gone away and explained to others that a cubic foot was a lump of wood. In these days they are better informed; and those in towns, as they have been for centuries, are really expert workmen.

In India an engineer has usually not only to do the earthwork and masonry, but to make the bricks and lime. The works are carried out either under his own orders through the subordinate staff in charge of coolies on daily wages or through the agency of contractors. In the days of the 'Seventies in the Punjaub the contractors were sometimes men who did not realise the meaning of a contract, and would sign agreements with only a vague idea of their contents. Many could sign only by making a cross or other mark, and were willing to give receipts without any question or check as to the quantities and amounts noted. Naturally, some of them became the dupes of others; and cases were known of a contractor receiving final cash payment and endeavouring to get out of the office by a back door to avoid meeting his partner, who was waiting outside to demand his legitimate share.

When the earthwork contracts of a canal were given out, one contractor might get a length ending opposite a milestone or furlong post, and another contractor's length would then begin.

When the work of two contractors whose limits had been marked in this way was being measured up finally, it was discovered that, during the preceding night, one of them had removed the milestone a hundred feet or so into the part of the other, and set it up neatly as if it had always been there. This he did to get that one hundred feet of length which had been dug by the other contractor recorded in his own length, intending to move the milestone back after the measurement. The other, however, had been too sharp for him, and the fraud was found out.

One dodge is to pile a few inches of earth on the top of the "dummies" left for measuring the depth of excavation. If, for instance, the average depth excavated is two feet, the addition of three inches gives an extra one-eighth of the total quantity, amounting possibly to hundreds of rupees in the payment. This added height might even be finished off with a piece of turf, the grass on the top being to indicate that it was the original ground-level. When the extra earth was scraped away the grass on the real original surface was brought to view and the trick discovered. Then would follow a shouting match, the contractor trying to prove that some one to whom he had given a sub-contract had been trying to cheat him, and the other throwing the blame on the contractor or some one else; the whole dispute being, may be, a piece of acting, the two being really in collusion.

The contractors and others used to send me presents of baskets of fruit and vegetables. These *dâlis* (or "dollies," as they are called) are sometimes given before contracts are to be tendered for, no doubt in the hope of keeping on good terms with the engineer in the prospect of favours to come; but they are as often given in ordinary politeness and goodwill, it being one of the customs of the country in making friendly advances. Aberigh Mackay, in his 'Twenty-one Days in India,' says, "They represent in the profuse East the visiting-cards of the meagre West." They may quite properly be received in that light, and it would be ungracious to refuse them when inexpensive and well within the means of the donors. The custom, however, opens the door for attempts at bribery; and, though I have never had a clear case of a bribe being offered to myself, other engineers have told me of cases. One, who was going to England on three months' leave, had the offer of payment of his passage-money. It was at first made tentatively, and my friend did not understand; but, when it became clear, the contractor had to beat a very hasty retreat.

The irrigation canals are more like rivers than like the narrow canals in England. When run first through a tract of country they divide the village lands, and it is necessary to have a bridge at every three miles or less, according to the proximity of important villages, to enable the villagers to move backwards and forwards to their fields on the other side of the canal. When one of these bridges had been completed and was made available for use, as Europeans and officials rarely came that way, a smart man conceived the idea of making a little money by representing that he was newly appointed as a toll collector. He stood for a few days on the bridge taking toll from the simple villagers who crossed, till he was discovered by some of the subordinate staff who had to patrol the canal banks.

Until I was well acquainted with the language I had to rely partly on my *munshi*, or head clerk, in talking to the villagers, whose language was rougher and more of a brogue than that of the better educated. Once, when asking questions through him, I understood enough to know that he was dictating to the villagers the replies they had better make.

The office work went quite smoothly. This was partly because the accountant was well trained, and both he and the clerk were intelligent, steady workers; and partly because the public works system is arranged so as to keep the records of transactions and the compilation of accounts in clearly defined grooves. At each stage of a work some special list or report or account has to be written, the earlier ones being the bases on which the later ones depend. The final records showing work done to date and expenses incurred are sent forward monthly to the examiner of accounts at headquarters, supported by copies or originals of the initial and intermediate accounts made up as the work progresses; and, after scrutiny by him, if satisfactory, they are passed. One of the most important of these initial records is called a "muster-roll," in which the names of the men employed are recorded daily so as to show how much each man is to be paid at the end of the month according to the number of days he has worked. If inspection is not frequent, in the hurry of work or through carelessness or laziness, the subordinate in charge may omit to write the list up for a day, or several days; and, if he gets into this habit, there may be at the end of the month no muster-rolls in support of the month's charges, and he then writes them up from memory. This leads in some places to the compilation of the month's accounts first, and then the writing up of a set of muster-rolls to suitably support them, fictitious names being entered, dates and daily signatures or marks being added.

In one case, when orders for the commencement of some works should have been signed before the works began, and the works had been completed without the written record of permission to begin, the error was discovered only when the completion certificate was about to be sent for scrutiny with the other accounts. A batch of these work orders were brought for my signature, some even dated before my arrival. On my explaining that it would not be right to sign orders for the commencement of a work after it was completed, and that dates should be only of the day on which the signatures are given, the clerk replied that the set of accounts would be incomplete, and that the examiner would make "unnecessary remarks."

This might almost be called a case of inversion of ideas. Such cases arise now and then. In Sind the bulls that draw the carts have a set of bells encircling their necks, and, as soon as they start on a journey the bells begin to jingle, and go on jingling as long as the bulls are moving. As soon as they stop, of course the bells are quiet. One evening an English traveller on one of the carts, being annoyed at the continual ringing of the bells, had the carts stopped and the bells removed from the bulls' necks. When the party again started the bulls immediately missed the usual music. They were so accustomed to associate it with the motion of their journey, and the silence with the fact of their stopping, that, finding the bells were not ringing, they decided that the proper thing to do was to stop. Each time they were started off again they stopped almost immediately. It was only by refastening the bells to their necks that they were induced to proceed.

The writing of Hindustani, when in the Persian character, which is mostly used, is from right to left; and, when in the Devanagri character, though then from left to right, there are some letters pronounced after those before which they are written. This is at least a case of inversion of letters if not of ideas.

All sorts of rumours get abroad when a census is to be taken. Fears arise that some of the children are to be appropriated, or that a percentage of the grown-up girls are to be taken away to act as attendants on the Queen of England. Among the Nagas of Assam, when a new road was constructed through their country and milestones erected, this distrust took the shape of a suspicion that the milestones were census-takers. The figures showing the mileage were all defaced, under the impression that they were counting the passers-by instead of the latter counting them,—as curious an inversion of ideas as can be imagined.

Items of interest of this sort were more often talked of in the early years of my life in India than at present when the country is more advanced. It was then only seventeen years after the Mutiny. One very old Sikh *chuprassy*, Sawan Singh, was worth talking to, as he had been through it all and in the Sikh War as well. He gave me a graphic account of the battle of Chillianwallah, of which, unfortunately, I made no notes at the time.

An interesting incident happened within a few days after my taking up my abode in the canal bungalow. This was a visit from about twenty Sikh headmen of the villages in the neighbourhood. They all rose on my going out to see them, salaamed, and offered rupees for me to touch in acknowledgment of their salute. Their dignified bearing and polite manner were difficult for me, young as I was, to deal with as I felt was necessary, for they were very old men. Sikhs do not cut the hair, and these men had masses of white hair and beard. As a group they made a striking picture. They explained that they had come to see me not so much as the new sahib but because I was "one of themselves," that is, an abstainer from flesh food.

VI.

THE DRY HOT WEATHER.

HOT DAYS AND NIGHTS—THE PUNKAH—MEALS—MUSIC—INTERRUPTED SLEEP—DUST-STORMS—IN CAMP IN A HURRICANE.

By the middle of April, only three months after there had been frost over the country, the weather had become unpleasantly hot,—much hotter than anything experienced in England. The nights were still fairly cool, but the days, after about nine o'clock and up to evening, were so hot that only the thinnest white clothing was needed. All green vegetation had become brown or had disappeared, except near the canal and at the edges of any pools of water not yet dried up. Clouds of dust arose when the wind blew or a conveyance passed along the road, and the trees were covered with it. The fields were hard, parched, and bare. Punkahs were kept going all day, and arrangements were made to cool the air as it passed through the bungalow.

Though the Punjaub is far north and nearer than the rest of India to the snows of the Himalayas, it is the hottest part of India, the hot season beginning a little earlier than in the Deccan. At Jacobabad, Sibi, and Sukkur, the highest temperatures are recorded—viz., 125° to

130° in the shade. During the hottest time the night temperature is seldom below 100°. This is due to the proximity of large tracts of sandy desert which store up the heat during the day and radiate it during the night. During April, May, and part of June it is a very dry heat, increasing in intensity till the monsoon bursts about the end of June and the rainy season begins.

Proper protection for the head when out of doors was now absolutely necessary. Very large thick hats are worn made of pith, that being light and a good insulator of the sun's rays. A fresh plantain leaf inside the hat helps to keep the head cool. There is something insidious in the attacks of the sun. The rays of the setting sun cause sunstroke by getting at the back of the neck and head under the margin of one's hat. It is a temptation to remove one's hat to cool the head in the evening rather too soon—that is, before the sun has quite set. New arrivals find it pleasant to go now and then bare-headed in the middle of the day in the cold season, and probably become the sooner sensitive to its hidden power. Sunstroke is said to be caused also by the glare passing through the eye to the brain. Blue spectacles are worn by those who suffer from glare; but these are not to be commended if they have not side pieces to prevent the contrast of the blue in front with the bright white glare which forces itself to notice from the sides. Blue glasses at the sides are therefore added, and then the difficulty is that free circulation of the air round the eyes is prevented.

Hats on the horses' heads are rarely or never seen in the north of India as they are in Calcutta and Bombay. Sunstroke occurs among horses, and they suffer in other ways from the heat. In the hottest months my journeys were seldom longer than twelve or fourteen miles in a day, and then it was necessary to change my horse half-way. At the end of that time he would be wet with perspiration. None of the lively and sometimes troublesome spirits so usual in the cold weather are found in horses in the dry heat of April, May, and June, or in the damp hot months, July, August, and September. Insects worry them in the damp heat, and some seem to exist specially for the torment of horses.

Though trying, the hot dry weather is usually healthy, if the right times for bathing, sleep, and meals are attended to, the diet frugal, and over-exertion in the sun avoided. Unfortunately Europeans are in the habit of eating far too much, and of foods which cannot fail to do harm, especially when much impurity exists in them and putrefaction is in progress. Frequent drinks of iced whisky-and-soda, and heavy meals of highly spiced and curried meat three times a-day, break down the working powers of the digestive organs and the liver. It appears not to have been so, at least not always, in the arduous times when the Empire was being built up under great difficulties. In Tennant's 'Indian Recreations,' written in 1798, he says that at Cawnpore the practice of feeding on beef, mutton, pork, and poultry among Europeans had not then been introduced. And one military officer, holding a good appointment as late as 1820, spoke of dining on porridge and plantains.

Many a hot restless night renders one less able to face the work of the day. People rise in the early morning, pale and jaded, and work through the trying heat in a listless manner, with little appetite for food. Pick-me-ups of whisky-and-soda, or "pegs," give a temporary feeling of restored vitality; but this is at the expense of the reserve strength, and there follows a relapse into depression. The whip does not give strength to a tired horse, but only causes him to draw upon any reserve of strength he may have left; and it may be found at last that no amount of whipping or whisky-and-soda will revive the exhausted body.

In the dry hot nights it is usual to sleep outside the bungalow and at some distance from it to escape the heat radiated from the hot brick walls. To touch in the afternoon any ironwork or stone masonry that has been exposed to the midday sun is painful, and may even cause a blister.

We leave the doors and windows open in the early morning up to about eight o'clock, that being the coolest part of the day. The bungalow is then closed and the air remains for some time cooler than that outside which is being heated by the sun. If, as is usual, a wind is blowing, hot wind though it be, the door on the windy side is left open and a closely fitting screen of thick *khus-khus* grass is put up. This is kept watered on the outside, and the wind, in passing through into the bungalow, is thereby cooled. At first it is refreshing, and the scent of the *khus-khus* is pleasant; but some people find the damp causes depression and fever.

The punkah is relied on more than anything else to keep us cool. A wooden pole is suspended horizontally across the length or breadth of the room by means of ropes attached to hooks in the ceiling. Hanging from the pole is a depth of two or three feet of several thicknesses of cloth, the lower end of which reaches down to just above one's head. A rope attached to the middle of the pole is passed through the wall to the verandah outside, where a man sits and pulls it backwards and forwards, causing the pole and cloth frill to swing across the room over the heads of its occupants. The breeze so created, though there is no lowering of the temperature of the air, causes a cooling of one's body by more rapid evaporation from the skin. It also keeps off the attacks of mosquitoes.

The men (or, in the south of India, women) who pull the punkah do so for three hours at a time, and are then relieved by others. Strange to say, punkah-pulling is a favourite occupation of the lower-paid coolies. They will even take a *punkahwalla's* post in preference to one rather more highly paid. They can sit down to this kind of work, and they even sleep while pulling steadily at the rope. The older men and women pull best. Now and then, but not often, a punkahwalla has dodges for evading the work. When we are obliged, owing to damp or dust-storms, to sleep inside the bungalow, it is common to have the doors open and to sleep in full view of the punkahwalla. Once I quietly watched him, as my sleep had been much disturbed and my suspicions were aroused. He pulled well till I was apparently fast asleep, when he gradually slowed down and stopped altogether. The heat and mosquitoes soon began to make me restless, and, on signs of my becoming awake again, he went on pulling. When waking up like that, hot and in perspiration, with mosquitoes buzzing in one's ear or biting one's hands, nightmare or alarming and eccentric dreams make matters worse. A night of snatches of sleep under such circumstances does little to fit one for the work of a hot tedious day; and my punkahwalla had to be dismissed for a more reliable one.

With closed doors during the day the rooms are darker than usual and rather gloomy. When a servant or visitor has to come in, the door is opened and shut as quickly as possible to prevent entrance of hot air from the outside. The contrast with the cooler air inside is so great sometimes that hot air from outside appears like a blast from a furnace. On going out into the verandah one gets quickly heated up and able to bear the temperature, and even to do hours of outdoor work in the midday sun, if carefully protected with a good solar *topi* (hat) and an umbrella thickly covered with white linen. Solar *topis* stuffed with paper instead of being made throughout with pith must be avoided.

Though the punkah is so useful and almost

indispensable if work is to proceed and health to be retained, still something can be said against the arrangement. It is annoying to find that, owing to the great heat and the effect of the breeze from the punkah, the ink on one's pen at times gets dry in passing from the inkstand to the paper one is writing on. Some kinds of paper curl up with the heat into the shape of a saucer, or become so dry that they easily crack across in any direction. At office many sets of papers are on the table, and have frequently to be referred to. To keep them from being blown about by the punkah it is necessary to use a paper-weight on each set of loose papers, and to keep one hand on the paper one is reading or writing on. The other may be used to raise a weight to get at some other document for reference. It is then that one finds that two hands are not enough, for, as soon as the weight is raised, a wave of the punkah may cause half a dozen loose sheets to sail away across the room. When a man has had a bad night and a few whisky-and-soda pegs, and comes to office in a not very placid state of mind, such occurrences do not improve his temper, especially if also the iron rings from which the punkah ropes hang squeak at every pull of the punkah through their not having been oiled. He then has to sit aside in perspiration and worried by insects while the punkah is stopped, a ladder is brought, and a man goes up to the ceiling to oil the hooks and rings.

At meals, fruit in the hot weather is a very

desirable item. Except at certain centres, such as Bombay and Bangalore, it is not to be had in much variety. As a rule, if one is near a town or larger village, fruit of some kind can be got at almost all seasons; but the supposed profusion of fruit in India is a myth. Mangoes are in the markets for only a few weeks of the year, and are expensive. Custard-apples, guavas, pummelos, pomegranates, jack fruit, and other specially Indian fruits are liked only by a few English people. The banana is more generally liked, and is more common in all parts. Figs, plums, apricots, pine-apples, leechees, loquats, apples, pears, and oranges are occasionally to be had. Grapes and walnuts are sold in the cold season by travelling Afghan dealers, who come from the hills with camels loaded with fruit and other merchandise. Soon after I had settled in my bungalow on the Bari Boab canal, one of these Afghan dealers came with a string of twelve camels, and I was glad to buy some of his grapes. I found that my servants were afraid of him; and one afterwards told me that those men never give them *dasturi*, or commission, on the amount of my purchases. He admitted also that they do not ask them for it. Certainly the Afghan was a man of striking appearance and not likely to be intimidated by them. Afghans have clear-cut and rather handsome features, but the expression of the face is always serious. Keen black eyes, a profusion of black hair hanging in curls over the shoulders, loose white dress with trousers tied tight at the ankles, the ever ready dagger in their belts, and the general air of independence, make up a remarkable combination. They are strict Mahomedans, *Shias* as a rule having a contempt for the less vigorous *Sunni* Mahomedans of India.

Fruit being not enough available, and not enough appreciated by Europeans when it is, resort is had to curries and chutnies to tempt the appetite, or at least to give a fillip to the jaded palate. Iced drinks frequently indulged in take away the wish for solid food. Butter melts to the consistency of oil, and the milk is bad or inferior, partly owing to the heat and partly because the cows can get no green food, the grass being burnt up by the sun. Tinned and bottled foods are much used, but some of the liquid ones and the more perishable soon go bad. Even the labels cannot be relied on, for those of the best firms, such as "Crosse & Blackwell," are taken from used tins and pasted on tins of inferior stores. Old tinned foods are sold by auction, especially when a household is dispersing, and are bought up by small general dealers. They may be exposed for sale for a year or two in distant villages before some luckless European in camp, or native living in European style, runs short of provisions, and his servants buy up these ancient "Europe stores," all unsuspicious of their deadly contents. Tinned meat, if not kept cool, like all dead flesh in the hot season, requires only one day or less to become putrid. The bulging of the tin is one indication of the awful state of its contents, if the odour on opening it were not enough. But some show has to be made for the expenditure, and not only native servants but Europeans too will mince such meat, if not very offensive, and curry it into an appetising dish.

It is after dinner, in the "cool" of the evening, when sitting outside the bungalow in the open air, that the quiet and the darkness and comparatively balmy air are refreshing in the dry hot months. Long arm-chairs are used to sit in, or lie in full length; and may be a small punkah can be rigged up. In the absence of the breeze from the punkah, especially if one indulges in iced drinks, a stinging eruption on the skin, called "prickly heat," is a frequent source of annoyance. It comes and goes, at intervals of a few minutes, on the arms, chest, and back. The feeling is as if hundreds of pins were pressing on the skin. Some say it is healthy, and is only caused by excessive action of the pores in profuse perspiration.

A pleasant evening indoors with a little music may be wished for. Suppose it is the piano or a stringed instrument or a flute that one plays, it cannot be under the punkah, for the leaves of the music may take wings and fly across the room. Or, if they are fastened down or held by the hand, the corners or edges may, at every swing of the punkah, flap up and down in a way to trouble nervous people. Being, therefore, necessarily away from the punkah, the musician soon gets into a perspiration and is the subject of attention from flies, mosquitoes, and other winged nuisances. If both his hands are occupied he may have to go on to the end of a piece with a mosquito biting some sensitive part or a "creature" crawling down his neck. Some of the winged ones make for the eyes and settle on the eyelash, a peculiarly sensitive part; and a musician may be seen shaking his head or working his shoulders sideways in the endeavour to drive off some one of these pests without having to stop in his playing or singing. It is strange to see him suddenly stop playing with one hand and frantically slap his face, perhaps involuntarily, and then go on again sharp, trying to give the full effect as if nothing had happened.

In dry heat woodwork shrinks and the strings of banjos and violins tighten and may snap with a loud report in the middle of the night. The frames split up and crack suddenly, and the flutes, if of cocoa-wood, do the same, but gradually. Piano-keys get loose and rattle.

This is not the only kind of interruption of one's sleep from musical instruments. May is one of the hottest months. It is also the month for native weddings; and the ceremonies and processions of a wedding-day are followed by sweatmeat feasts, nautches, and tom-tom music the greater part of the night. To Europeans the tom-tom is the most monotonous of all musical instruments; and its incessant, to our ears, single note for hours at a time causes us to wake at intervals and some to use bad language. If any of the servants have been to the *tamasha* or show, they may return late at night and settle in the verandah outside one's bedroom for a chat and a smoke at the hookah, neither the chat nor the strong scent of the hookah being conducive to the sleep of Europeans. In the south of India there is a very small bird with a very loud voice, which at intervals of two or three minutes in the silence of the night calls out "Brain fever! brain fever!" in a mournful tone, most irritating to those who are trying to sleep.

In the dry heat the clothing becomes charged with electricity, and, on passing one's hand over the sleeve, it is followed by a series of bright electric sparks. This is very noticeable when removing one's clothes at night.

Our habit of sleeping with open doors in the hot season has some disadvantages. In the moonlight it is advisable not to sleep outside, but just inside the doorway in shadow. Open doors and windows enable stray village or pariah dogs to come foraging about the room, or an occasional inquisitive monkey in the early morning. When living at Ajmere in Rajputana, I had a very unusual visitor one night. My bungalow was on the outskirts of the station (that is, collection of houses forming a town or settlement of any importance, however small), and near a native burial-ground. Jackals dig up newly-buried bodies to feed on, burial being at only a short depth below the surface. One night, as it was bright moonlight, I had my bed in shadow inside the house. In the stillness of the night I was awakened by the breath of a jackal on my cheek and his harsh strident chuckle of pleasure, sounding something like "Hech, hech, hech." I sprang up quickly, awake enough to recognise him as a jackal as he bolted from the room, no doubt in terror. He had placed his forepaws on the side of my bed—of this I was conscious at the moment of waking — and, finding me wrapped in only a white sheet, no doubt inferred that this was a fresh corpse. Next would have come the familiar cry, "Here lies the body of a dead Hindoo-oo-oo," had not the animal been scared away.

One of the most annoying things in the dry hot weather, and yet an event in some respects to be thankful for, is a dust-storm. In May and June storms of wind with volumes of dust and sand occur in the Punjaub, Rajputana, and Sind; and, after the break of the monsoon at the end of June, with heavy rain instead of dust. In the arid tracts the dust-storms come at any time from May to September. They may be looked for during spells of three or four days at a time of more intense heat than usual.

The first I experienced was in May 1875. Nearing the end of a ride I was walking my horse leisurely, as the bungalow which was my destination was in sight only about half a mile away. The heat was very great, the air still and oppressive, and the sky above and ahead quite free from cloud. There was the brilliant glare usual in the dry hot weather, and the trees and landscape were in perfect repose. A few puffs of wind from behind made me look round, and the strong contrast of the scene behind with that in front was one never to be forgotten. Across the sky was a sharp division between the bright unclouded part and the rest, which, just behind me from above to the horizon, was a mass of dense threatening clouds, as black apparently as ink. Below the clouds and reaching to the earth was a thick haze in a state of violent commotion. The trees and shrubs beyond, about half a mile behind, were waving frantically as if agitated by strong conflicting winds, while those nearer and all around were perfectly still. Having heard the character of these storms, I immediately put my horse at full speed towards the bungalow. Only just in time, for the storm followed fast, and the darkness closed over us almost at the moment of reaching the door where the servants had run to meet me. My bearer was standing with his hand on the door, which was fast becoming hidden in the darkness. He was calling to me, "Jaldi, sahib, jaldi!" (*i.e.*, "Quick, sir, quick!"), and he opened it just enough to let me in and closed it quickly so as to exclude the volume of dust being blown into the bungalow, thick as the rolling clouds of smoke sometimes seen at a city fire. The darkness then became complete, and the roaring of the wind and the swishing sound of the sand, and even small pebbles carried along by the storm, added to the confusion, which lasted at its height for perhaps five minutes. As it subsided the air became sensibly cooler, but for some time afterwards the wind and gloom remained. After one of these visitations there is a fog for three or four days, due to dust particles suspended in the air, hiding the landscape beyond about a mile and allowing the sun to shine through with only a dull glow. The satisfactory part is the comparative coolness left by the storm, and the fall for a few minutes after it of large drops of rain.

If caught in the open in one of these duststorms the only thing to do is to select the most favourable place in which to stand still through it, something firm to hold on by, and, if possible, something to stand behind. When the darkness has begun the horses stand quite still with their tails to the storm. Until then they are inclined to bolt away; and once, as it was not possible to get to shelter in time, I had to dismount at a tree as the best stand-by, before my horse became too excited and got away, as he was trying to do, into quite level country with no trees or other refuge. It was only by winding the reins two or three times round a post that I managed to hold him. His *syce*, who had been left some distance behind, must have followed up very fast, for, just as it became so dark that I could not even see the ground, he managed to find us, helped by the neighing of the horse and what assistance I could give him by shouting between the noises made by the storm. The wind becomes so strong that one's breathing is affected, the breath coming and going in short gasps. To avoid this, and to protect my neck from the sand and pebbles, I used to draw my coat over my head and keep it buttoned, remaining in a stooping position with my back to the wind till things were quieter.

So sharply defined is the boundary of the storm that, at Sukkur, I once rode as fast as the horse could take me just outside the black mass of flying dust almost parallel with the direction of the wind. But not quite parallel, for when I had got only half-way to my bungalow it came at me sideways, and, though near a friend's bungalow, I had to dismount before reaching it and wait till the darkness was past. It was at this place that one of the police-officers, sleeping on the roof of his house, was caught by a storm of this kind so suddenly that his bed was turned upside down before he could get away to his rooms below.

In a bungalow after one of these storms there is much discomfort for some time. Owing to the heat the doors and windows shrink and leave large chinks which allow the dust to enter. The whole place and everything in it become thickly coated. Here and there, according as the wind has set, there are articles of furniture with an inch thickness of dust over them. It is everywhere—on and in one's clothes, down one's back, in one's boots, up the sleeves, and in the eyes and ears. Little use to wash, for the basin, jugs, soap, and towels, and even the water, are black. Everything one touches is coated to some degree. For days afterwards new hiding-places of the dust come to light in one's boxes, desks, and cupboards as they occasionally come into use. If dinner was under preparation when the storm broke, dust and sand are in all the food, and every mouthful carries with it a share of gritty matter. For a time, however, there is a respite from the flies and mosquitoes, thousands of which are probably killed and others carried away by the storm.

In tent the discomfort is rather less than when caught in the open country. In the North-West Provinces, when my sleeping tent was only about twenty yards from the bungalow, I had some difficulty in finding my way through the clouds of dust to the door. At first I lost my way, the furious wind having carried sideways the voices of my servants who were trying to guide me by shouting. My intention had been to stay in the tent through the storm, but the hullabaloo made me think it might be carried away.

When in camp with papers and books lying about, it is an exciting time when the first puffs of wind come and the servants are heard running about to make things snug for a coming *andhi*, as the dust-storm is called. "Sahib, ata hai!" ("Sir, it is coming!"), they call to me. Papers, books, glassware, crockery, and all light articles must be hastily collected and put safely in boxes; the pegs to which the ropes of the tent are fastened must be driven firmer into the ground with a few extra blows of the mallets, especially those on the side from which the storm is approaching. When it does come the noise is even worse than usual, as the flapping of the canvas and outer door coverings and the whistling of the wind among the ropes make the din louder and more discordant. Now and then there is the clatter of tin canisters, earthen jars, and cooking utensils that have been caught by the wind and are carried rapidly past into the jungle. At times apparently nothing can save the tent from coming down as the poles bend and creak and the canvas sides bulge in. Once I had four men inside my tent pressing with their whole strength against the foremost pole to help the ropes in keeping it up. My custom was to collect a sort of barricade of the heaviest furniture and boxes in the centre of the tent, with a refuge in case of need underneath, for I did not want to be enveloped in the canvas should the tent fall.

One of my worst experiences was in the Deccan in 1893, in the country of H.H. the Nizam of Hyderabad. My tent was pitched fortunately on rising ground and near a large tree. Conditions are very different in the Deccan from what they are in the north of India, as will be described in more detail afterwards. The *khlassies* and servants had, all except the cook, gone to sleep in the village not far away. There ought to have been three or four at least sleeping at the camp,—and, if it had not been for the storm waking me, the fact of there having been only one would not have come to my notice. It was in the middle of the night that it came, not with dust as in the Punjaub, but with torrents of rain. The wind was so strong that I decided to get up and dress to be ready for emergencies. This was not easy, for in the growing confusion it was difficult to find things. No candle or lamp would remain alight for even a few seconds, had it been at all possible to light one. Fortunately there were vivid flashes of lightning alternating with the peals of thunder. In my hurry I managed to secure a waterproof coat, a flask of brandy, and the books containing the results of my survey. On stepping out of the tent to see what my servants were doing and to send them off for shelter to the village about a quarter of a mile or less away, I received a douche of water down my back inside the waterproof, and the wind caught my breath and twirled me half round before I could collect my senses. By means of the lightning I saw that the *shouldari*, or small tent in which my cook and table servant usually slept, was lying flat on the ground. After helping the cook to crawl from under the canvas, we both took shelter on the leeward side of the large tree. The prospect of staying there was soon too ugly to be faced, and we decided to make for the village, where some shelter would be obtainable. This we could do, as the lightning was so frequent and so vivid that the village could be plainly seen. Half-way to it we were wading knee-deep in a rapid stream, passing over what had been dry ground during the day and where there had been no sign of a watercourse.

On arrival at the village in a state of exhaustion I told the cook to knock at the nearest hut and inquire where there was a place of any kind where shelter could be had till morning. Immediately he had done so there came a series of screams from the interior of the hut, and he explained to me that the inmates were terrified at hearing a knock at that time of night and in such a storm. They thought it must be *shaitans* about. As I had noticed a bullock-cart standing not far away with straw in it and a bamboo cover over it, I decided to get into that, telling the servant to make himself snug in the village somewhere without troubling about me. The straw was very wet, and so was I; but I curled myself up in it, and, after drinking a little brandy, as the storm abated got some snatches of sleep till daylight.

The scene next morning was dismal in the extreme. All the lower parts of the tent had been blown away to some distance, and the central pole and upper part of the canvas were standing very much askew and battered about. The direction the storm had taken was marked by a long line of my clothes, papers, and small articles of furniture, all mixed up with mud, leaves, and branches of trees. The men of these parts are slow and not so willing in difficulty and emergency as are the Sikhs and Purbeahs and other Northern races. It was, therefore, a long time before we got straight again: and I well remember what a very long time it was before I could get anything to eat.

VII.

LIFE DURING THE MONSOON AND RAINY SEASON.

ARRIVAL OF THE MONSOON—CONTRAST WITH THE DRY HEAT—INSECTS—BIRDS—SNAKES—THE MONGOOSE—FLOODS—TRAVELLING UNDER DIFFICULTIES—SOLITUDE.

FROM early in June in the Punjaub the newspapers are consulted daily for news of the monsoon having arrived at Colombo in Ceylon. Once having burst there, its progress can be traced through the south and centre of India; and by about the middle or towards the end of June, if the monsoon is an average one taking its usual course, it can be predicted to within a day or two when it will arrive at Lahore or Amritsar or other large towns. Its advent is eagerly looked for, as the heavy rain it brings cools the air and soaks the parched country. If continued through July, August, and part of September, in good quantity and well distributed, it prevents the failure of the next season's crops and fears of famine are allayed.

The monsoon winds blow from May to September from the south-west. They are caused by the hot air rising from the heated earth and the compensating inflow of cool air from the Southern hemisphere, which is in its winter. The wind blowing from south to north is deflected by the earth's motion from west to east, the motion in the tropics being more rapid than in the temperate zones; and the resulting direction is south-west. As it comes over thousands of miles of ocean it is loaded with moisture by the time it strikes on the Western Ghauts and Nilgherries on the Bombay and Malabar coasts, and (after crossing the Bay of Bengal) on the eastern end of the Himalayas. The condensation produced by the impact and pressure on reaching these mountain ranges results in heavy downpours of rain during July, August, and September. This rainfall extends over the north and central parts of India and along the western districts. The east of Madras is not so much affected by it as it is by a return north-east monsoon blowing from November to March with a much lighter rainfall.

The cooling of the air is at first delightful. It is not only that the strong wind does this, but there is an actual fall of the temperature of ten or fifteen degrees or even more for a time. The pleasant feeling does not continue long, though the temperature never rises again to the high figures recorded in the dry heat. During the first fall there is a seething hissing noise as the rain-drops reach the ground and are quickly absorbed in the hot earth. It appears as if the soil were hot enough to cause the first rain to become steam, and to make the same noise as when water falls upon a hot iron; but it is really due almost wholly to the soaking of the rain into the very parched earth and the crumbling and expanding of the clods. Steam rises at first insensibly, but after a few days the air becomes very humid. Though the temperature is lower than in the dry heat, it is soon found that the damp heat is almost as disagreeable, if not at times more so. The skin can no longer throw off the perspiration freely into dry air, and, failing this safety-valve, the other purifying organs are called on to do more work. Headache, languor, depression, and small attacks of feverishness are more frequent.

In the dry heat the sky is, except during and after dust-storms, clear and with a strong glare. It has not a blue expanse as in Europe, but rather a brassy or burnished appearance, the sun itself being difficult to see in the brilliant blaze except by using deep-blue glasses. During the rainy season it is rarely seen except in the breaks of the monsoon. Its rays during those breaks pass through the purified air with great power, and must be carefully avoided. The temperature rises, and there is a return of prickly heat and general uneasiness. The breaks are, as a rule, not long, and the sky may be densely overcast and the sun hidden for weeks at a time. On the arrival of the monsoon it is pretty to see the gathering of the rolling clouds of all shapes and sizes and variations of colour, from different shades of grey to deep black. During the breaks the sunsets are fine.

Unpleasant as the monsoon season is, owing to

the rain and heat, it is made worse by the insects, which are more numerous and troublesome than before. The damp penetrates everywhere, and cannot be got rid of as can the dust left by a dust-storm. One's clothes are damp day and night, and cling about the body in a most unpleasant way. In some parts, *e.g.*, Bombay city, it is usual to keep large open wicker-work baskets inverted all day over a charcoal fire, and to hang over them the linen, such as one's night-dresses, which it is specially necessary to keep dry. Another way is to keep the linen required for the night between dried blankets, so that the damp air cannot get at it. Mildew is common; and our clothes, papers, books, trunks, shelves, and cupboards, must be frequently inspected and brushed.

The punkah is at times even more necessary and pleasant than in the dry heat, but sometimes it is a source of discomfort and even unbearable. This is caused by a chill preceding fever or tending to lead up to fever, or when a peculiar depression, special to the rainy season, has got a hold on the nerves. Away from the punkah, large drops of perspiration collect on the hands and forehead and round the neck. It is disagreeable, but much safer than if no perspiration came at all.

This condition of the hands is troublesome when writing. The paper itself is damp; and when envelopes are to be used it may be found that they are all fastened up, the moisture in the air having caused the gum to stick. Instead of doors and windows having shrunk and being too small for their frames as in the dry heat, they are now swollen and are too large. Owing to this swelling of the wood, if a window is shut it is difficult to open, and if a door is open it may have become so large that it cannot be closed. Where wood-work has been glued it comes apart. Screws have to be used instead of glue, and they serve well during the rainy season; but in the next dry hot season some woods split up where the screws are driven.

Musical instruments are also affected differently. Instead of the piano keys being loose and rattling, they swell and become so large that they press against one another, and one note on being struck will carry with it several adjoining ones. Pianos must be well protected with cosies, like those used for teapots, and with saucers containing chemicals absorbing the moisture inside. Insects attack the softer wood-work, the strings, and the padded parts. Rats, bats, frogs, lizards, centipedes, white ants, scorpions, snakes, and other creatures fond of secluded spots, may occasionally be found among the internal arrangements of a piano or harmonium above and around the pedals. It might be thought that a musician has a lively time now and then with such an audience during the dulness of the rainy season, but they do not all come at once, and one gets into the way of not minding the harmless ones and hoping that none of the others may be about.

Of the smaller insects the common house-fly

is annoying. Especially in the hills in the dry season, flies are troublesome owing to their numbers and the way they have of settling on sensitive parts of one's skin and of swarming over articles of food. In hot weather in the plains they settle on the hand or elsewhere, not with a sting, but with a peculiarly irritating touch A lively fly or two may circle round and round one's head and alight on the neck, ear, or nose, or bob at one's eyes as if it were an exciting game they were playing. There are some very small ones, called "eye flies," that hover about in groups of three or four at about a quarter of an inch in front of the eyes, especially of people whose eyes are bright. It is useless to try to get rid of them, and the nuisance must be borne till the season or weather or local surroundings change. They were found most troublesome in camp when my tents were pitched under mango trees.

Very pretty are the fire-flies, especially when seen, as I once saw them, by thousands on a dark night. It was where there were many trees, and as they moved slowly about among one another, now and then with their light apparently extinguished for a moment as they passed behind a tree, the effect was as if there were tiny stars twinkling and moving gracefully all round.

The mosquito not only stings badly, but approaches the ears with an exasperating singing noise growing louder and more irritating as it gets close up. There is no knowing till it gets quite close whether a sharp slap on the side of one's head will be properly timed to dispose of the creature. The nerves are kept at tension till this is done, for it is difficult to judge how far off the mosquito is, and a slap too soon may only be punishment to oneself while the mosquito escapes sideways. In Assam the mosquitoes are unusually large, and the newly arrived European is treated to wonderful stories of shooting-parties made up to exterminate them. Close-fitting nets are used at night to surround one's bed so that the mosquitoes cannot enter; the mesh of which the nets are made being such that the free circulation of air is not impeded.

Other winged insects collect in the rainy season,—moths, flying-ants, beetles, and some which bring with them an offensive odour,—besides creatures which leap or crawl. Dinner is served about eight o'clock; after dark being the pleasantest time for that meal, when the day's work is over and the heat is somewhat modified. But it is just then that more insects are attracted from outside by the lights in the rooms. They gather round the lamps and can be seen, helpless and wriggling, in the kerosine oil which oozes from the wicks and lies about the base of the globe. Sometimes dinner is a difficult task, as they may even make the table-cloth more black than white—so numerous are they in the hot damp evenings. They settle on the food as it is being passed from one's plate to the mouth, and the fork or spoon has to be

COPRIS ISIDIS.

shaken to drive them off before the mouthful can be taken. They fall into the soup and the pegs, and may be found by dozens in the jam and marmalade. They get mixed up with the folds of the dresses of the ladies, whose costumes in the hot evenings are loose and just suitable for such visitors; and occasionally a lady has to leave the table hurriedly because a *poochi* has fallen down her back.

One of the amusements during dessert is to invert a tumbler or wine-glass over some unusually large or ugly beetle or mantis that may be roaming about the table. The creature is examined and discussed, and some interesting, if rather incredible, stories are told of its habits. It is extraordinary what the beetles shown in the illustration can do in the way of carrying weights. To those uninstructed as to the cause, it is rather uncanny to see one's plate, apparently of its own accord, travelling slowly over the table in an irregular course. This is caused by a beetle underneath crawling along with the plate on its back.

Of the other interesting insects attracting attention at dinner the most curious is the mantis, about twice or three times the size of an ordinary grasshopper. It keeps its front legs elevated above its head in the attitude of prayer, probably to enable it the more readily to catch its prey. It lives on trees, and has the same colour, so that it is able to hide from its enemies. Another is the "stick" insect, with a long body like a piece of stick, and three pairs of wire-like legs almost invisible when on the ground unless special attention is drawn to them. Once, when dining by myself, I noticed the animal shown in the illustration sitting just on the other side of my plate watching me. I became interested and watched him for a few minutes, till suddenly he sprang at me and settled on the end of my nose. His claws seemed to be like hooks, and it was with some difficulty I pulled him off.

These are harmless insects, though troublesome at meals. Another interesting and quite harmless one is the vanishing butterfly. It settles on the ground or a leaf or elsewhere, and, if alarmed, immediately assumes the colour of the object on which it is resting, so that it cannot be detected. Another is the *shikari* (or hunting) spider, which jumps from a long distance and alights unerringly on the insect it wishes to capture. One kind of spider is fond of a small apple when it is rotten; and, as he prefers to have it on the tree, he winds his web firmly round it and the tree before decay sets in so as to prevent its falling when rotten. When quite rotten he lives inside it and uses it as his food.

The ground-lizard is another harmless creature. It is useful on the walls, as the frog is on the floors, in catching mosquitoes; and, for this reason, both lizards and frogs are left unmolested in houses. Some of our kerosine-oil lamps are hung close to the wall. It is not usual to paper our walls, as, in the damp season, the paper would get mildewed and discoloured and peel off in patches; and the only covering is the whitewash, either alone or

SCHIZODACTYLUS MONSTROSUS.

with a coat of colour over it. Round the wall-lamps, attracted by the light, numerous winged insects, including mosquitoes, collect, and lizards come to feed on them. When on a tree the lizard imitates the shape of a twig, and stands out from a branch quite motionless until some luckless insect comes within striking distance. The tongue is forked and pushed out rapidly, the action being like that of the tongue of the chameleon, only that, in his case, the insects are secured by a sticky substance on the tongue. The "blood-sucker" variety is said to be dangerous to sleeping babies.

The most numerous of all insects are the ants, black, red, and white. The red and black are known to engage in battle, with leaders and lines of soldiers. The black are large, and bite the red ones in two. The red are small and more numerous. They swarm round a black one and tear off his legs till he is disabled. Both kinds are fond of sweet things, and are often found in such numbers in our jars of preserves that these may have to be thrown away after having been only partly used. Sugar basins are kept standing in saucers filled with water, the ants being unable or unwilling to swim. It is said that, when baulked in that way, they will leave the table, drop on to the floor, cross it, climb the wall, and travel along the ceiling till vertically over the sugar basin, and then drop into it.

The white ants are very destructive. They eat into the wood-work of houses, the door and window-frames, ceiling supports, rafters and beams.

As they eat inside a beam, it may appear from the outside to be quite sound though really hollow and about to fall. They are fond of paper, cloth, and leather, and sometimes eat important documents and small articles of clothing so quickly as to destroy them in a single night. One's leather trunk, if left unprotected and not examined for some time, may be found to be full of holes when wanted for use. Relying on their character for destructiveness, a cashier, who could not account satisfactorily for a deficiency in his cash-chest, made an excuse that the white ants had eaten the rupees.

Ant-hills are common and often very large. When they are small and, perhaps, level with the ground a horse may put his foot in one and be tripped up. No doubt there are many useful purposes served in the economy of Nature by these clever and hard-working insects. For example, the cultivation of the ground-nut in Southern India is much dependent on their operations. The stalks of the plant, after flowering, curl downwards and force the pod into the ground where the nuts (or peas) ripen; and, though the nuts are not eaten by them, the ground is prepared by red ants softening and pulverising it so as to facilitate the movement of the pod.

Centipedes, tarantulas (a kind of spider), and scorpions are found in houses, in out-of-the-way corners and under the matting, and cause severe pain when they sting. The centipedes and tarantulas leave a trail over the skin showing where they have crawled, and after a time this becomes red, swollen, and painful. Scorpions are yellow when young and black when old, the sting of the latter being much the worse. It is poisonous but not deadly, except, perhaps, to a very young child. They live in hot, dark, and damp places, and under stones. On the night of the fine show of fire-flies, when crossing with bare feet from my bedroom to the verandah to get some cooler air, I was stung by a yellow one. In the darkness my fear at first was that it was a snake; but the natives found and killed it. They told me that, as they had killed the scorpion, the pain in my foot would become much less than if it had been allowed to escape. As it was, though I rubbed the part with ipecacuanha and ammonia, the pain was severe till early morning, and affected not only the foot but the leg up to above the knee. After it had gone it was some time before the depression caused by it passed away. A friend of mine, on being stung, mounted his horse and rode hard for several miles in order to divert his attention from the pain.

"Ticks" are minute insects which burrow in the flesh, folding the skin round themselves to form a nest. They cause much pain and are difficult to get rid of. Kerosine oil rubbed over the skin is a partial remedy.

Bees are plentiful in the hills, and hill honey is good. They are dreaded by the natives when found in the plains, as, when disturbed, they are rather vindictive. Wasps and hornets are rare. At the Sikh temple at Nandair in the Deccan, while I was taking a photograph of a group of

Sikhs, a number of hornets came out from inside a tree close by and attacked me. They stung me on the neck and face, and inside the coat sleeves. It was some weeks before I quite lost the painful effects. They did not attack any of the natives, of whom there were many present. The Sikhs said it was my dark coat which was obnoxious to the hornets, they themselves being all in white. The same thing occurred when a bull in the North-West Provinces singled me out and came several times at me before the natives could pacify him. In that case also they told me that it was my dark-coloured coat that annoyed the animal.

Of the birds, the commonest are the sparrows, crows, and parrots. The sparrows come in at the open doors and windows, and make themselves at home inside the bungalows. They collect on ledges and bars which form parts of the inner structure of the roofs or ceilings of most rooms, and descend now and then to help themselves to crumbs on the table, even when meals are in progress. It is not uncommon at meal-time to see the table servants chasing the sparrows about the room, endeavouring to drive them out while some one holds up the "chick" or bamboo net which covers the doorway. Crows stay outside on trees or other high places to keep out of reach of the dogs, and always ready to swoop down after stray bits of food when the coast is clear. There is a red variety which keeps to the jungle. Green parrots fly past by dozens or more. They are not kept much as pets in cages owing to their shrill note, but are used, instead of pigeons, by sportsmen to shoot from traps. "Polly"-shooting it is called. Where life is held very sacred among the natives, and especially among those who believe in the doctrine of transmigration, a certain amount of indignation is caused though it is rarely expressed strongly. One rich Hindu employed a number of boys to search the fields and jungles for parrots, in order to forestall the boys sent out by those who supply the sportsmen. He had a large cage in which he collected them for safety. Those who practise trap-shooting do so in order to become perfect shots, and it is becoming customary to use pigeons or pollies made of clay, in order to avoid hurting native susceptibility.

The game-birds are duck, wild goose, partridge, quail, snipe, and some less common, such as bustard, pheasant, and water-fowl. The peacock is sometimes shot for its flesh, but it is a sacred bird and is prized more for its feathers. It is a favourite with native noblemen who usually keep a few in their grounds. When staying at a Rajah's house, Europeans find their shrill screams of pleasure at the approach of sunrise too piercing to be agreeable.

Other handsome birds are the golden oriole and the blue jay; and there is the bulbul, which has a rich singing note. When sitting outside my tent alone one evening I heard one, and so beautiful was the song he sang in a tree only a few feet above me that I sat as motionless as possible for fear of disturbing him. The "maina" is a kind of starling and is kept in cages and much petted by the natives for its talking powers. Another variety is heard now and then in the jungle calling out "Did you do it? Did you do it?" There is one something like a snipe which the natives call "Nothing at all."

How real and great the danger from snakes is may be judged from the fact that there are 20,000 or more deaths every year from snake-bite alone. In 1899 the number was 24,619; and in 1901 it was 21,380. They live in holes in the ground, remaining there through the cold season in a torpid state, and appear above ground as soon as the hot season sets in. As they are so much hidden and prefer damp swampy places and thick jungle, it is out of the question to try to exterminate them. All that can be done is to keep down their numbers and to take such precautions as are known to be effective in guarding against their attacks.

That so many natives are killed annually is due partly to their habit of going about with bare feet, even into long grass and other places where snakes are likely to be found. In hot weather many natives sleep out of doors on the ground; and, as snakes go about at night enjoying the cool and in search of eggs, frogs, lizards, and other small animals, it is frequently the case that they crawl over or close to a sleeping native. If he is not disturbed no harm may be done, for the snake is not specially aggressive towards human beings. If, however, the touch of the snake causes the sleeper to move so as to hurt it, he gets a bite which is or is not fatal according as it is from a cobra, a krait, or other kind. My own experience is that many natives do rely on "Kismet," and are firmly convinced that nothing, not even snake-bite, can cause death till the day appointed for them to die. It is this belief that their day of fate is irrevocably fixed, and that nothing can hasten or delay it, that makes fanatical Mahomedan soldiers so brave. Dervishes, Ghazis, Moplahs, and the followers of the Mullah in the Soudan believe in Kismet, and fling themselves on the bayonets of the unbeliever in the hope of Paradise.

In Assam, when riding back to my bungalow one morning, I noticed a crowd a short distance off the road. In the centre of a ring of spectators was an Assamese boy holding a krait, a deadly poisonous snake. He was deliberately passing it through his hands and round himself. Possibly the snake was comfortable and enjoyed the soft warm touch and gentle handling. Kraits so much appreciate warmth and luxury that they have been found under people's pillows in the morning. A little rough treatment or anything startling might have caused the boy to be bitten, and he would have had little chance of recovery. I spoke to some of the leading men of the village whom I knew, for the place was within a quarter of a mile of my bungalow, and pointed out the danger, intending to contrive some means of rescuing the child. They replied that he was quite safe because there was a sacred stone in his mouth, and that as long as it was there the snake dare not harm him. In many of our dealings with natives our efforts to help them are paralysed in some such manner. It is often better to let things alone for fear of making them worse. Had I pressed the matter, something might have been attempted which would have irritated the snake and caused one or more people to be bitten. The boy had himself caught it in the jungle in a friendly way and probably would let it go in a similar spirit, the snake all the time understanding that no harm was intended. I therefore cantered on home to my breakfast, and learnt afterwards that nothing serious had happened.

More deadly than the krait is the cobra di capello, a snake of three or four feet in length. When angry it raises its head a foot or less from the ground and the neck swells out into the shape of a hood. At the back of the neck are two marks like a pair of spectacles. It was a cobra that afforded me my first experience of Indian reptiles. One Sunday morning after breakfast, when I was settling down for a long read in my solitude, my table servant ran in calling "*Sâmp, sâmp!*" (*i.e.*, "Snake, snake"). I made sharp for my riding-whip and followed him to the bottle *khânah* (*i.e.*, pantry). He pointed to a corner under some shelves, but not seeing the snake, I stooped and tried to turn him out with my whip—a rash proceeding, but I did not know it at the time. A shout to me from several natives, who had collected at the door, made me rise, and in doing so I fortunately also moved a step backwards. The snake had climbed from the corner below up to the third row of plates, and as my head came up level with him he rose with a hiss and his hood distended. Had it not been beyond his striking distance and the shelves too shaky, he would have, no doubt, killed me; for there is no recovery from a cobra's bite. It was a fine sight to see him in his full power, with extended hood and bright blazing eyes, which I remember as looking like precious stones. He fell to the ground and was immediately pinned by the natives with several long bamboos, a far safer and more appropriate weapon than the short riding-whip I had used in my inexperience.

It was also in my first hot weather that I saw, in the distance, the Mahomedan accountant escape, but very narrowly, from the attack of a snake he had disturbed; and one night my syce's wife was killed by one.

There are the cobras, the ophiophagi (snakes that eat snakes), and the vipers, and of these there is only one—the hamadryad, a snake-eater—that will chase a man. Sir J. Fayrer, in his 'Thanatophidia,' says that the flesh of a person who is bitten does not seem to be affected; but that the blood is poisoned and the poison seems to act through the circulation, paralysing the nerve centres and thus destroying the vital force. The low-caste men who attended at his experiments always took away the poisoned fowls and ate them.

In many districts Government offers a reward for the destruction of snakes, varying, but generally about four annas (fourpence) per snake. It has been found in some parts that this was remunerative enough to induce some enterprising natives to rear them specially for the reward.

When a snake has been killed, if taken into the open air and thrown up high two or three times, by probably the third time of falling it is caught before reaching the ground by hawks or vultures that fight for it in mid-air, and are seen flying away with the pieces in their claws or beaks. In the bright glare the vultures are at first not seen, but soon after the first throw may appear as mere specks in the distance. They rapidly approach, and arrive with a rush and a whirring sound of the wings as they swoop down together in great curves at the falling snake. They have wonderfully keen sight, and are said to be always hovering at a great height watching for dead or dying animals.

When on a long survey in the Hyderabad State I was bitten by a snake which I may have hurt or startled as I stepped down into rather long grass to cross a ditch. The sharp pain at the moment suggested to me an unusually bad thorn; but immediately there was a cry of "snake!" from the men behind me. They used the flag-poles and other things to try to kill it, but it got away in a swamp. In making inquiries as to the kind of snake, for I had not seen it myself, two or three minutes passed, and I then knew that at least it was not a cobra, for I should have been nearly insensible by then. Sharp pains, however, came on, and finally, such numbness of the leg that I could not feel if it was on the ground or not. At first I had walked about quickly to keep the circulation going. My tent was five miles away, and no ammonia or other antidote was available. After about an hour the pain and numbness left me. There were two highly inflamed pin-points, about an eighth of an inch apart, where the teeth had made their marks. Probably only a trace of poison followed the teeth which, as they had first passed through the cloth of the trousers, had been thereby kept clean, the poison not having passed through the cloth, or at least very little of it.

Mosquito-nets, if packed well round one's bed at night, are some protection. Tarring the legs of the bed would probably be a good thing, but I never tried it, having relied on permanganate of potash and carbolic acid powder scattered about the corners and doorways of the rooms. It is said that a snake will not cross a row of geraniums round a house.

One of the best safeguards is in one's dogs, especially the fox-terriers. If a snake is about they soon find it out, and bark at a safe distance till attention is directed to it. But the best of all, when available, is a mongoose, the Indian ichneumon, an animal something like a ferret but much larger. Snakes of all kinds seem to be quite overmatched, even in rapidity of movement, by these wonderful agile and keen-eyed creatures. In a *melée* the mongoose at last grips the snake by the back of the neck, kills it, and makes a meal of it. They are excellent pets as long as chained, but, unfortunately, when let loose they have a propensity for roaming, and disappear for days at a time in search of eggs and other food. As appears to be the case with all the true carnivora, they have the power of fascinating or hypnotising their prey, and probably also of thereby deadening the senses and emotions as well as the will. That was so in the well-known instance of Dr Livingstone when in the power of a lion. I once saw a rat run hard from a place of safety direct into a bull mastiff's mouth, the dog having been watching it and standing quite still at the time. On another occasion I saw a rat running at full speed to escape a mongoose that was following comparatively leisurely. The mongoose apparently took no trouble, and was probably exerting his hypnotic power, for the rat suddenly stopped and waited quite motionless. The mongoose walked quietly up to it, caught it by the back with his sharp teeth, probably thereby breaking the spinal cord, and carried it off with its head hanging down on one side of his mouth, and its tail on the other side.

In Madras my attention was called to a whip-snake climbing up the side of the bungalow, probably to his home in the thatched roof. That kind is very thin and something like whip-cord. Another time, at Bolarum in the Hyderabad State, when returning home late in the moonlight, I saw a long snake cross my path and disappear into my bedroom. Then followed an hour's cautious hunt over every room and corner, but no snake was found. All the rooms and the outhouses were sprinkled with carbolic acid powder; and I had to sleep in a room where it was possible that the animal was coiled up in some hiding-place difficult of access, though it was more likely that he had passed through the room and out into the open on the other side. Twice I have at evening noticed in time a snake in the middle of the roadway with his head towards me, apparently waiting for me, but, may be, merely alarmed and taking up an attitude of defence. One was a small snake, the name of which I never learnt, but probably the *Echis carinata,* which arranges itself in the shape of a cone with its head on the top. It waits in that position till the person or animal it fears or wishes to attack is near enough, and it then springs at him and gives a serious bite. This, however, is not often fatal, but injures the sight so much that some people go blind. An old Irish terrier I was keeping for friends was killed in this way. A story, probably quite true, is told of a lady who, sitting in tent by her child in a cradle, on looking up from her reading saw a snake hanging from a rope with its head quite near the child. This was alarming enough; but there was no danger, for all the snake wanted was a drink of the milk standing in a cup close by.

A story was current in the Punjaub of a police-officer who woke one night under the impression that burglars were in his room. As several burglaries had occurred at other houses, he was anxious to catch the men, and, being a man of courage and powerful build, he rose in the darkness and carefully felt about the room, keeping his eye on the door, through which no one could go out without his seeing them. Having examined all parts and come to the conclusion that no one was in the room, he lit his lamp and discovered a cobra among some newspapers he had been reading before retiring. As he had been walking about with bare feet he had been in real danger.

This story also is probably true; but I now give one about which some have expressed doubt. The ophiophagi (snake-eating snakes) have teeth pointing backwards, thus enabling them the more surely to prevent their prey from escaping. It is said that they are obliged to swallow anything they have caught, as their teeth prevent its rejection. The story I allude to is of two such snakes playing with one another. One, by accident or in play, caught the tail of the other in his teeth, and the other in retaliation did the same to him. Both had to go on swallowing till each had eaten the other and nothing at all was left.

There is no knowing what the natives of India may consider a fit object of adoration. Some worship images of stone, wood, or clay; others worship rivers, others the pen they use, and some worship alligators and even snakes. The illustration opposite is of a snake idol which I saw natives bow to and leave presents for at

A SNAKE IDOL.

Hampi in the Madras Presidency in 1901. The expansion above the head of the idol is a representation of the hood of a cobra.

But, besides the heat, damp, fevers, the insects, and reptiles, there are other annoyances in the rainy season. At intervals the rain is excessive. The heaviest fall known is at Cherrapunji in Assam, where the Bay of Bengal branch of the monsoon first strikes the Himalayas on a bold projection of the Khasia hills about 4500 feet above the sea. It stands near the edge of a line of cliffs rising abruptly to about 1000 feet above the plains immediately below. In 1850 there was a fall of thirty inches in twenty-four hours. As nearly the whole of the rainfall occurs within about three months (July, August, and September), the smaller vegetation and loose soil are washed away by the deluge and carried over the cliffs. At the foot of these can be seen for miles a mass of boulders and *débris* filled in with rank vegetation, and said to be surrounded by an atmosphere of deadly gases in which no animal can live.

In the north of India there are many very large rivers. The Ganges, Jumna, Indus, Sutlej, and others rapidly rise when the heaviest rain falls, and extensive floods occur. Some of the floods in the valley of the Beas in the Punjaub I have seen spread over the country as far as the eye could reach, the mud villages, trees, temples, &c., standing out as if floating on the expanse of water. It is then that even large rivers cut for themselves new channels, and on the subsidence of the floods may be found to have abandoned their former beds, and to be flowing far away from the old channels for some miles before coming again into the original course. Whole villages, metalled roads, and cultivated fields may be swept away and much loss inflicted on the owners. Expensive bridges over the old watercourses have sometimes been left standing on dry land. Dera Ghazi Khan, a town of 20,000 inhabitants in the Punjaub, is now yearly threatened with destruction by floods of the Indus river.

During my first rainy season, one rain-gauge in the Punjaub recorded twenty-two inches in ten hours; and at Allahabad, in the North-West Provinces, twenty-six inches were registered in twenty-four hours. This was on September 7, 1875; and one result was that 1500 houses in Amritsar fell, and several lives were lost. In twenty-seven miles of the railway between Amritsar and the river Beas, where my sub-division of the canal ended, many parts were either wholly or partially destroyed. Shortly before the breaks occurred I passed over that part in what was probably the last train, and saw the great expanse of water on one side of the line high above the country on the opposite side, the railway being in embankment. The water was rushing through the bridges and culverts with great rapidity.

On returning from Amritsar I had to travel by the Grand Trunk road, which is parallel with the railway and not far from it in this part of its length. It is the finest road in India, and extends from Calcutta to near the Afghan border at Peshawur. It is thirty feet broad and well metalled. But as it is down-stream of the railway, it had been exposed to the full force of the torrents coming from the bridges and breaks in the embankments, and was in such a state of chaos that no wheeled traffic could pass along. Here and there the *kunkur* (road metal) had been so well rammed that it had resisted the destructive action of the water, though the earth beneath the metal had been washed away. The road metal remained in position, resting on nothing at all immediately below it, being held up simply by its adhesion to the adjoining stretches of road remaining intact. This result had arisen at first from the water finding its way under the *kunkur* through small channels,—rat-holes possibly,—which became gradually wider as the earth got saturated and was carried away. There were dead goats and fowls lying about round the villages, the inhabitants in some places having had enough to do to look after themselves and their oxen and buffaloes, and being unable to rescue all their live stock. Some of them told me that the snakes had been flooded out of their holes in the ground in great numbers, and had been hanging from the branches of trees till the floods subsided.

The earthwork and bridges of my sub-division had only lately been completed, but the heavy rain and the maximum discharge of flood through the canal before the earthwork was consolidated enough for so great a strain, caused several breaks in the banks and much damage throughout. At one of the inspection bungalows, though it was on rising ground, the height to which the water had risen was well defined by the mark left by the muddy water, inside and out, on all the walls one foot above the plinth and floors, which were themselves eighteen inches above the ground. At the Raiya bungalow, near the Beas river, the compound was still submerged; and it was amusing to see the office clerks floating about on planks, trying to catch with sticks various articles of lost clothing. At the breaks on the railway the permanent way had remained unbroken, though the bank had been destroyed. The rails, held together by the fishplates and bolts, with the sleepers still attached to them, were hanging across the breaks in curves.

In the most rainy parts of the monsoon travelling is more uncomfortable than at any other time, especially when inspecting the state of the works. The new unsettled earthwork and rough roadways become full of holes and swamps, and it is hard work for the bulls when carts are used. Extra labour is thrown on the servants, as they sometimes have all to join together, even in heavy rain, to push the carts or help to lift a wheel out of a mud-hole or deep rut. In the Punjaub and North-West Provinces the men work with a will, and seem to think little of getting their clothing saturated with rain and covered with mud. Many a long ride I had in the muggy damp heat and the rain, arriving before my men and carts, and unable to say how long they would be delayed. My work took me along the canal banks or roads at the side where a horse could pick his way or easily walk through pools of water or mud, while the men and carts would go by the best village roads they could find. It was tedious waiting at the inspection bungalow with only bare furniture, perhaps without comforts, wet through, and with a touch of fever coming on. With the *bundhobust*, or set of arrangements, properly made, there should be some comforts sent ahead the day before in case of a breakdown; but it cannot always be said till just before starting when or where one has to go, and the best laid schemes "gang aft agley." So, having arrived ahead, one can only lie in a long arm-chair and wait in damp clothes, and, as evening comes on and no carts have arrived, fall into a fitful sleep, waking up with a start when the jingle of the bells of the bulls is heard.

The rainy season is the time of illnesses. The Medical officer of Amritsar told me that before the heavy rainfall of September 7, 1875, he had in hospital 400 cases of cholera, and that soon after the downpour there were only nineteen cases. Fever is common, and there are frequent outbreaks of dysentery and cholera. Towards the end of the monsoon, on the approach of the cold weather, the temperature falls rapidly. After six or seven months of exposure to first the dry heat and then the damp heat, people are not so vigorous and able to resist depressing influences. It may be hot and stuffy at bed-time, and one goes to sleep with only a sheet as covering; and, if during the night the temperature fall suddenly, towards morning one may wake up shivering and glad to add a blanket or two. This chilling at night while asleep, if prolonged, may cause fever or dysentery.

For those whose headquarters are in isolated parts, and for days at a time obliged to remain mostly indoors, the solitude occasionally becomes oppressive. One cannot read and write much for pleasure, especially after some hours of office work or preparation of plans. The horses and dogs are valuable then as chums; but to get at the stables involves perhaps careful dressing up in waterproofs and a run through a swamped compound. Music is out of the question, as the instruments are probably unfit, and even if they are in fair order the tunes sound dismal under such circumstances. A talk now and then with some of the natives is good, but it is rarely interesting for long. Sometimes I held imaginary conversations with imaginary people, and at other times I would shout out loud to break the intolerable silence. One's nerves get out of order, and such trifles as the chirruping of the squirrels outside on the verandah roof or in the trees, or the too rich scent of the lime-trees, may irritate them.

But by about the middle of September the rains become lighter and people remark, "Quite a cold weather feeling in the air to-day." The sun appears more often and not so hot, and the clouds gradually disappear. There is, in the North at least, a prospect of five or six months of real cold weather, and a pleasant time of camping and solid progress in the season when work can proceed without such interruptions as storms, floods, and illness. As the pleasant time sets in our spirits revive and we begin to forget the troubles of the past few months, and to agree that India is not such a bad place after all.

VIII.

LIFE ON IRRIGATION WORKS IN THE NORTH-WEST PROVINCES.

TWO INTERESTING EVENTS—CONSTRUCTION OF IRRIGATION WORKS—NARORA—HEAD WORKS OF THE LOWER GANGES CANAL—THE COOLIES AT WORK AND AT REST—INCIDENTS—ALLIGATORS—BEGINNING OF THE FAMINE OF 1877-78.

THE cold weather had returned at last. Though work has to be done at all times of the year, this is spoken of as the working season. There are no floods or heavy rains, and as the rivers are low, foundations of bridges, masonry dams, and other works can be constructed more easily and quickly, and at least cost.

The works of my sub-division had been far advanced when I joined it, and little more was now to be done besides repairing the damage caused by the unusual floods. I was then transferred to some very large irrigation works in progress in the North-West Provinces. Before I left the Punjaub there were two interesting occurrences,—one a journey to the low hills of the Himalayas, and the other the visit of the Prince of Wales, now King Edward VII.

Though my trip was only to the foot of the low hills, I had a nearer view of the snows and saw some pretty scenery. There was not time to go to the interior, nor was it the season for doing so. A wolf was the only wild animal I saw. A ride of about eighty miles in the five days' Christmas leave and a few climbs afforded an enjoyable excursion. Occasional short leave, when not interfering with duty, is freely given, on the ground that it enables a man to gain health and become better able to do his work.

The visit of the Prince of Wales was a great event at Lahore. The processions of troops, native and European—the Rajahs, Maharajahs, and Nawabs, with their curiously dressed body-guards and followers, the numerous elephants in handsome trappings, and the native crowd in its wonderful variety—made up a picturesque scene. But sometimes to see the processions we had to wait for hours in the hot sun and the thick dust raised by the crowds. A *levée* in the morning, also with tedious waiting, was interesting in the collection of native gentlemen mixed with the Europeans.

Far more enjoyable and, in a different way, more picturesque was the ball at the Montgomery Hall. The costumes of the native chiefs, some adorned with much colouring and precious stones, the dresses of the ladies, and the great variety of uniforms of the officers of the British and native regiments, were in good contrast to one another, and to the black attire of the civilians. In India the decorations of shrubs and flowers can be more profuse and ornamental than in England, and the military bands are some of the best.

There was a firework show at the Golden

Temple. The natives are good at such displays; and this one was better than usual, as the temple, standing out in the coloured lights, and its reflection in the Pool of Immortality, added an unusual and pleasing effect. The return home was in strong contrast as one passed along the curious, narrow, crooked, dark streets amid the crowd of native sight-seers.

My transfer to the North-West Provinces was 350 miles southwards. One horse I took with me by rail in case of need for my work; the other travelled by road. This is a common thing when a horse is not immediately wanted. The syce (horse-keeper) walks with the horse from twenty-five to thirty miles a-day. The baggage is light, being a blanket each for the horse and syce, a few ropes and brushes, and the bucket; and these are not too much for the horse to carry. They start each day before sunrise, and walk, say, twelve miles or so, then rest during the heat of the day in some pleasant spot, and travel another twelve miles at evening.

My new headquarters were on the Ganges river at Narora, where water was to be diverted into the Lower Ganges canal to irrigate the country between the Ganges and the Jumna rivers. Massive head works were under construction, the coolies employed being sometimes as many as 4000. I found myself one of several assistant engineers under the orders of Colonel J. H. Western, R.E., who was in charge. He and other irrigation officers of the North-West Provinces — Scott-Moncrieff, Garstin, Willcocks, Ross, and Wilson—

afterwards went to Egypt, and all were decorated for their good service there. The two last died, and Wilson's was the sixth death among the fifty students who went out with me in 1874.

Many things have to be carefully considered, not only in designing such a work as the Lower Ganges canal, but also before sanction can be given to it. Will the value of the increased produce of the irrigated lands be enough to justify the outlay? Are the character of the soil and the physical conditions of the locality such as admit of effective irrigation? The position of the head works where the canal is taken off from the river is one of much importance. It would be a great loss to the nation if, after the canal had been constructed, and especially if irrigation had already begun, the river should leave its course and select a new bed for itself. As the dam would cause the flood-level to rise for some miles up-stream, there might be a danger of the spread of the flood-water over parts of the country hitherto unflooded, and even of an inducement being thereby offered for the river to seek a new course. Though the site chosen was one at which the river was likely to be permanent, it was found necessary to protect the country with an embankment for four miles. The course of the river below the weir had also to be anticipated; for interference with the normal conditions of flow gives rise to all sorts of possibilities of unexpected results. Costly training and protective works were required. The levels of the bed of the river, of the highest known floods, and of the surrounding country for some miles up-stream and down-stream of the proposed site, the amount and character of the silt brought down by the floods, of the salts in solution, and of the weeds, of which the river brings down the seeds from the hills, and many other data, had to be collected and considered by expert irrigation officers. The possibility of draining away the water when it has irrigated the fields is an important point, for there is the danger of its collecting and forming unhealthy swamps.

The Ganges at Narora is more than three-quarters of a mile broad. In flood it discharges 300,000 cubic feet per second; and it is said that, owing to the many tributaries it receives in its course to the sea, the flood discharge at its mouth becomes as much as 2,000,000 cubic feet per second. Some idea of this volume of water may be formed by comparing with it the discharge of the Thames, which is only 40,000 cubic feet at its highest flood.

In the cold season the amount of water passing down the river at Narora falls to only a little over 5000 cubic feet a second, and the canal was designed to take off nearly all this. As at its commencement it has a bed-width of over 200 feet, and when full is ten feet deep, it has the appearance of a fine river; and as it flows through hundreds of miles of country, and has a roadway and rows of trees throughout on each bank, it is a picturesque addition to the scenery. Of course it is smaller in the lower parts, because as the water is drawn off to irrigate the country provision is made to carry only the reduced quantity, and at its end it becomes little more than a large ditch. Many bridges over the canal had to be made to carry the road traffic, aqueducts to carry the canal over the rivers, and several masonry falls to adjust the levels. 600,000 acres are fertilised by this canal, and at the time of its completion about a million and a half acres were already being irrigated by the Upper Ganges canal and other canals in the North-West Provinces. The total would raise food enough for 8,000,000 people for eight months.

The work at Narora was very different from that on the Bari Doab canal. There it was done by small contractors and gangs scattered over many miles. Here there were numerous large gangs crowded together in a comparatively small space. The scene was animated and, of its kind, picturesque. There were hundreds of wells being sunk and filled with concrete, the earthwork excavation of the canal, the brick and stone masonry of the weir and sluices, ramming, pumping, pitching, river-training, dredging, brickmaking, lime-burning, pile-driving, temporary bridging, and minor works. In the midst of all this was a tramway over which ran trains carrying the material to all parts of the work. In odd places were stalls of the small traders who sold parched peas, sweetmeats, and fruit; the huts of the native contractors and coolies and their families, and small offices where the initial accounts were kept by subordinate officials in charge of sections of the work.

The subordinates were some of the best in the Public Works Department. A few were sergeants of the Royal Engineers, whose services had been lent; and smart, well-educated, and intelligent men they were. The native clerks and draughtsmen worked well. All had plenty to do, and, partly for this reason and partly owing to the better supervision possible when all are together, there were not the irregularities I had found in the Punjaub. The smaller contractors had now and then to be watched—for instance, when purchasing quantities of thick manilla rope: as it was bought by weight we found it necessary, before weighing, to spread it out in the sun for a few days under lock and key to get rid of any water with which it might be saturated.

One of the best petty contractors, especially for earthwork, was the "Purbeah" of Oudh; but, though he worked well, he was rarely contented. He seemed to be never clear in his mind as to whether he had made a good bargain or not. A trifling concession now and then usually met his case, and was enough to induce him to go on contentedly for a time.

The coolies and artisans, though at times working indifferently, were on the whole satisfactory. They could, and would when necessary, work with a will and very effectively. When, for instance, an iron girder had to be erected or an obstacle removed, they pulled well together if properly supervised; and especially if there were among them one to lead a chorus such as English workmen sometimes use. They sing "Allavelli,

allavelli," as they ram the concrete or work with the crowbars; and, at the moment of successfully completing a trying bit of work, they shout "Jee kee ja!" which takes the place of the English "Hurrah." They may, however, get excited and noisy, and pull in wrong directions if not properly handled. A native gang, if all the members are not trained or accustomed to work together, is a troublesome team to drive.

At dusk, when they came away in crowds from the work, many were covered with mud and wet lime, for they are not particular about either themselves or their clothing when at work. A wash down soon put them fairly right; and, though they might be damp for some time, they cared little as they settled down with their caste people or other chums to the long-looked-for evening meal. Many small fires were scattered about in the darkness, and round them groups of men and women preparing *chupatties* and enjoying their leisure and hookahs. After the meal some of them sang or, more rarely, played tom-toms and stringed instruments. There were, even among the poorest, men who sang well and improvised their song. One evening, knowing their language, I recognised, fairly well adapted to the tune, a description of my own doings during the day, and of those of other engineers.

During my two years' experience at Narora, and near it, some interesting incidents came to my notice. It was not a pleasant sight in times of flood to see the dead body of a man or of a bull or buffalo floating down the river with a vulture perched on it in anticipation of a meal. One day, on coming to where a high bank of sand was being removed, I found the coolies digging frantically at one spot. They had been undercutting the bank to cause the top part to tumble down without their having to dig at it. It had fallen, but they had forgotten that a baby belonging to a woman on the work had been left lying just below. The baby was entombed, and the trouble was to know exactly where, and to avoid hitting him with the spades in their excited efforts to remove the sand before suffocation occurred. He was dug out uninjured, and with a stolid self-possessed look on his face, as if he had been the least concerned in the affair.

When large bridges are to be constructed—as was the case when the railway bridge over the Ganges at Benares was begun—there is sometimes a scare and a difficulty in getting labourers, because reports get about that a number of children of the adjoining villages will have to be buried alive beneath the foundations for luck.

Once, when riding along a jungly road, I disturbed a group of women who were sitting in a circle and all crying aloud. On my passing by they stopped a little, and then went on crying. They were mourners for some one lately dead, probably professional mourners hired by the relations for the occasion. A friend of mine told me that when he was travelling by steamer on the river a similar party of mourners were on board crying till sunset, when their leader said, "Now stop, my children, and we will begin again to-morrow morning at seven o'clock."

At the workshops at Narora was a blast-furnace, and the flames at night, in the monsoon season, attracted numerous insects. The heat was so great that they never actually reached the flames, but fell dead or senseless when within twenty or thirty feet from them. Each morning a ring of dead insects was found at about that distance round the foot of the furnace.

On the banks of the large rivers of India alligators may often be seen lying motionless and with their mouths wide open. The rows of jagged teeth stand out clearly against the sky. It is said that they sleep in that way so that insects may fly or crawl into their mouths and collect there till they awake and snap their jaws on the accumulated meal. Some say they are not asleep at all, but only pretending.

A sad thing was related to me as having occurred in Burmah, where a father and son were returning to land from a row on the Irrawaddy. The boat having grounded, and there being a few feet of shallow water between it and the shore, the son sprang out to pull it close up for his father to land. His leg was immediately seized by an alligator, and he was gradually dragged under in spite of the efforts of his father to save him.

There are two kinds. One, the "ghurial," is long-nosed and feeds on fish; the other is the dreaded "mugger," which is snub-nosed and lives on dead animals, occasionally also seizing a goat, a dog, or a man. It makes its way slowly across strips of dry land from one piece of water to another. The tail is used as a weapon as well as the teeth: and one of my servants, when bathing, had his leg badly cut by the stroke of an alligator's tail.

While walking along a footpath on the bank of the Ganges, a *chuprassy* (messenger) with me stopped and pointed ahead to a dark mud-bank close by which we should have passed. I could see nothing at first, even though looking directly at the spot where a large alligator was standing. At last the outline, and the outline only, appeared; and it reminded me at the moment of one of Doré's pictures of a rather malignant-looking antediluvian creature of the same class. It had either chosen that bank because it was of the same colour as itself, or it may have had the power of assuming the colour of the background, as in the case of the vanishing butterfly and other creatures. We gave it a wide berth.

Towards the end of the dry hot weather, when, about the middle of June, the burst of the monsoon and then heavy floods in the Ganges were expected, we looked forward to a slack time and comparative rest, though at an unpleasant season. This we had in 1876; but, in 1877, June passed and then July and the other monsoon months without the usual heavy rains. The deficiency at first caused famine in Madras, and this gradually spread to the North. Extra work, instead of rest, was then our lot, and at a trying time of year. The long hours of standing about in the hot sun and the glare, the clouds of sand blown from the sand-banks, and the many depressing influences of the famine which followed, could not fail to have serious results on the health. So severe was the strain that some of the hard-working subordinate officers suffered much for years afterwards. Narora became a centre at which food was distributed to the famine-stricken, and work given to those who were able to earn money.

It was pitiable to see the state of exhaustion in which some of the villagers arrived from distant parts. If they came during the night they would lie down to sleep till morning; and several times, in the early morning, my attention was directed to dead bodies behind stacks of bricks or near the lime-kilns, where the men had gone for warmth. Apart from our regular work we all helped in various ways, one of which was to personally superintend the feeding of some hundreds of old men, women, children, and others who could not earn their food. My share included about two hundred, and these I had to see fed in the evening. Some called me "Baboo ji," the highest term of respect they were familiar with. Others were full of complaints, and, strange to say, it was sometimes the quality of the food they grumbled at, apparently on the ground that, as it was given by Government, it ought to be of the very best.

IX.

FAMINE.

CAUSE OF FAMINES—RELIEF WORK—GRATUITOUS RELIEF—THE JUBILEE FEAST AT DELHI—POPULATION—GOVERNMENT MEASURES—MOVEMENT OF GRAIN—RAILWAYS—SPECULATION.

THE first alarm of an approaching famine is when, about the middle of June, the monsoon either has not broken at all at Colombo or has begun with only weak winds. From then till about the end of July there is always hope that the wind may increase, and the clouds roll up from the south-west and burst in a satisfactory rainfall; but if August is reached with a weak monsoon or one which is giving all the rain to Assam, Burmah, and other parts where it is not wanted, or the rain is falling mostly on the sea instead of on the land, the result must be either a famine or scarcity.

There are parts of India where want of rain is never felt. At Cherrapunji in Assam the normal fall is about 480 inches a-year. In 1861 the total fall was 805 inches, of which 366 inches fell in July. This may be compared with that of England, which is from twenty-five to seventy inches *in a year*. In Assam, Burmah, parts of Bengal, and tracts of Bombay near the coast, the country is well watered or water-logged, or the climate is humid enough. But most parts of the interior are dependent on the heavy south-west monsoon rains of July, August, and September. The deserts of Rajputana and the Punjaub get practically no rain, and there are some well-populated places, such as Dera Ghazi Khan and Dera Ismail Khan, where the rainfall is only from five to ten inches yearly.

There are, of course, many theories of the causes of famines,—from that which suggests a connection between them and the spots on the sun to one which attributes them to bad administration by the British Government, and the theory of a bishop of Madras that they are God's punishment for the sins and idolatry of the people. On the first hypothesis the famines should recur when the sun-spots are at a maximum, about once in eleven years, and persumably not in one part more than in another; but statistics do not support it. On the second theory it is sought to show that the natives are impoverished by British rule, and are thus rendered less able to pay higher than usual for their food when prices rise. To this it is replied that famines occurred long before British rule, and that they were more destructive than now, as there were not then the means of mitigating them we now have. Though in late famines the number of deaths was large, it would have been much larger had the irrigation works and the network of railways not been on the ground, and if the British Government organisation and the relief sent out from England had not been available. Much of the difficulty in preventing deaths lies in the fact that relief can only be given on a large scale at towns and the more important villages, and on engineering works, which are the centres at which the famine-stricken collect to earn money to buy food or to receive gratuitous relief. Over the area of more than a million square miles in British India there are scattered 1500 towns and 550,000 villages. In the Native States, containing about 680,000 square miles, there are 694 towns and 178,000 villages. Of the total population of nearly 300 millions, about 260 millions live *in the villages.* Some of these villages are in forests and jungles, and in waste, rocky, or swampy tracts where communications are slow. The people are of many religions, castes, and tribes; and they speak altogether about eighty different languages. The workers would have to be a hundred or more times as numerous as they are, in order that all the villages be visited as soon as famine appears, to ascertain where distress exists, and to induce the villagers to come in to the centres where relief is distributed. There are probably tens of thousands of old villagers who have lived in and near their own villages all their lives. I have several times found old men who had never been as far as ten miles from the village in which they were born. These people are frightened at the prospect of going far from home. They hear sometimes of a murder having been committed in a larger village, say twenty miles away, and speak with dread of going to such a place; or vague rumours reach them of the animosity of opposing sects, extortion of petty officials, highway robbers, plague, earthquake, the black water (as they call the sea), and the powers for good and evil of those in authority. In one part of Assam the villagers had heard of no larger place than Gauhati, a town on the Brahmapootra river, and were under the impression that of course the Queen of England lived there. At the Delhi durbar in 1877, when the Queen was proclaimed Empress, it was understood by some that the herald who made the proclamation was the Queen's husband.

The magnitude of the task can be only incompletely estimated when it is considered that, in the famine of 1896, the numbers in receipt of relief were, in June, four millions, and in August had risen to over six millions. In that of 1900 there were in British territory in July nearly five millions, of whom about half were in receipt of gratuitous relief. There were also a million and a half in Native States.

Relief is given by Government to the able-bodied by provision of work, chiefly on construction of earthen banks for railways or dams and collections of road metal; and to those unable to work it is given gratuitously. This is supplemented by the efforts of the missionaries and of others who distribute the funds collected in England and India by private subscription. It is necessary to be careful to give no more than is needed to keep the men alive and in good health, otherwise the relief might attract labourers from parts where they are able to get work and food, and the famine would thus be intensified. Complaints have at times been made by the usual employers of labour that their own operations have been interfered with by the withdrawal of their labourers to go to the relief works. There is also a tendency with a few even to remain on famine work after the necessity has passed away. Men, apparently able-bodied, may be reduced in health by having for some time had less food than usual, and they are not able to do a full day's work when on relief; a minimum wage is therefore fixed and is paid to every worker, however little he does for it.

It is usual in ordinary times to get the earthwork and the collection of road metal and railway ballast done by contract, the contractors engaging the coolies on their own account. In time of famine this will not answer, because the contractors, having to make a profit, will engage only the able-bodied who can do a full day's work.

Among many misrepresentations, it was at one time said that Government made use of a famine to get work done at less than usual rates. The fact is that, for the amounts paid, the work done is only a fraction, sometimes only a small fraction, of what it is at other times; and famine work is very expensive. It has often to be employed on parts of projects which would not otherwise be undertaken at the time, but which would have been put in hand at some future day, the work done having afterwards to lie waiting till more important projects are finished.

As might be expected, the labourers on the relief works do not show interest or energy, and work in a listless way. It is right to get the able-bodied to work a little for the subsistence pay, and probably good for their health. Those who can do so earn extra by doing piece-work or a fuller day's work than the rest. Besides the men, the women and children also work, doing as much or as little as they choose. A man, woman, and two or three children on piece-work, may together earn enough for a much better evening meal than if they relied on the subsistence wages. In ordinary times a man often earns enough to support himself and the members of his family as well. On some famine works there was a large proportion of old men, women, and children, and these, though doing only nominal work, added the minimum famine wage of each to the usual earnings of their bread-winner, making a total which might be greater than was usual at the best of times.

Some of the men reached the Narora works in such a state that at a short distance they looked like skeletons, every rib and the bones of the elbows and knees standing out in sharp outline, and the face appearing like a death's head. I was startled one morning, on riding up to a place where a gang of men were about to move a winch, at being appealed to by one of those who had just arrived to be allowed to join the gang to earn a little money. The overseer remarked that the man was "done for"; but he declared he could pull on the rope. Of course I sent him sharp to where food was distributed free. Many such died of cold or of any illness that came,—fever, pneumonia, and cholera being common; yet some who seemed to be too far gone recovered, while others, apparently well nourished, died soon. Families arrived much exhausted and only just able to creep along, and they brought with them babies with faces like those of very old people. Some of the children when born were merely skin and bone.

When the women were employed on large or scattered works, it was sometimes necessary to make special provision for the care of the youngest children in their absence. One method was to label them to prevent disputes as to ownership. An inspecting officer in 1900 arrived at one of the offices of a large famine camp in Berar, and had brought with him a typewriting machine. The news of this extraordinary novelty spread among the workers, and a crowd of women returned in great haste from the works and hurriedly appropriated their children. The rumour had got abroad that the machine was to be used to operate on them. Probably the scare was a side result of a former visit of the vaccinating officer with his lancet and vaccine tubes.

The cattle suffer dreadfully and die by thousands. It is important to preserve them, if only for their services in ploughing the fields for the next crop and drawing water from the wells when they have any water in them. It is painful to pass in one's rides across the bare parched fields with nothing green left on them, and to be approached by the bulls and goats that move towards us as possibly bringing them some assistance. In the famine of 1877-78 in Madras, the thatch in the roofs in villages was used in a desperate effort to feed and save the cattle.

In the North and in some parts of Southern India the cattle have to go through a time of scarcity every year. For about six weeks during the hottest part of each year, before the rains set in, the country is bare and brown. They get only straw, roots, and leaves to eat, and, if their owners can afford it, a little grain. Within two days after the first fall of rain the country becomes green and the cattle get relief. With the best of monsoons the crops could not be raised without the ploughing, carting, and irrigating done by the bulls and buffaloes. In 1901 there were forty-two million bulls and buffaloes and about the same number of cows and calves. Fourteen million ploughs were in use, and three million carts.

It is sometimes asked whether the natives are grateful for the efforts made on their behalf. Some examples are given in the 'Annual Report on the Progress and Condition of India for 1899-1900.' The majority appear to be indifferent, owing probably to their very passive character; but there are many who do show gratitude in their own quiet way, which may easily be misunderstood by those who have not lived much amongst them. Both in the famine and on occasions of illness I have known cases in which their thanks have been freely given; but it is more usual that they are expressed in a quiet, perhaps almost unnoticeable, manner. When I was travelling in the Himalayas, a man and woman, living in an isolated hut, brought a young child losing its sight and asked for medicine for the eyes. I could do no more than advise frequent bathing, cleanliness of dress, and living much in the fresh air. On leaving I almost missed seeing the slight movement which was intended as a mark of their appreciation of the interest I had shown. A common reason given by beggars to induce one to give alms is that "Your name will become great"—*i.e.*, as a benefactor; and really disinterested sympathy does not always get its due. Of course it is an unimportant point; and in India we never inquire whether gratitude is felt.

The rulers of the Native States do what they can, and rich men distribute food and funds, generally on a fixed day of the week. A mistake often made at this weekly distribution is that it is left too much to head servants or petty officials who distribute injudiciously. A crowd collects, and if there is not intelligent personal supervision, it may be that those most in need, being the weakest, are pushed aside by the stronger, and much of the relief goes to the abler-bodied. When travelling on a length of railway in my charge in the Punjaub during the famine of 1900, I found one Sikh station-master had a small famine fund which he and the station staff had collected among themselves and were administering very well. Their personal supervision ensured the relief going to those who really needed it. Many of the famine-stricken brought out their hidden treasure to be sold. At the Bombay mint in May 1877 as much as £80,000 worth of silver personal jewellery was converted into cash. Some try to get into jail, because there they will at least be fed. In country districts weeds and shrubs not before used for food were eaten. The prickly pear, for example, which grows wild and is used for hedging, was found to be, though inferior, a food for cattle when chopped up and for men when boiled.

As an illustration of the difficulty a casual cold weather visitor naturally finds in understanding the conditions of life in India, it may be related that in the famine of 1877 at one camp there were 1300 or 1400 destitute people collected for shelter and relief. Many visitors came to offer sympathy and assistance; but the natives refused milk and other food offered by ladies and other philanthropists, and clamoured to have the provisions prepared by their own caste people. Knowing the feeling of the natives in the matter of caste and pollution of their food if touched by us, English people settled in India do not offer assistance in the shape which appears natural in the eyes of casual visitors from England, and they sometimes get charged by them with want of sympathy.

The really effective efforts that are being made are not seen by tourists. The able-bodied being provided for by enabling them to get work and wages enough to live and keep in health, those less able are not at all forgotten. In addition to the gratuitous relief given by Government, there is that provided from the funds collected in England and India by private subscription. These are used for subsidiary relief to add small comforts in the way of clothing and extra food for the sick, infirm, aged, children, and destitute widows; to provide for orphans, to relieve the thousands of the poorer *purdah* women and respectable persons who would rather endure great privation than come to the relief works, and to help to restore to their homes and their original position people who had lost their all in the famine. The helpless orphans left by those who had died before relief could reach them were, in some cases, placed in missionary orphanages. One might think that the missionaries could hardly use their funds in a better way; but, though a perfectly natural and humane proceeding, it laid them open to the charge of making use of the famine to proselytise. One feels inclined to ask if the missionaries should have left the children to die.

A free meal or feast is so unusual that, when one is offered, it is eagerly looked forward to and long remembered. If a public one, crowds come to it, wait for hours, and go to great inconvenience to secure it,—even some who are fairly well to do. During the famine of 1897 I was stationed at Delhi and was able to do something, as did many other English residents, to help the Rev. Stephen Thomas, of the Baptist Mission, on the occasion of a feast given to the poor on Queen Victoria's Jubilee. He also distributed Rs. 18,000 in famine relief to *purdah* ladies and respectable families, who were unable to work. Three-quarters of these were Mahomedans, the Hindus of Delhi being better off. The Hindu families relieved had often to break their caste even by merely accepting the tickets for relief. Much contempt was expressed for some of the richer Hindus who had refused to assist in the relief, though some had subscribed at first owing to panic, as they feared the famine-stricken would riot and loot their property.

Mr Thomas had started special shops at which he had grain sold at low prices to those to whom tickets authorising them to purchase had been distributed. These tickets enabled them to buy sixteen *seers* (equal to thirty-two pounds) of grain for one rupee, the market price at the *bunnias*' (grain-dealers') shops being only eleven *seers* for a rupee. It was found that the men in charge attempted to make money by giving light weight, and that some of the people relieved were not really in want, but had taken the tickets in order to sell them to the *bunnias*, who bought the grain at the reduced price and sold it again at their own shops at famine prices. One strange result of the famine in Delhi was that at one time the rate for *coarse* grain rose higher than that for the usually more expensive wheat, because the coarser grain was being bought for seed for the next crop.

On 23rd June 1897 the Jubilee feast was given in the Queen's gardens. Up to twelve o'clock upwards of 8000 had come in, and there were crowds at the gates. To some it was merely a show and a gala day; but to the poorest it was a real boon. Many of these no doubt were shut out. In the press of the crowd several were hurt, and there were some very aged, some deformed, and a few lepers. More police than usual were present, as a rush was feared: and faction fights have frequently occurred at Delhi. They kept the crowds seated in rows while waiting, and in line as they passed on to the place where the food was distributed. Some had to wait for hours for their turn, but in the end were served with a really good meal.

White tickets had been given out for men and brown ones for women. Several men came with brown tickets, their women probably fearing to come, and having sent some of their male relatives instead; or some of the men may have stolen the women's tickets. Some tore their tickets in half so as to admit two instead of one. Others, finding that a white piece of paper had the power to ensure admission, brought any piece of old newspaper roughly about the size of the tickets, and tried to get in with it. There were also several attempts to get in a second time.

The cause of famines being primarily the failure or partial failure of the monsoon, it is probable, seeing how often this has happened in late years, that in earlier times there were many famines and years of scarcity which have not been recorded. They were, in some cases, probably much more severe owing to want of proper communications; and in others they may have been mitigated by the fact that the grain locally raised could not be freely exported as it is now. There have been serious famines in China, Persia, Egypt, and Ireland; and in India there were famines before the British took over the government. The first of which there is trustworthy record was that of 1769-70 in the lower valley of the Ganges, when practically one-third of the population of Bengal perished. In 1780-83 there was the great Karnatic famine: and there were nine others before 1860. In none of these was there much done by the State in the way of relief, and little of the country was under British control.

After the Mutiny in 1857 the British took over the government; and the first famine they had to deal with was that of 1860-61, when relief was organised on a large scale. In that of 1865-66, in Orissa, relief was given at a cost of £1,700,000; but about a quarter of the population died, because Orissa was isolated, and no importation of food quick enough was possible either by land or sea. In the famine of 1873-74, in Behar, the area was comparatively small, and it was found possible, by expending £6,500,000 sterling and importing a million tons of rice, to save all lives. Then came the famine of 1876-77-78, at first in Madras, but afterwards also in the North-West Provinces and other parts. There had been no such complete failure of the crops for forty years. Government spent about £10,000,000 to meet it, and had heavy indirect losses. The system of relief work had not yet been fully established, and three-quarters of the famine-stricken were relieved gratuitously. In response to an appeal originated by Mr Digby, £800,000 was subscribed in England. 268,000 tons of grain were imported by land and 166,000 tons by sea. How serious such a famine is may be judged from the fact that in Madras alone the births fell from 632,000 in 1876 to 348,000 in 1878.

Since then there have been two other serious famines—viz., in 1895-96 and in 1900, besides an occasional year of scarcity. In 1895 a deficient monsoon was followed by failure of the winter rains. Early in November it was estimated by the Government of India that an area containing eighty or ninety millions of people would be affected. Though a little rain fell in December and January, famine set in over tracts containing forty-four millions, and by June 1896 there were over four millions in receipt of relief. That of 1900 was even worse, for by August of that year there were six and a quarter millions.

The cutting of timber for use on railways and public and private works, the burning of forests and long grass by nomad and hill tribes, and other minor matters, have a small influence on the rainfall; and they are trifling compared with the great forces acting between the two hemispheres. The Forest Department is engaged now in preserving forests and planting trees. An influence much farther reaching is that of the action of the grain-dealers, who, for their private and, in the present state of the law, legitimate gain, keep back the stores of food they have in hand in the prospect of the scarcity increasing and their being able to command higher prices. There are large stores of grain in the granaries of the rich *bunnias* (grain-dealers), and the poorer natives know it. Riots and looting of these stores are at times a danger. The course of trade cannot well be interfered with. When a famine breaks out, much of the grain on the spot may be already sold for export to foreign countries or other parts of India; and cases have been known of grain being imported from distant parts of the country to meet the famine, while other grain was being sent away from the same place to comply with agreements already made.

An agricultural population is generally a poor one; and as three-fifths or more of the natives of India are agriculturists depending on the seasons, and many deeply in debt to the money-lender, there are millions who have little margin to meet emergencies. A rise of prices therefore means that less food can be purchased. For this reason it has been said that the famines are money famines rather than food famines; and famine relief is nearly always given in the shape of money. Famine is really only a weak check on population. Births are fewer. The necessity of living on less food and coarser kinds lowers the vitality; and pneumonia and fever in the cold weather, cholera and dysentery in the hot weather, more easily affect those with badly nourished bodies. Reckoning over long periods of years, the extra deaths caused by the famine are only about two per thousand; but cholera, dysentery, fever, and plague carry off about thirty per thousand each year.

A famine never affects the whole, and rarely even the greater part, of India. Of the 1,762,000 square miles, more than a million are under British administration. Of this about 200,000,000 acres are waste and uncultivable and forest land. 70,000,000 acres are devoted to rice cultivation, 107,000,000 acres to other food grains (wheat, barley, millet, pulse, &c.), and 39,000,000 acres to other crops (oil-seeds, cotton, jute, indigo, opium, sugar, tea, tobacco, &c.) In the famine year 1899-1900, the total area under crops in British territory fell to 180,000,000 acres, and under rice and grain to 165,000,000 acres. In that year, £50,000,000 worth less than usual was raised of the total of £270,000,000, the average annual value of the crops.

Some of the tracts in which these crops are raised are well watered and always free from famine; and of the rest about 33,000,000 acres are irrigated. About 100,000,000 or 120,000,000 acres of the cultivated area are dependent on the monsoon; and as this area is scattered over the Punjaub, North-West Provinces, Bombay, Bengal, and Madras, it is highly improbable that the whole would be thrown out of cultivation at the same time by total failure of the monsoon over every part.

Though the areas liable to be affected are small in comparison with the area of the whole country, many of them are densely populated, for they are the homes of the agricultural classes. So far from the famines depopulating the country, the statistics for British India show that in the ten years ending 1901, during which there had been two severe famines, the increase was more than 10,000,000, or 4½ per cent. Over Bengal the average density is 413 per square mile, and in several large agricultural districts the villages are so near that the density is from 600 to 900 to the square mile. Even this falls much short of the density in one of the Taluqs of the Cochin State, where there are 1920 per square mile. In that district, however, there is heavy and regular rainfall,—the serious consideration in Bengal being the liability to failure of the rains. The average over the whole of British India is 213 per square mile, and in Native States about 90.

Famine time is one of anxiety for Government, and excessive work for the officials. The measures for meeting it have to be rapidly organised; and what this means among the scattered villages, the enormous areas, and the millions of people accustomed to a fixed simple daily routine, can be known only to those who have dealt with them. The existing administrative and executive organisation must be, to some extent, diverted from their usual duties; and these have to be carried on by officials who may have already as much as they can well attend to. The kind of relief works most suitable for each part affected, the agency by which the works are to be executed and the relief distributed, the hurrying up of the food supplies from the distant markets, and all the other arrangements for coping with the dearth, have all to be carefully considered at Calcutta or Simla by the administrative authorities, and then energetically put into working order by the executive officials.

In 1900, when famine came, Lord Curzon offered loans on easy terms to the Native States that wanted money, and the services of engineers and doctors. Some of the Maharajahs of Rajputana availed themselves of the offer; and much extra relief to Rajput, Bhil, and Marwari peasantry was thereby made possible under the good management of Sir Pertab Singh and other Native ministers, aided by experienced English officers whose services were lent for the purpose. Nearly a million pounds were lent to the Native States of Rajputana and Bombay, and a guarantee was given for the repayment of another £700,000, borrowed in the market by other Native States.

The principles on which it is best to proceed have been enunciated from time to time in the light of experience of several famines. In 1875 it was said, in a Government of India Resolution dealing with the scarcity of 1873-74: "It is only where there is a great deficiency, and there is also reason to believe that traders will be unable to meet that deficiency, that it is right for the State to interfere for the purpose of supplementing the general food supply"; and Lord Northbrook's Government decided that famines can no longer be treated as abnormal or exceptional calamities, but must be recognised as to be provided for as ordinary charges of the State. It was decided that, in making provision for the wants of the administration, yearly provision against possible famine must enter into the calculations.

In his Financial Statement in 1877-78, Sir J. Strachey said that a fundamental maxim of Government is "to abstain absolutely from all interference with trade, and that this is the only way in which we can feel confident that everything which it is possible to do to bring food to the starving population will be done."

He stated that, Government having acted on that principle during the 1877 famine, the result was an immense activity in the grain trade and "railway stations in districts two thousand miles away encumbered with grain awaiting the means of transport, and our ports filled with ships destined to bear to the starving millions the plenty of happier regions. Not only traders, but people of all classes rushed into the grain market and bought up food for future need or for future sale. In this way prices went up very suddenly, it is true, but high prices are at such times the salvation of a country. Consumption, not essential, is sternly checked, and the reduction of stocks is lessened until a rise in prices with the accompanying prospects of profits to producers and traders leads to importation from without."

The arrival of the new supplies of grain may,

however, be much delayed by congestion of traffic on the railways. In the meantime famine prices rule, and the poorest suffer. When in September 1877 Sir R. Temple was pressed by the townspeople to establish a fixed price of grain and compel all shopkeepers to adhere to it, he very properly replied that the Government would not interfere, for the immediate result would be that no grain would come into the market, and the last state would be worse than the first.

The main principles in distributing Government relief are that, as a rule, no gratuitous relief be given to persons able to work, and that, when given, it shall only be such as is required to keep a non-labouring person alive and in good health; that all who can do so shall perform a certain reasonable task for the relief given, and that extra comforts are not to be provided except for the sick. The subsistence quantity of food was estimated in 1877 as a pound and a half of grain per man per day; and Government keeps a close watch on the health of the people in the relief camps and, as far as possible, on the condition of the cattle. After the famine Government still assists the cultivators by making advances to enable them to buy seed for the next crop and cattle for ploughing, and by remitting or suspending the rent due for land. Government is the chief landlord, and the land tax (or rent) is the chief item of Government revenue. In 1902, £1,300,000 of land revenue was remitted. In addition to these heavy expenses and the wages paid on the relief works and in gratuitous relief, there are losses of railway receipts from goods and passengers and of customs dues owing to paralysis of trade in Manchester goods and other imports.

Under pressure of high prices the cultivators naturally endeavour to borrow money and will agree to pay exorbitant interest. There are plenty of money-lenders ready to take advantage of them where there is a prospect of their ultimately getting a large proportion of the interest. The chronic indebtedness of the small landholders is intensified, and there is a tendency for the land to pass out of the hands of the agriculturists into those of the money-lender at unfair low rates. It is difficult for Government to interfere as fully as could be wished; but there has been some legislation to prevent this growing indebtedness of the ryots and the disposal of their landed property.

By means of "protective" railways, as distinguished from productive ones on which profits are expected, and by means of a large extension of irrigation, much has been done already, and is still being arranged to mitigate the severity of famines. The Famine Insurance Fund was started in 1878. It was decided to put aside yearly a million and a half sterling for construction of protective works whenever a surplus large enough was available. In years of deficit or special demands absorbing all surplus, the fund was of course not available. When that was so there was no appropriation of the Famine Insurance Fund for other purposes, as was once charged against the Government of India by people who were either prejudiced or unable to understand the Budget figures. It simply did not exist.

The cost of a famine being each time several million sterling, it would be interesting to find out what, over a number of years, is the average cost per year per thousand of the population, and to compare it with the cost of relieving paupers in England. Apart from the expenditure on famines, there is practically no indoor or outdoor relief of paupers by the State in India. The natives look after their own poor without resort to the State. At the time of the 1877 famine, which cost more than ten millions sterling, the charge for pauper relief in England was seven millions sterling per year. In 1900 the figures were four and a quarter millions sterling for famine relief in India, and about eleven millions for poor relief in England.

That the normal course of trade should not be interfered with by Government action was not a principle with the rulers in old days. There are still the remains of a huge granary built at Patna in Bengal, with the inscription, "For the perpetual prevention of famine in these provinces." In Pondicherry, the French Government in famine time strictly forbid the export of food grains, and they suspend the duty on imported grain. The Government of India prefers to rely on high prices naturally inducing the grain-dealers to pour grain into the districts where famine exists, and in thus competing with the local dealers to force them to lower the prices of the grain on the spot.

Before the famine of 1877-78 about 6000 miles of broad-gauge railways had been constructed and 1000 miles of metre gauge, at a cost of more than £100,000,000. They were, however, only equipped for ordinary traffic, and had not sufficient rolling stock and other necessaries to meet the sudden huge demand, and they were therefore unable to carry all the grain offered for immediate consignment to the famine districts. At some stations the platforms were for weeks loaded up with grain awaiting transit.

In that year it was estimated that a million and a half tons of food grains were carried into the famine districts from other parts of India, and that the producing and trading classes of those parts made by it a clear profit of six millions sterling. As Sir J. Strachey remarked at the time, these railways saved millions of lives. The export of wheat, however, to Europe was in that year larger than ever before.

In later famines the exports of wheat have fallen considerably, owing probably to the greater facilities now available for supplying the affected districts by rail. Instead of there being only 7000 miles of railways as in 1877-78, there are now 25,823 miles laid down and equipped at a cost of about £225,000,000, and there are 2440 miles more under construction or sanctioned. The excessive high rates of grain which prevailed in former famines were unknown in that of 1900-1; and this, together with the fact that the exports of wheat fell from 10,000,000 cwt. in 1899-1900 to only 50,000 cwt. in 1900-1, showed that the railways were working well. Instead of exporting their normal quantity of 250,000 tons of grain, the British provinces affected by famine imported 2,500,000 tons, and the Native States of Rajputana and Central India imported 800,000 tons. Such a movement of grain would have been impossible without the railways.

The beneficial results in famine time of this large extension of railways are now apparent, and the foresight of the administrators in the 'Seventies in refusing to interfere with the course of trade is being justified. In those times the producing and trading classes were enriched, and the poorer agriculturalists and those with fixed incomes suffered. Speculators seemed then to be able to do what they liked with the market, and caused loss of life by suddenly raising prices beyond the means of many of the consumers. In November 1877 it was reported in the 'Civil and Military Gazette':—

> "Not an hour passes without constant messages on the subject of grain; and money, with a ten per cent rate on it, is so continuously remitted by telegraph, that in one telegraph office in this province (Punjaub) a clear profit to Government of Rs. 2000 was made in one day. In the neighbouring station a fall of rain in the morning lowered the price of grain from 16 to 20 *seers*, causing great activity in speculation. A further fall to 26 *seers* occurred at midday on receipt of a telegram that rain was falling heavily in the district to which the grain was mainly

sent. A merchant who had bought dear and held back for a fall is reported to have committed suicide. Two hours after news came that the rain had cleared off, and bright sunshine came out. Up rose the price again to 20 *seers:* and another merchant boasts that he had cleared in three hours over two lakhs of rupees (£13,333). The amount may be exaggerated, but there is no doubt that speculation and profits have of late been enormous."

In some Native States the *bunnias* (grain-dealers) have not the power allowed them under British rule, and get punished for trying to corner the market. Refusal of Government to interfere in the course of trade will probably be best in the end; but it does seem hard that in the meantime, when lives are at stake, Government has no power to buy up at normal rates for use on relief works a part of the increased crops raised by irrigation. Irrigation works on a large scale have been constructed at great cost, specially in view of the need to meet famines; yet speculators have the right to raise the price of their grain, and to send abroad as much as they please even in famine time.

In the famine of 1900 in one town of the Punjaub, after heavy rain had at last fallen, I inquired from some of the local grain-dealers if prices had been reduced, and was informed that they had received orders from Calcutta not to reduce the price yet.

There is a little interference by Government, as grain consigned to the famine districts is given preference over all other traffic on the railways. When it is considered politic to do so Government does interfere, as in the matters of the currency value of the rupee, the coolie emigration to the tea-gardens of Assam, and the seizure of the tools of the agriculturalist for debt.

In one part of Madras a successful experiment was made with long lines of men carrying food-supplies on their heads from Bellary to the Kaladgi relief works, a distance of 140 miles. Lines of bullock-carts are probably used in the same way in parts where railways do not serve.

In future it may be possible to foretell sooner and more accurately than hitherto the approach of the famine. That of 1900 was predicted early by Mr Hutchins, a meteorologist of Cape Colony, who had studied the atmospheric conditions there with reference to their probable effect on the monsoon rainfall of India.

X.

LIFE IN TOWNS.

OFFICE WORK—CLUBS—MESSES—TOWN *VERSUS* JUNGLE—HOTELS—BUNGALOWS—TRANSFERS—OFFICIALS—THE DOCTOR—LITIGATION—COMMITTEES—NATIVE GENTLEMEN—ACCOUNTANTS AND CLERKS—EURASIANS—SOCIAL GATHERINGS—COOKS—THE BAZAAR—SHOPPING—*TAMÂSHAS*—JUGGLERS—PROCESSIONS—WEDDINGS—WIDOWS—FAKIRS—LEPERS—CHILDREN—SCHOOLS.

THE life we lead in towns is very different from that already described. Early rising and retiring are not so necessary, and only those who have outdoor work as well as office work need be early risers. Still, especially in the hot weather, the hours kept are earlier than usual in England.

The chief occupation of the day being one's office duties, which begin nominally at ten o'clock and end at four, there is plenty of time available for recreation and social gathering, except when, as often happens, the work keeps one later at office, and even requires attention at odd times during the evening. For some, but these are rare cases, there is little leisure from morning to night. Every one, however, has to hold himself ready to attend to urgent work at any time; the first and most important object being to keep the affairs of each department and each branch of it current, up to date, and in good working order. Arrears and confusion in one may interfere with work in other branches and cause far-reaching inconvenience.

As a rule the routine works smoothly, and that gives most of us leisure for the early morning ride, and leaves us free in the evening for tennis or racquets or other amusement before dinner, and a game of cards or billiards, and perhaps some music, afterwards.

Those who are not very liable to sudden orders of transfer to long distances, and who feel fairly stationary for a year or two, settle down in comfort in one of the houses usually available. There is always a garden attached, generally one of considerable size, and a set of stables adjoining the servants' quarters. Those whose stay is uncertain, besides bachelors and those married men whose wives are in England or up in the hills, often find it best to live at the Club or an hotel, if there is one worth living at.

In the hottest months and the most unhealthy ones most ladies go to the hill stations, and then town life is not so bright: but there is always something going on, tennis or billiard tournaments, whist or bridge, and when the weather will allow, races and sports. Where there is a regiment stationed these matters are well looked after, and the band is an addition to the pleasures of life. In the cold season, when the ladies have returned, the "At Homes," dances, garden-parties, and other pleasant gatherings are frequent.

On arrival at one of these "stations," as they are called, where officials are located, whether in large numbers in towns or only a few in isolated parts, a man's first duty, after taking charge of his office, is to make the acquaintance of those already there. In the larger places are a Governor or Lieut.-Governor, or a Chief Commissioner, Collector, or other official of the Civil administration, a General, and others on whom one should call by recording one's name in their visiting-books; and, in smaller places, the chief magistrate and other leading officials. After calling on them, one drives round the station to call on others whose acquaintance is wished for; and these, in the smaller stations, consist of all the officials and non-officials one is likely to meet at the Club or elsewhere. If a *persona grata*, or even if only "not a bad sort," invitations follow to dinners, "At Homes," and other social gatherings. There is a genial friendly welcome, and so one becomes a member of the community. Some one puts you up for the Club, and you may be honoured with an invitation to consider yourself an honorary member of one or more of the Messes.

In calling it is usual, but in some parts only, to leave a card for the sahib and one for each member of his family—or it was at one time. One new arrival wanted to know what he was to do when calling on a native gentleman. He was told by a professional joker that he should do the same; and as in one case a Nawab in the station had eighteen wives, he was of course to leave nineteen cards. At Calcutta, Sunday is the day for calling, and when visiting there

I was shown the cards of the Chinese ambassador and his party, who had just gone. They were much larger than a lady's card, and the names were printed small in one of the lower corners, the rest of the card being blank.

Some there are who prefer camp life, or, at least, life in the more solitary parts. They care little for the society of ladies or for Clubs, and prefer the opportunities for activity and sport to be had in the jungles. Others find station life expensive, or object to the inconvenience of routine and the formalities and regularity required. One's house must be well furnished, the garden kept in good order, the servants properly dressed at one's own expense; one's clothing must be of a kind not so *néglige* and comfortable as can be worn in camp, and a good and perhaps expensive dog-cart or other turn-out must be kept.

Whatever individual opinion may be, it is probably admitted by most people that a social life is better than isolation. At the Clubs, the Messes and the gatherings, one exchanges ideas and learns a good deal, besides having the hard corners of one's own individuality rounded off. There is less likelihood of becoming morbid or out of sorts, and the extra pleasure of life among friends adds vigour to one's vitality. In the jungles the risk of illness is greater, or, at least, the risk of its being allowed to weaken the system too far before effectual medical aid can be obtained.

At the Clubs and Messes it is interesting to

meet leading public men and to hear their well-considered and matured opinions on public questions; whereas in the jungles, the newspaper, arriving irregularly perhaps, is the only source of such information. Towards the end of a long service it was rather strange to meet again at these centres the friends and acquaintances of twenty or more years before, whose paths had deviated from my own, and who had, in the meantime, developed from young "griffs" into staid, courteous, and experienced old Collectors or Colonels.

It is rarely dull in a station unless one has become run down in health by too long a spell of work in a trying part without a trip to the hills or a furlough to England. There are so many ways in which amusement and interest can be found apart from one's duties. Even a walk through the bazaar may afford new and curious examples of Eastern life, however often one may have been there before. Such a diversion, however, is seldom resorted to if others are available. Hobbies—and most Europeans in India have one or more—are a good stand-by as an antidote to ennui. For those who paint or take photos there are innumerable opportunities; and one can be in few parts of India where the collector of curios need be at a loss for occupation.

Some useful extra work in the interests of one's own set of friends or of the community may be taken up. There are the library, the public gardens, the photographic and other societies to be kept going, the Volunteer movement to be encouraged and organised, local branches of missions to be helped, and philanthropic efforts in the shape of Friend-in-need societies, Women's workshops, Y.M.C.A., S.P.C.A., and Lady Dufferin's fund. If required to serve on a District or Cantonment Committee, even there not only interest but amusement too can be found.

Living at hotels is to be avoided, as the rooms, the meals, and the servants are inferior. Even in hotels it is usual to keep two or three of one's own servants to ensure fairly satisfactory arrangements. One's own bungalow is far more comfortable; but there is the risk of receiving any day an urgent telegram to proceed some hundred of miles away on transfer to a new station. This may be rendered necessary by the sudden illness of another official whose duties require early attention, and for whose post no one else is available. It means, however, having to pay up a month's rent, selling off one's furniture at a loss, and sometimes one's horses and trap. A little compensation may come in extra allowances in the new post or a temporary promotion. The most annoying case is when the new post proves to be only an officiating one for a few months till a new permanent holder is appointed; and one is then ordered back again to begin afresh, uncertain whether for a stay long enough to make it worth while to go to the expense of setting up again in comfort, or whether it is better to live in "camp style" or at an hotel and to depend on hired horses and conveyances. If the latter is decided on, it may be found that one's stay is prolonged, and it would have been as well to take a bungalow.

If one is fairly settled in a place the bungalow can be made cosy, and the garden filled with handsome shrubs and flowers which would be much admired could they be grown in an English garden.

It often happens, as in my own case, that it is only two or three times in one's service that such comfort is to be had,—our lives being too much ruled by the need to move about over great distances and at short notice. Those whose duties locate them for long periods in one part, and who do get home comforts, have several times told me that they envied my style of life because I had the opportunity of seeing so much. Certainly there are advantages in both kinds of life; and in the course of my travels on duty, or transfer, or leave, I have been able to see most of the interesting towns and scenes of India.

There are certain officials, some or most of whom are always found in a Civil station: the chief Civil authority, who is a Deputy Commissioner or a Collector, and his assistants, the Medical officer, the Engineer, the Postal and Telegraph officers, the Forest officer, and the Police Superintendent. From them useful information is got showing the workings of Government in matters outside one's own special branch. The Medical officer is the one who has all of us in his charge in matters of health and leave on medical certificate. A visit now and then with him to the jail is instructive. He is in charge of the jail, as he has to look after the health of the prisoners and the sanitary arrangements generally. There may be some troublesome characters in hand, such as dacoits or Thugs; but generally speaking the prisoners are quiet and easily managed. It is thought by some that they are too well treated, for many of them are apparently as contented in jail as out of it; and it is a standing joke that when a prisoner is troublesome, the most effective way of making him behave himself is to threaten to turn him out of the jail.

The doctor's duties are at times arduous and constant. His hospital and dispensary, jail and daily rounds, must afford almost daily troublesome cases requiring attention to offensive details. The poorer natives go freely to the dispensary for medicines, but they look with horror on the hospital as a place where people get their arms and legs cut off. In some towns there are the training hospitals established by Lady Dufferin, to teach native and Eurasian women to become doctors and nurses, and so ensure qualified attendance on the Zenana ladies; and there are the homes of the "Nursing Sisters," established by Lady Roberts for attention to sick English soldiers.

A visit to the Court of the magistrate or judge is not altogether enjoyable. The atmosphere is never pleasant, owing to the crowd of all sorts collected in the rooms and outside. The work of the magistrate must be tedious, and at times exasperating. The time of the Court is much wasted by pleaders and witnesses; and the task of getting at the truth is often almost hopeless. Apart from the natural inaccuracy of the lower classes of natives, and their tendency to work round and round the point at issue, there is the trouble caused by professional false witnesses. In 'The Calcutta Review' of April 1895, Baboo Kailas Chunder Kanjilal, B.L., writes:—

> "The Courts are infested by a set of touters or pettifoggers who corrupt the very fountain of justice by distorting the facts of evidence, and by other nefarious practices, which, despite stringent penal provisions, these detestable pests carry on with impunity."

It has been said that the natives of India are very litigious; but this has been denied, the large number of cases being considered as not out of proportion to the population. Not including those relating to the rent law and immoveable property, there are annually 1,200,000 suits for money and moveable property in British India alone, and numerous appeals. In 1900 there were nearly a million sentenced to fines and terms of imprisonment, most of the fines and periods being small; but 45,000 were sentenced to be whipped, and 592 to death. In one way the free and full use of the power to litigate is an excellent thing, for it familiarises all classes with the fact that justice is available; and the poorest, and those who before were defenceless, need not now submit tamely and hopelessly to rapacious petty officials, money-lenders, and other tyrants.

Local Committees control the expenditure of Municipal and other local funds, and see that the communications, sanitary arrangements, water supply, and such important matters are properly attended to. There are native members on these committees, and some of them take much interest in the work. On the Cantonment Committee at Secunderabad there were several, and they were really interested and useful. In some of the largest towns the committees are almost wholly of natives, especially in Bengal, where the Baboos are well educated and take interest in local affairs. There is, however, among them a certain want of business aptitude, and their zeal is at times neutralised by spells of apathy. The final result is sometimes meagre compared with the apparent effort, the state of the district roads and the sanitation not being such as to warrant the expenditure incurred, and the intentions expressed in speeches at the committee meetings. They have not yet full ability to work together,—religious and caste prejudice interfering, and their too great deference to custom. This will gradually right itself; but, in the meantime, Local Self-Government is only a partial success. It is not wholly the fault of the members of the committee, but partly owing to the dislike of the masses of the people to the necessary changes, especially when inspection of their private premises is to be made in the interests of sanitation. British methods refuse to recognise the family claims of hereditary office-seekers, who may be quite unfit to deal with local matters in a practical way, and give rights to low-caste people which they never had before. There seems to be in some parts much more racial antagonism towards one another than towards Europeans.

Sanitary measures are resisted most by the poor and ignorant. At first towards the measures taken to check the plague there was strong opposition even on the part of the more educated and intelligent; but this gave way before the evident need for them and the utility of the methods adopted, and segregation and disinfectants are now approved by the leading men. In another matter there has been an advance in Bengal, more real and radical than could have been hoped for, in the rejection of idolatrous rites, and the distinctions of caste by the progressive Brahmins, led by Baboo Keshub Chunder Sen and the Brahmo Samaj.

The native gentlemen we meet—the educated Baboos of Bengal, those of the North among whom the term Baboo is not used, the Hindu Rajahs, and Mahomedan Nawabs,—all are most polite in their manner towards us. When we go to their houses on business, or as guests at one of their entertainments, they treat us as if our visit had been a long-expected pleasure. In some places it is the custom to offer us small presents, such as a bottle of scent, and to put garlands of strong-scented white jasmine flowers round our necks.

Some of the older established houses of the native noblemen are on antiquated lines, and, though interesting, are not attractive. There may be a handsome gateway leading into a courtyard, with carved pillars and cornices and ornamental walls, and a verandah round an open space in which are a fountain and a few shrubs and birds. But the ornamentation is broken in places and discoloured, the fountain is small and untidy, the shrubs poor and straggling. In one of these yards the birds I saw were well-kept parrots in costly cages, and a handsome peacock; but there were also two or three naked children, a hookah, a very ugly bedstead belonging to one of the servants, and a heap of refuse which should have long ago been cleared away. The houses are badly lighted, the windows being few and small; and the general arrangements give no promise of comfort. There is usually in the centre of the main room a good chandelier with hanging glass prisms; and there may be costly pieces of furniture side by side with English penny prints and coloured supplements of Christmas numbers in good frames. There is sure to be a musical box, and often an ancient piano or harmonium, or both.

The owners of such houses are not of the advanced modern type of native gentlemen. In the houses of those of modern tastes everything is good, comfortable, and up-to-date. It is a pleasure to visit them, and to talk and dine with them. With those of the older school there are various formalities anxiously considered: for instance, how far it is correct to advance in welcoming or parting from a guest, whether to the door of the room or to the top of the staircase or farther, according to his degree of importance. There may have been details of conduct expected by them from their guests which, through ignorance, I failed to comply with. Those of the later school have no such formalities, and welcome a guest heartily just as an English host would: and brandy-and-soda and cigars take the place of scent and *âtta* and *pân*.

Some of the native gentlemen are good sportsmen, polo-players, and cricketers; but few play tennis or billiards, though the markers become first-rate at these games. I only heard of one native gentleman taking to billiards at a club in the North-West Provinces, and he, it is said, never won because he considered it best fun to aim at the pockets.

At the Government House "At Homes," and at the levées and durbars, native gentlemen are seen in their best array. They come in numbers to these gatherings and to the garden-parties; but unfortunately they cannot bring their wives and other female relations. It is to be hoped that this tyranny of the harem and the zenana will soon pass away: and it is known that several native gentlemen are in favour of giving their ladies some of the social pleasures and freedom which English ladies enjoy. They, however, cannot move in the matter while the majority are strongly opposed to the change.

In our offices the accountants and clerks work steadily, and are reliable as soon as they have mastered the rules and routine. Once they have done so they themselves insist strictly on what may or may not be done; and no deviation from the Code rules is, in their opinion, even to be thought of without at least a Government order from authority higher than that of the officer under whom they are serving. This is well; and we can rely on irregularities being brought to notice. Any necessary latitude is therefore checked, and is only passed on proper authority. The office routine goes on like clockwork except in case of some special disorganising occurrence. So regular is some of the work that I have had a messenger, one little removed above an ordinary coolie, when bringing papers to me for signature, point out the place where the Baboo said my signature was to be. The man had probably noted the blank spaces, had seen what was usually done, and looked on the officer in charge as the final automaton in the series.

The men are regular in their attendance except when some family event requires that leave be applied for. Besides regular leave they are allowed casual leave when urgently required, as in case of a birth, death, or marriage in their families. Sometimes the written applications are amusing, and, on rare occasions, they are evident attempts at shirking work. Cases occur in which the reasons given on former occasions have been looked up over a long period, and it has been found that a man has already several times had leave on account of the death of his grandmother, a very important member of the Hindu family circle.

For bad carelessness or other default a small fine is now and then imposed, but occasionally remitted on representation of large family expenses or indebtedness. In one case a clerk pleaded for remission of a fine of one rupee, on the ground of his having a large family to support, and a few days afterwards he spent some hundreds of rupees on fireworks, sweetmeats, and dinners to the Brahmin priests on the occasion of his son's wedding. These heavy expenses they are obliged by custom to incur though they can ill afford them, and even have to go into heavy debt for life.

There are generally in the larger offices a few English and Eurasian subordinates who manage some of the more important sections and the preparation of plans and estimates. The word "Eurasian" is the first half of the word "Europe" prefixed to the word "Asian,"—Eurasians being those who are partly of European and partly Asian parentage. Though they are born in India and stay all their lives there, yet they live like Europeans and speak of England as "home."

The higher classes of Eurasians are well educated, and obtain Government posts or engage in farming and trade. Naturally they have only crude ideas of life outside India, for they rarely travel. One Eurasian gentleman told me that, from pictures and descriptions, he felt sure he had a clear idea of what the sea is like. I found, however, that he was much astray, and that it was better not to try to undeceive him. He also told me that he would not like to be then (in 1878) in London because of the Whitechapel murders. Another, a tea-planter who had never left India, had made money, and decided it was time to see England. On being asked what he would do when he got there, he replied that he had quite decided to buy tents as soon as he arrived and go up country.

The poorer Eurasians are rarely robust or active, and are in an unenviable position, as they have to live more among the natives and much in native style. Some, on account of their partial European descent, assume an attitude of great superiority towards the natives, with the result that they incur their dislike and contempt.

Besides the larger social gatherings, there are the meetings of friends at one or another's houses for tennis or badminton before dinner, and music or a game of whist afterwards. These are some of the pleasantest of my recollections. Had it not been for them many more of the evenings alone in my bungalow would have been dreary, as indeed they often were. At the houses of the married folks are the English children not already gone to England for their education. They must be sent home in time to avoid any permanent ill effects of the climate, and certain bad influences they are subject to in mixing, as they must, with the native servants. In an article in vol. xcv. of 'The Calcutta Review' on "A Girl's Life in India a Hundred Years Ago," Mrs Sherwood speaks strongly of the evil put into her mind by the native servants, which she was never able wholly to forget. In the more healthy parts, on the plateaux and in the hills, the children of purely English parents are vigorous enough, and are a terror to the natives, whom they worry, and who do not understand such independence and mischief in young folks. As a rule, in the plains the want of the bracing air of England or the hills is seen in the pale faces and listless or fretful manners of the children. In old days, when England could not be so easily reached, they stayed late or altogether in India; and the results are seen in their numerous graves in the older churchyards.

Once, but once only, I went to a nautch. It was given by a *sowcar*, or small merchant, on the occasion of his daughter's wedding. As each English guest arrived a brass band played a few bars of "God save the Queen." It was not easy to recognise the National Anthem; but natives tell us that we do not understand music. They have delicate ears; and quarter tones are common in their music, while ours only has half tones. Even in the tom-tom, which to us appears to have only one note, they recognise variety, and will listen to it for hours. We were decorated with small garlands, and sat round the room to see the dancing. It was done by a dozen or more gaudily dressed girls, who shuffled their feet about in a monotonous style to a dismal tune; and, after about half an hour, we were glad to get away. Native gentlemen do not dance themselves as a rule, but pay professionals to do it for them. When English people have a fancy dress ball, the natives next day say that the sahibs all went mad last night.

The servants of the North-West Provinces are a little, but not much, different from those of the Punjaub. A few hundred miles south of Allahabad a change in their character appears, for we then get into the zone of the servants of Bengal and Bombay. Those of the North are good to their relations, and much of their earnings goes to support not only near relations but others who have little claim on them. The result sometimes is that they gradually collect in the servants' quarters a crowd of hangers-on, and they will, if not checked, soon make the compound and garden a playground for their children and generally noisy and untidy. They do their best for us, but this cannot be said of those of Bengal, Bombay, and the South, though some of them also are really good.

On engaging a new bearer when on leave at Simla, I, as is usual, got the servants of one of my friends to find one for me, and said he was to be a "Purbeah." The men happened to be Mahomedans, and of course wanted one of their own set to have the post; so they brought me one who they said was a Purbeah named "Allah Buksh" (a pronounced Mahomedan as indicated by his name). I amused myself by asking a few questions, such as "How long has he been a Purbeah?" and why he became a Purbeah. If not carried too far, this is an effective way of meeting a trivial deception; and the men soon recognised that I was not new to the country and got me a real Purbeah.

Some of them have little idea of propriety of time or place, and will speak loudly and very openly to us in the presence of ladies about things it is not usual to mention before them. For ladies they have no great respect, and will sometimes, when the ladies are unprotected and of a mild disposition, speak disrespectfully to them, using the word "*tum*" (*i.e.*, you) which is properly used in speaking to one on a lower social plane or an equal among themselves.

When English people leave all arrangements of the meals to a head servant or cook, the kitchens are wonders of confusion, and should not be visited before dinner, or even after. A lady lately out from England went to see the making of the curries she found so good at meals, and refused to touch any meat dishes for a fortnight afterwards. Strange to say, the cook himself evolves order out of all the apparent chaos; but it is at the cost of much extra work and frequent long delays. A hostess at her dinner-parties is at times annoyed by a long wait between the courses due to some of these haphazard ways. On looking in at a kitchen one may see near the door little piles of constituents of the courses under preparation all on the floor; and, mixed up in between, are various heaps of egg-shells, cabbage-leaves, dirty plates, bowls of dirty water, empty sardine-tins, refuse parts of fish and meat, feathers, heads and feet of fowls lately killed, and beyond these, in the thick smoke, the dim forms of the cook and his assistants all but naked and hard at work. Some ladies are energetic in supervision of their kitchens, and insist on the cook's preparing everything on the tables instead of on the floor: and then things are done better. Hotel kitchens and those of travellers' bungalows are often badly supervised or not at all; and there is much risk of illness from the food supplied and prepared there.

On cold nights it is common for cooks and other servants to collect in the kitchen where there is a large fire, and at times to block up the small window, and even the door and the chinks round it, to keep out the cold air before going to sleep. At Lahore, when I was visiting a friend, he kindly gave the one servant I had with me a small room for himself for the night. The man lit a fire in it to cook his food and then blocked out all ventilation and went to sleep. Next morning, as he was late and did not answer, the door was burst open. Finding him senseless, I had him taken into the open air and restoratives applied; but it was some time before he showed signs of life, and for three or four days he was in a dazed condition. A native doctor told me that there are often such cases in Lahore.

In the North-West Provinces one habit of all kinds of the lower classes which gave much annoyance to General Gordon when in India was the constant "watching," as he called it; that is, their way when waiting for orders or simply standing about, of keeping their eyes fixed on

IN THE BAZAAR.

the sahib's face. Some do it openly, but others stand behind the verandah pillars and the corners of the house so as to be just hidden themselves, except that enough of the face is shown to allow of one eye being kept on the sahib. Should he move about, the native makes a corresponding move so as to keep out of view, just as squirrels do when they hide behind the branches of trees. I have now and then found I was not alone when I fancied I had been for some time.

When wishing for leave, some have a way of arranging that letters or telegrams reach them from a friend in a distant place, giving an urgent reason for their presence being required. In such cases their eagerness to point out the postmark or other proof of its being genuine might well arouse suspicion, only that inquiry in the matter is not worth making, it being better to give leave if possible when a man is anxious for it.

A walk or drive now and then through the bazaar is instructive and amusing. It is there that the town gossip is retailed and many an absurd rumour gains credence. Fanaticism, caste prejudice, and race hatred cause occasional faction fights. Delhi, Amritsar, Lahore, Benares, and other large towns have been the scenes of such disturbances; and, on the occasions of great fairs and religious processions, the authorities have to be vigilant. When the Hindu *Holi* and the Mahomedan *Mohurrum*, which are movable feasts, happen to fall on the same day and the processions of the opposing religions meet in the street, a disturbance is most likely to occur.

The Hindu temples and mosques are scattered through the bazaar, and some may be approached only by going up dark, narrow, and offensive side streets. On some a flag flies at the top, and I do not think I ever saw one of these flags fixed properly. They were always askew as if blown out of position by the wind. Some of the finest pieces of architecture stand side by side with tumble-down old buildings and in squalid disreputable surroundings. At night and odd times during the day there are gongs and bells sounded, not so much, in the case of Hindus, for prayers, as to call attention to the temple and the presence of the priest, and for driving away evil spirits. In the Mahomedan mosques, of course, there are the usual calls to prayer at early morning and evening.

There is strong contrast of light and shade, except in the rainy season, in all Indian towns and villages. In a medium-sized town the medley of people, shops, bulls, and carts, with a few camels and now and then an elephant, with no particular arrangement or rule of the road to go by but mixed up anyhow, gives an orderly person the idea of a general muddle. A bull or buffalo may lie down in the middle of the road, or a couple of men may sit there to have a chat and a smoke, or children play and dogs quarrel just where carts and buggies are likely to pass at any time. If there is room to squeeze by on one side pedestrians do so, and seem to look upon the monopolising of the greater part of the road in that way as nothing reprehensible. But when carts come along, or a *tum-tum*, there is a good deal of shouting and a stoppage before the road is cleared. A friend once drove me through a bazaar at a rather rapid pace, on the principle that the natives should learn to get out of the way sharp, and trusting to his good driving; but though the people cleared off, some only just in time, they left their bundles lying in the road, and he had to dodge them or stop till they were removed. A bull that had made himself comfortable for the night had to be treated with more respect, for nothing but a stop and the use of a stick was of any use. Some natives walking ahead well out of the track of a horse and trap will, on hearing the sound of the hoofs, run sideways to escape being knocked down, but without looking round first to see if they are in danger. They thus run from safety right into danger in front of one's horse, and sometimes do so just when the driver is almost abreast of them and it is necessary for him to pull up sharp or cause the horse to swerve.

At the shops, most of which in England would be called stalls, and many of them mere holes in the sides of the houses, there are seen the poorer natives buying their daily quantity of flour, pulse, butter, and condiments, generally unvarying in amount from day to day, and receiving, at the side of the leaf on which the *ghi* or butter is placed, a pinch of salt, which is the "extra" usually given them by the *bunnia* or shopkeeper. It is a sort of retainer to induce the customer to return daily to that particular dealer. "I have eaten your salt" is a saying meaning that a binding obligation is felt by the person who has eaten it. The quality of the food, however, is an almost daily matter of dispute between the customer and the dealer; and if there is the least rise in price, the commotion among them is, to our minds, out of proportion to what it need be.

The shopkeepers do not press the passer to buy or to come into the shop except in some quarters of the largest towns. In Calcutta the China bazaar is well known; and to go shopping there is an extraordinary experience for one whose servant or guide is aware of his intention to make purchases. The guide passes the word to the dealers as to what sort of sahib it is as far as his inquiries have gone or his imagination suggests. If he is living at a good hotel and perhaps about to proceed to England, and therefore presumably looking out for curiosities to take with him, the prices asked are high; but even then it depends partly on the time of day, the dealers being more anxious to sell in the early part of the day "for luck" during the rest of it. At first the inferior classes of curios are produced and first-class prices asked. There is a little by-play and dramatic nonsense sometimes: for instance, when a customer evidently wants an article but hesitates to give the price mentioned, the dealer may ask him to say how much he offers. On his naming a figure, he need not be surprised at the dealer's sudden look of astonishment and his beginning to pack up his wares, apparently in a state of indignation. Let him stick to his price and prepare to leave the shop. The dealer will relent in time to stop him and propose to halve the difference or to toss for it, or will finally accept the lower figure.

On driving once to this bazaar, as soon as I entered it my *gharry* (cab) was surrounded by the smaller dealers selling, as seen in Cheapside, toys, penny novelties, and curios. Many hands were thrust through the windows on both sides offering the cheaper curios for sale. The babel of voices and the crowd made it impossible for me to understand anything said or to get out of the *gharry* in comfort to pass into a shop. Several small Japanese dolls, silver filigree ornaments, silk handkerchiefs, and other Oriental wares were thrown in at the windows in the hope of my being pleased with them and of their owners afterwards sorting themselves and getting paid. At one time I was throwing them out as fast as they came in, to convince the men that I could not do business in that extraordinary way. It was true I had gone to pick up curios before going to England, and the hawkers probably thought they had got a rich globe-trotter to deal with. It was of no use my calling to the *gharry* driver to drive on, for the din was too great for him to hear me. Probably, also, he would have taken care to find too many difficulties ahead, as for anything I bought he would expect a small douceur from the shopkeeper, as would also my servant and the guide. The shopkeepers of Calcutta are not so trustful as the smaller outside dealers, and they require cash before delivery. It is said that they do not trust one another; so much so that cases are known when, there being two partners in a shop, each one has a key, and the shop cannot be opened till both are present, each to keep an eye on the other.

Nothing like this occurs in the bazaars of Northern towns. There, if it is known that you have come to see the sights or buy curiosities, and you go on foot, a small crowd will follow you about; and, if you have no guide, one of them will constitute himself your mentor and pilot you along, at the same time keeping the rest of the crowd from pressing too near. When the purchasing is complete they come round to offer to carry the packages to your hotel, and so make a few pence for themselves,—those not getting such employment asking for *baksheesh*. It is safe to hand over the packages to any of the men and boys to carry to the hotel. They will be found awaiting your arrival there.

Some of the smaller traders are gamblers in their ways of doing business. If the price asked for an article is too high, and no agreement can be come to with the customer, it is not unusual for the shopkeeper to offer to toss whether the buyer shall pay double or have it for nothing. Some purchasers have the gambling propensity in them and like the idea. If the shopman loses he parts with his goods without any show of vexation, and probably makes his profit in the end by as often winning as losing. I have known dealers who came to sell curios to the passengers on the ocean liners at Colombo, go so far as to allow passengers to buy their wares and carry them off to Australia or to England on payment by cheque. It appears at first rather simple or foolish; but they judge fairly well of the character and position of those whom they are trusting, and it is rare for them to be swindled. Their profits also are possibly comparatively large.

Gambling is seen in the bazaar in other shapes. Card-parties of four or less are found in the midst of the crowd of buyers and sellers in awkward corners with barely room for the players to move their arms. Various kinds of gambling are indulged in on a large scale,—for instance the rain gambling, when there is much excitement, on the approach of the monsoon, as to the day and hour when the first drops of rain will fall. In Bombay, when the Back Bay scheme for reclaiming an extensive area of the sea was on the market, there was heavy speculation in the shares. At the Diwali festival it is said that when their transmigration takes place the souls of those who do not gamble will enter the bodies of donkeys.

At times one hears above the hubbub of the bazaar a curious noise made by a man with a small drum-shaped rattle in his hand. Inside are a few peas, and by a quick movement he produces a sort of toy-drum accompaniment to his voice as he tries to collect a crowd to admire the antics of his pair of monkeys,—one riding a goat and the other leading it. In a less crowded part there may be a troupe of tumblers: and these are amusing, not so much in their performance as in the ways they have of advertising themselves first.

One man struts about, puffs out his chest and beats it with his hand in a defiant way, as if indignant at the thought of any one daring to suppose himself his equal as an expert tumbler or wrestler. Others make mysterious preparations in a serious but ostentatious manner, as if the *tamâsha*, or show, was to be something most unusual. And when at last it comes off it is of the tamest kind, and stops when one is still wondering when the interesting part is going to begin. The crowd always seem quite satisfied.

There is another performance which, when described by English people from India, causes much surprise and incredulity. Even in the streets in India the basket trick and the mango-tree trick are freely shown when the right sort of juggler is performing. Instead of being kept as something very special to be shown on great occasions and to make large sums of money, they are put forward for a few pence in the open street.

The mango-tree trick is the simplest of them, and is a clever piece of legerdemain. Though I had not the opportunity of examining closely, I saw the whole performance from a verandah a short distance above. The conjurer had an empty flower-pot into which he put some dry earth. In this he placed a seed, and then threw a light cloth over the whole. After a few minutes he raised it, and a small mango plant was seen a few inches high in the flower-pot. Again he threw the cloth over, and, after another few minutes, removed it, and it was seen that the plant was eight or nine inches high, with branches and leaves. A third time, and it was about a foot or more in height; and the performance was over. Throughout the quarter of an hour or so during which it lasted there was no one but the performer in the open space, surrounded by a crowd of sight-seers. The man himself sat far enough away from the flower-pot while covering it with the cloth and uncovering it again; and, as he himself was lightly clothed and with almost bare arms, and evidently had no paraphernalia to work with, the trick was exceedingly well done. We all know that at evening parties at home amateur conjurers can produce flowers from apparently nothing at all; and this can be done by means of springs which expand flattened paper imitations. It might be thought that in some such way the mango-tree was made to grow; but in this case a seed was used and apparently nothing else, and the plant was real.

The basket trick is even more mysterious. One performance of it I watched throughout, and I can vouch that the descriptions usually given of it are correct. In an open roadway, with a clear space of fifteen or twenty feet all round between him and the spectators, the performer placed his basket on a spot selected at random to suit the convenience of myself and a few other European spectators. There was, therefore, no trap-door as has sometimes been supposed. The basket was of two parts, each being hemispherical, and one fitting on the top of the other. Both parts were of light common wicker-work, and quite empty. Into the lower one a boy was placed, and there was only just room for him to curl himself up in it. The upper half was then put over him and fixed down. After a few movements of the basket, due to the boy's settling himself more comfortably, the juggler began a conversation with him. The boy's answers seemed to irritate him, and at last, apparently in a rage, he plunged a sword through and through the basket. The boy's screams, the man's angry denunciations, and the sword covered with blood, were all realistic enough,—so much so that some of the spectators ran forward to interfere. On opening the basket it was found to be empty, while the boy himself came running towards us from some distance behind the crowd.

As in the case of many other well-shown tricks, puzzling though they may be to the spectator, the explanation is probably simple enough.

At feast-times the streets may be blocked by processions or by amusement-seekers who get up an impromptu dance or other diversion. A crowd collects, and the police on duty join them to look on at the fun. This also happens when a Hindu wedding procession passes; for it is generally on an extensive scale, as required by the Brahmin system of extortion. However poor a man of caste may be, the wedding of his son or daughter must be the occasion for large, or comparatively large, expenditure on processions, feasts, and presents to the priests and their myrmidons. Sometimes the stream of elephants, horsemen, carriages, and brass bands, with people on foot, all decked out in expensive array, though only that of a commoner of low degree, is more like what might be expected at the wedding of a prince. A Rajput bridegroom has an easy way of avoiding much of the expenditure he might have to incur in tipping the numerous dependents of his father-in-law by sending, instead of himself, a sword—to which the girl is married—as quite the same thing. A maid carries the sword by her side, while the bride walks round some cooking-pots placed on bamboos. After that she leaves her home for good and joins her husband.

May is the chief month for weddings. The rejoicings at night have plenty of "tom-toming" mixed up with them; and, as the sound of the tom-tom travels far and clear, any Europeans near are much disturbed. In most cases of Hindu weddings, or at least of betrothals, the bride is a child, often a very young one. If of good caste, should her husband die, child though she be, she becomes a widow for life, and is treated harshly by her relations, and almost as if she were an outcast or a criminal. She may no longer play with her brothers and sisters nor have her meals with her family; and she is dressed in coarse material. There are 17,000,000 widows in India; and when caste Hindus, they are not allowed to remarry. In former days it was a meritorious act for a widow to throw herself on the funeral pyre of her dead husband and be burnt with him; but the British Government made it illegal, though by doing so they interfered with the native custom and religion. The evils attending child marriage and the prohibition of the remarriage of widows are so great that among Hindus there have been attempts to break through the tyranny of custom and Brahmin dictation. Mr Justice Telang, some years ago, led an attempt at reform of these abuses; but custom and the priests were too strong for him, and he had to agree to the marriage of his own daughters at the ages of ten and eight.

In an address by Sir Monier Williams on January 27, 1898, it was said:—

> "For a child widow to look plump, healthy, and happy would be a disgrace to her whole family. So she must be deprived of her hair and ornaments, she must be reduced to emaciation by severe penances, by allowing her only one meal a-day, by turning her into a domestic slave or household drudge, and by obliging her to keep well out of the way in all seasons of rejoicing. For the mere sight of her is a bad omen."

Some of the sights of the bazaar are sad and repellent. There are the grown-up widows who have to get their living anyhow, and there are the religious beggars who have vowed to do no work, and to live on unsolicited alms. These *fakirs*, as they are called, go about almost naked, with their hair dyed and matted and their skin rubbed over with white ashes. Or there are lepers, perhaps white all over with the disease, some having lost all their fingers, which have rotted and fallen off. A missionary may now and then be seen preaching in the open air, and sometimes a rival meeting held by a learned

Hindu or a Mussulman Wahabi. Blind people are not numerous, but there are some in nearly all the bazaars. In some bazaars there are many blind children.

Of the novelties introduced from Europe, nothing has been so quickly adopted as the sewing machine. It is everywhere, and, no doubt, is found to be a lucrative investment by the *derzis* or tailors. Not only in the shops of the tailors but in shops of all sorts, the fashion-plates from England and the illustrated drapers' lists are exhibited as ornaments and attractions. Linen garments are exposed for sale in all bazaars. The best are of Manchester make: and the end of a piece on which the Manchester trade-mark is stamped commands a higher price than the rest. It is looked on as a desirable ornament. The end of a *pugaree* hangs loose from the head, and flutters in the wind as the man who wears it walks through the bazaar. The owner of one on which the trade-mark is stamped on the flowing end is proud of the distinction.

The children about the streets and alleys seem to play at nothing in particular. There are no shouts of laughter, no running about, no real fun or mischief; only sitting about, and the occasional aimless flourishing of a stick, and, in a few places, some kite-flying on a very small scale. Their large eyes give them the appearance of being always in a state of wonder, which, however, leads to no special curiosity or wish to investigate. They will follow a visitor, and a few run ahead to drive stray dogs out of the way, or even to order big men to move aside for the sahib. They pat their bare stomachs to indicate that they are hungry, and ask for *baksheesh* (money) to buy sweetmeats. Women and children are employed to keep the roads clean: and it is usual for them to have the worst kind of such work, using their hands freely in collecting refuse.

In all towns and most fair-sized villages there are schools, the total number in British India being about 150,000. Those who can read and write or are under instruction are only 1 in 10 males and 1 in 150 females; and there are twice as many Hindu pupils as Mahomedan and others. In British India there were 4½ million pupils in the year 1901, and this was an increase of about 700,000 over the number of 1891. In the technical schools studying law, medicine, engineering, art, &c., there are 30,000 pupils. The women have little education. Those of the higher classes are kept much in seclusion, the rest are workers in the house or the field; and for both classes education is deemed superfluous.

JAIN TEMPLE AT DILWARRA (MOUNT ABU).

THE EYES OF THE CENTRAL IMAGE ARE OF PRECIOUS STONES.

XI.

TOWNS AND TEMPLES.

ALLAHABAD — THE MUTINY — LUCKNOW — DELHI — CURIOS — AGRA —AJODHYA — BENARES — CREMATION — ABU TEMPLES — JEYPUR —ULWAR — INDORE — ROCK-CUT TEMPLES — PRESIDENCY TOWNS— BENGALI BABOOS — SUNDERBUNDS — EARTHQUAKES — MADRAS— CATAMARANS — TEMPLES OF THE SOUTH — CONJEEVERAM — CUMBACONUM—TRICHINOPOLI—JHINJI—THE BRITISH SOLDIER—AT THE RAILWAY STATIONS—LOAFERS.

To every one in Government service one month's leave on full pay is granted each year, provided he can be spared from his duties and some one else can be appointed to take them up during his absence. The leave may be refused by Government, or he can defer it himself till a more convenient time, accumulating it from year to year up to three months but not more. This is short leave, or "privilege" leave, as compared with "furlough," which is given on half-pay once in four or five years, if applied for, at the rate of one year after every four in the case of those on the more favourable rules. Short leave enables us to go to the hills for a change in the hot weather, and the long leave to visit England and other countries after each spell of a few years of service. Only a small part of the long leave counts as service towards pension, the rest having to be made up by staying longer on duty before final retirement. It is good policy on the part of Government to arrange leave in this way, as it enables officials to keep themselves in good health and therefore in good working trim.

On leaving the Irrigation works at Narora, I was transferred to Allahabad, the capital town of the North-West Provinces. It has no special attraction for a tourist, but for one settled in India it is a desirable station on account of the conveniences, and the garden-parties, dances, and other gatherings at Government House and at the Club and Military messes. The North-West Province Club is one where many of the leading men in India are met; and the dinners there, the billiards, the card-parties, and the general air of good comradeship, were like a tonic to the jaded office-man and those who could get a change from Mofussil or jungly life.

Allahabad is close to where the river Jumna joins the Ganges; and the junction is, as usual in the case of large rivers uniting, a sacred spot. In the month of May there is a gathering of hundreds of thousands from all parts at the *Magh mela* or fair, at which the Brahmin priests probably are the chief gainers. At the fairs at Benares, Hurdwar, Ajodhya, and other sacred spots on the large rivers, there is much bathing as a religious duty; and money is given by all to the priests and to the numerous beggars. Fakirs do a good trade, especially those who have become deformed in the course of the penances they have been through. Some lie on beds made of a board supporting a number of iron spikes, their only mattress.

A useful institution was the "Eye Hospital," supported by voluntary contributions, for treating destitute natives suffering from affections of the eyes, and superintended by Dr Hall, whose services were much appreciated.

Allahabad was the scene of one of the sad events of the Mutiny. The sepoys revolted on June 6, 1857, and massacred several officers and civilians two hours after an evening parade at which the thanks of the Governor-General had been read to them for their offer to march against the rebels at Delhi. Ladies and others got safely into the fort, where they remained till the mutineers marched away and General Neill arrived, and then General Havelock, on the way to the relief of Cawnpore.

When I was living for a few months at one of the hotels at Allahabad, one of the residents was General Hicks, who related to me an incident which then happened. He and a companion were too late to reach the fort, and found themselves isolated and intercepted by the rebels. The only way was to wait till dark, swim the river, and then go down-stream on the other bank till opposite the fort and swim across again. This they did, disguising themselves by discarding their clothing and rubbing themselves with mud so as to appear like natives in the dim light. The river is infested with alligators at this part; but they gained the fort in safety. For some time, however, they were refused admittance, as it was thought they were natives: and it was only on General Hicks inducing those inside to send for his wife to identify him that they were admitted.

The North-West Provinces was where the Mutiny broke out and the more important events occurred. It began at Meerut on 10th May 1857, and rapidly spread,—many of the outbreaks being rendered more easy through the confidence the British officers had in the loyalty of the native regiments under their own command.

At Lucknow the Residency, which was besieged by the mutineers and was relieved, first by Havelock and Sir James Outram, and afterwards by Sir Colin Campbell, still has the marks of the bullets on the walls. At Cawnpore are the Memorial Church, the memorial over the well into which the mutineers threw the English women and children, and the *ghat* at the river where the Europeans, leaving under a promise of safe passage to Allahabad, were massacred by order of Nana Sahib. The well is covered up, and a statue of an angel stands over it—the whole being in an enclosure into which no native is allowed to enter. A painful event happened there a few years ago,—a British soldier becoming so excited at the story that he killed one of the natives standing near. He was tried and executed.

It was the very vigorous and determined action of General Nicholson at Delhi at the right time that decided the course of events in our favour. The Sikhs had sided with us and had been very useful and loyal; but it was feared that even their loyalty might not stand the test of further misfortune. General Nicholson, on the night of 13th September 1857, insisted that Delhi must be taken without further delay. Next morning six British officers and men of the Royal Engineers and eight native sappers placed the powder-bags against the Cashmere Gate, two officers losing their lives in the act. A breach was made, the town was stormed, and the troops got inside at last. In the street-fighting that followed General Nicholson was killed. His name is remembered among the Sikhs with the greatest respect: and they boast that in scaling the walls a Sikh was at the top as soon as the first Englishman. Both, however, were immediately killed. The names of those who lost their lives are recorded on two tablets on the Cashmere Gate, and there are many tablets in the Memorial Church at Cawnpore.

Round Delhi there are numerous places of interest. The ridge where the British camp was during the siege, the fort, the large Mahomedan mosque (the Jumma Musjid), built of red sandstone and marble, the mass of ruins of old Delhi, extending over several miles, the Kootub (a high ornamented tower), and the tomb of Nizam ud din, are the best worth visiting.

Here, on the great plain to the west, some of the greatest battles were fought against the Mahomedan conquerors from the North and by the Moguls against the Mahrattas. In the year 1001 A.D. Mahomed of Ghazni established the faith of Islam at Delhi by force. In 1398 Tamerlane, after conquering from Samarkhand up to the Caspian Sea, came down through the Punjaub, massacring the inhabitants of the towns and villages, and took Delhi; and in the sixteenth century the Mogul empire was established there by Akbar. It was from the Jumma Musjid that the holy war against the infidels was preached at the time of the Mutiny, the Mahomedans having for a time joined with the Hindus against the English; and it was on the plain between this Musjid and the city wall that the proclamation of Queen Victoria as Empress of India was made in 1877.

At one part of this plain there is a well into which boys jump, one after another in rapid succession. At the level of the water there is a hole in the side of the well through which they scramble out and then come up a slope to the top again. The jump is considerable, the impetus carrying them some distance beneath the water. As there are sometimes half a dozen in the water at once, all mixed up, some descending, others rising, and some also in mid-air, it would appear impossible for accidents not to occur in such a confined space. They do it over and over again for a few pice (farthings).

It should be arranged that on the drive back from the Kootub, a visit be paid to the tomb of Nizam ud din at evening, when the Mahomedan call to prayer is being sounded. The old priests in their picturesque Mahomedan garb, the sonorous deep musical tones of their voices answering one another, together with the deepening shadows of the finely-carved pillars and doorways, give an impressive and rather solemn effect.

Inside Delhi the Moti Musjid, a small mosque in white marble, is very handsome; and the Dewan-i-Khas (Hall of Audience) was much admired by Mr Prinsep for its raised patterns and inlaid work. This hall is part of the palace of Shah Jehan, and is well located on the river-bank. Round the roof is the well-known inscription—"If there is a heaven on earth, it is this—it is this."

The curios for collectors are numerous and varied. The silver filigree work, miniature paintings, and the muslin embroidery are exceptionally good, and show that some of the native artists have great patience, keen sight, and good taste. The *phoolkaris* are shawls spangled with tiny mirrors, and are ornamental as table-covers or curtains. They are made by native women of the towns and villages, and are worn by them on great occasions. At one time it was the fashion for tourists to prefer those that had been actually worn by the natives, as being, for that reason, so much the more interesting to their lady friends at home.

At Delhi and other large towns there have occurred serious religious riots when the ill-feeling between Mahomedans and Hindus became acute. Some years ago a dead pig was tied to the priest's reading-desk inside the Jumma Musjid, —an insult that could not be overlooked, for pig or pork is unclean to the Mahomedans as well as to the Jews. The Mahomedan population was quickly roused, and in the riots which followed several Hindus and Mahomedans were killed.

The handsomest of all the Mahomedan buildings is the famous Taj Mahal of Agra, a mausoleum built by the Mogul emperor, Shah Jehan, in memory of his wife. It is built on the bank of the river Jumna, and is of white marble and red sandstone. Its external symmetry and the handsome trellis screens and other decorations inlaid with precious stones recommend it to the critical artist and even to those who usually care little for such things. One should go several times to it, as it is said to be more attractive after the first or second visit.

The fort of Agra, built by Akbar, of red sandstone, like that at Delhi, contains a Jumma Musjid and a pearl mosque of white marble, both of the time of Aurungzebe—that is, of our Queen Elizabeth. A few miles away are some fine specimens of architecture at Futtehpore Sikri. Pretty models of the Taj and other buildings in soapstone, ivory carvings, jade daggers, enamelled and inlaid work, are made at Agra and places near.

Ajodhya, a sacred city of pilgrimage on the bank of the river Gogra, is interesting as the birthplace of Buddha, who was born in the fifth century before Christ. He was a prince who became an ascetic, and a reformer of the licence and false doctrines which had grown up under the Brahmin rule. He began his reforms at Benares, and his teachings gained the ascendancy for about a thousand years before Brahminism revived.

A GATEWAY AT JEYPUR (RAJPUTANA.)

Benares is now the most sacred city of the Hindus and the home of 20,000 Brahmins, who have authority over the temples and other sacred places, and receive offerings from all classes,—princes, successful traders, pilgrims, and even the poorest contributing to their support. The town is on one bank of the Ganges, and has an imposing river front of palaces, temples, mosques, and private houses. The short spires of the Hindu temples, the minarets of the mosques, and the numerous flights of stone steps from the high ground to the river; the crowds of devotees, priests, pilgrims, bathers, and beggars; the boats, the burning *ghats* where the dead are cremated,—all together make up a curious, picturesque, and extraordinary mixture. People come to die there and be buried in the sacred river. Bisheshwar is the ruling god of the place, though of course all the deities are worshipped. The great mosque, the Buddhist tope of trees, the monkey temple, the "well of forgiveness," and many other freaks of human folly, are here to be seen in the quaintest variety. Monkeys are worshipped, and scamper about in full possession of the trees, the roofs, and those parts of the streets they care for, stealing, grimacing, and playing pranks on one another and the passer-by. They cause much loss to the poorer natives, whose food they sometimes appropriate. It is only in keeping with the absurdity of the whole system that these mischievous creatures are believed to be incarnations of former saints. The "well of forgiveness" is supposed to be full of the sweat of the benign god Vishnu, and thousands bathe in it each year. All crimes, even the worst, are supposed to be thus expiated. It is in a fetid state, as is said to be also that at Mecca. Mr W. S. Caine, in his 'A Trip Round the World,' relates that, when he saw it in 1887, he found the contents "as thick as gruel from constant bathing and the flowers which each worshipper throws into it, to decay uncleansed." A priest was "dispensing ladlefuls to a crowd who drink it up eagerly."

There are interesting Buddhist remains, and an old observatory with arrangements for noting the sun's altitude, the declination, latitude, the right ascension of stars, and other astronomical details. One of the most prominent buildings is the Mosque of Aurungzebe with its two minarets. It stands high, and is best seen from the river. When spending a few days at Benares, I tried to get a photograph of the town so as to show these minarets to the best advantage. To have taken the camera on to the river in a boat would have made it almost impossible to get a view owing to the continual movement of the boat, and I therefore tried to get one from the edge of the water, that being as far back as possible on dry land. Having left the man who carried the apparatus on the river-bank to stay in charge of the parts not required, I moved the camera along the sand close to the river from place to place in the endeavour to get the best view. In doing so I passed the end of what appeared to be only a spur put up to keep the river from encroaching when in flood, and had proceeded several yards past it when a native on the bank above begged me not to go farther. I had been watching the minarets more than anything else, and now found out that I had come beyond the enclosing boundary of the burying-ground, and was within the forbidden area. The man was there to stop trespassers, and his protest, as I was a sahib, had been deferred till I had gone so far that he was frightened; and even then it was only a mild appeal. I immediately began to collect my camera to retreat, but had time to see some strange sights. Just ahead were many stacks of wood, some with dead bodies on them and already alight. Amid the smoke from these were the low-caste men (*Dôms*), who are employed to burn the dead, running about arranging the faggots; and as they were nearly naked, dark skinned, and begrimed with smoke, the work they were doing appeared gruesome and hideous. This effect was increased when the flames began to reach the bodies. As they heated some parts before others, the result was that contortions of the bodies took place. They began to twist about as if still sensitive. One suddenly sat up as if startled; another whirled an arm about rapidly in a circle. When the heads had become hot the skulls exploded with a small report. What terrible scenes there must have been in the old days of suttee, when the living widows were burnt with their dead husbands!

At the time of my visit the "Durga Pooja" fair

was in progress. This is the time of worship of the savage vindictive goddess "Kali," and is more a Bengal feast than elsewhere. Most religious feasts are degenerating, or are becoming elevated into holiday fairs, when the people, though still supporting Brahmin priests and mendicants, take care to enjoy themselves. There is a brisk trade in idols, many made for the occasion of mud, and wonderfully well constructed, painted, and gilded. They are worshipped for three days, and on the last day there is a procession to the river in which the idols are "drowned."

Some of the curios sold here are good, especially the brass-work. Of this there are three kinds; and the third or inferior kind is easily sold off to tourists who do not know how to judge. All kinds are pretty, but the first class is much superior. There used to be wood carvings of quaint patterns; but some one made the mistake of having cups and saucers and other crockery carved in wood, and the artisans abandoned for a time their old pretty designs and produced only the new ugly ones, thinking probably that they would be more pleasing to tourists.

There is a large importation of English cotton goods and Birmingham ware. Many of the smaller native bankers make a good harvest by providing borrowers with money at high interest to spend at the fairs. There are several schools and a Government college—a sort of university where Sanscrit and English are studied—and important missions of the Church of England, the London Missionary Society, and the Baptists.

JAIN PRIEST AT MOUNT ABU RAJPUTANA).

Of the other towns north of Bombay, those of Rajputana and of the Mahratta countries governed by the Maharajahs Scindhia, Holkar, and the Gaikowar are most interesting. Jubbulpore in the Central Provinces has a sight worth seeing at the marble rocks on the Nerbudda river; but the group of towns to the west, containing handsome temples, palaces, and ruins, are much more visited and admired. North of Bombay are Surat and Baroda, the former now and for centuries past an important centre of trade in grain, cotton goods, and silk; and the latter the capital of the Mahratta ruler, the Gaikowar.

Farther north, in Rajputana, are Ahmedabad, Abu, Jeypur, Ulwur, Oodeypur, and others, all with special attractions. They have remains of Jain architecture, some in good condition; and some of the temples now in use are in charge of priests of that very ancient form of religion. Ahmedabad, the first reached in travelling northwards, is full of mosques, tombs, and gateways of an unusual style, being a mixture of Jain and Mahomedan. Here also is one of the *pinjrapols*, or homes for old and sick animals, supported by the Jains. In Broach one of these is maintained at a cost of £530 a-year.

The prettiest specimen of Jain architecture is the Dilwara (or Dewalwara) temple at Mount Abu, a sight missed by many visitors, as it is about fifteen miles off the line of railway and up the hill. The journey, however, is made comfortably by 'rickshaw. The stone of the temple is white marble, carved, and with a profusion of ornament. At p. 208 is a photo of a part of this temple, which the Jain priest allowed me to take. I wished to get a nearer view of the cross-legged figure, but this was not allowed, as the place was considered too sacred. The image is that of a *Tirthankar* or deified man; and there are twenty-four of these in the Jain system of worship. There are many ruins of Jain, Buddhist, and Brahmin temples here and at Ajodhya, their destruction being attributed to Aurungzebe, Tamerlane, and other Mahomedan conquerors.

Jeypur is a well-kept and picturesque town, and a centre of production of works of art. Fine enamelling, marble statues of Buddha, curious daggers, and other Rajput arms, carvings in ivory, sandalwood, soapstone, and clay, all of a superior kind, are on sale in the shops and at the School of Art. The Museum is as interesting a one as can be found in India; and, as far as specimens of the best Indian work go, it is perhaps the best in the world except that in the Indian section of the South Kensington Museum. When I visited Jeypur first, as it happened to be a holiday, the School of Art was closed, and my opportunity of securing good specimens of native work seemed lost. A boy, however, at the hotel offered to take me to where some old arms might be got. He led me to a blacksmith's workshop, and, among the lumber of old iron, parts of cart-wheels, ploughs, and other odd bits of iron waste which the blacksmith was about to put through his forge,

SHRINE OF BAKTAWAR SINGH AT ULWUR (RAJPUTANA).

were some old Rajput arms, rusty and apparently useless. Some villager, perhaps hard up for cash to pay the money-lender, had brought them in and sold them for a trifle; and the blacksmith was no wiser as to their value in the eyes of collectors. There were a sword in the shape of a serpent, or, as the natives call it, a flame-sword; a dagger, apparently with one point only but exposing three points when a spring was pressed, the two extra ones and the cutting edges acting sideways to enlarge the wound; a *kookri;* and a battle-axe with a stiletto hidden in the handle. All were ornamented, some with carved figures of men and animals. The equivalent of five shillings was asked for the lot, and at that price I bought them.

Near Jeypur is the half-deserted town, Amber, where there are more ruins of palaces and temples. There are several deserted towns in India still in a fair state of preservation. One may well feel sorrowful when walking through the streets of these desolate places with the ruins of former grandeur all round, and many of the houses and temples still standing. It may have been a massacre by some conquering tyrant, a ravaging visitation of cholera, plague, or famine, or even the intolerable increase of deadly snakes, that made the inhabitants abandon their ancestral homes. It is sad to think of the excessive misery caused by ignorance of sanitation and hygienic laws, fanaticism, and the superstition and cruelty rampant in the past.

At Ulwur and Oodeypur are some handsome

temples and palaces built round large lakes. At the shrine of Maharajah Baktawar Singh, at Ulwur, when taking the photo shown at preceding page, I had, as usual, a man holding an umbrella over me, as, especially when working at an instrument, the sun's rays behind are annoying and dangerous. Some of the Brahmins requested me to lower the umbrella, as it was not polite to some one or other of the deities; but on my explaining that I could not do without it, a reference was made to a head priest, and it was decided that there was no need to close the umbrella.

At Indore, the capital of the Mahratta prince, Holkar, the Europeans are few and live near the Residency, some distance from the native town. The palm scenery is pretty, and, in the absence of many opportunities of social gathering, boating on the river was resorted to in addition to the usual rides and an occasional game of tennis. Rowing or canoeing in the hot season amid the palm-trees where the river expands into small secluded lakes was healthy and restful, this part of India being high and comparatively cool. At the time of my being stationed there one of the Public Works subordinates was Din Diyal, then commencing to practise photography, which he has since followed as a profession so successfully that he has become one of the leading photographers in India, and has had the honorary title of Raja conferred on him by H.H. the Nizam of Hyderabad.

A visit to the native town of Indore was

ROCK-CUT TEMPLE AT THE KARLI CAVES (BOMBAY PRESIDENCY).

amusing. In those days Europeans entered the capitals of some Native States—Indore and Hyderabad for example—only with permission of the Resident; but to-day there is no longer need for this precaution. The passing of some of Holkar's troops was strange enough, for they marched just as they pleased, in irregular rows, and with apparently little discipline. Their uniforms were irregular, and their arms rather miscellaneous. There was little of smartness in their appearance; nor was there anything to suggest that they have the martial ability of which the Mahratta nation has shown itself possessed in the wars against the Moguls, the Sultans of Mysore, and the British. Since then the new arrangement by which the Imperial service troops of the Native States are now drilled by British officers has introduced more method.

Some tourists, when they land at Bombay, are induced to take the local steamer across to the caves of Elephanta. These, though interesting, are not nearly so good as the rock-cut temples at Karli, Ellora, and Ajanta. In those are shown groups of gods and heroic figures cut in the solid rock. The caves at Karli are entered through a door in the side of a hill, and have figures of women riding on elephants at the top of each of the imitation pillars. Those at Ellora and Ajanta have representations of gods and heroes, inscriptions and rich carvings, cave-temples, and monasteries with cells; and there are paintings of devotees, crowds of men in procession and in battle, elephants, snakes, ships, &c. The figure shown opposite is Indra, god of the firmament, and there is one of the savage god Siva and his wife Durga (or Kali). Siva is piercing a child with his spear, and his wife is catching the blood in a cup.

The three Presidency cities—Bombay, Calcutta, and Madras—have much in common, in that they have been considerably influenced by trade with Europe and by their proximity to the sea. But the populations differ widely. The Mahratta and Parsee of Bombay, the Bengali of Calcutta, and the Tamil of Madras, are in strong contrast. The population of Calcutta is one million, that of Madras only half a million. The trade of Calcutta is even larger than that of Bombay, and the exports are not of grain and cotton as at Bombay, but of rice, tea, jute, indigo, opium, and sugar. There are fine buildings, merchants' houses, docks, tramways, esplanades, and gardens as in Bombay and Madras, and a closely-packed native town. The approach from the sea is up eighty miles of river and among troublesome shoals.

The Bengali Baboo is a man of many-sided character. The best prominent characteristics of Bengalis are their memory and quickness of intellect, enabling them to pass examinations, take degrees, and succeed as merchants, lawyers, doctors, newspaper editors, accountants, and clerks. There is apparently, at times, a want of loyalty among them, but this was not the case during the Boer war. They are not a martial people, most of them being rather the reverse in their

INDRA, GOD OF THE FIRMAMENT.

manner, physique, character, and dress. Their costume is unlike that of any other class of natives, especially when they wear a loose white dress with short drawers showing long white stockings and patent-leather shoes. They live much on rice, and are fond of very hot condiments: and they nearly always have a great number of relations. Bengal itself has an area of 151,000 square miles, and over this the average population is 413 to the square mile.

When one is in Calcutta in the cold season visiting in comfort the various sights, and listening to the band in the pleasant evenings at the Eden gardens before dinner, it may be forgotten for the time that not far away are some of the wildest and most wonderful scenes in Nature. The Ganges and Brahmapootra both fall into the Bay of Bengal, and mingle their waters in the great swamp of the Sunderbunds. Here there are vast shoals, extending over an area of about 5000 square miles, forming the delta through which the water flows in many channels, the islands between being covered with vegetation, feverish, infested with alligators, and the home of fierce tigers. Higher up the Brahmapootra is Assam with its many half-civilised hill-tribes, its wild jungle, and variety of game. In about eighteen hours of journey by rail northwards Darjeeling is reached, and from there can be seen what is probably the grandest mountain view in the world.

Calcutta has had still nearer illustrations of the powers of Nature of a different sort. Plague, earthquakes, and cyclones are to be reckoned with. So bad was the plague in 1898 that a quarter of the population emigrated to the country parts, and trade was much interfered with. In June 1897 the earthquake which destroyed Shillong in Assam was severe at Calcutta. Some of the church steeples were thrown out of the upright position; roofs, walls, and masonry bridges were cracked and rendered unsafe; parts of the Eastern Bengal State Railway were twisted about; there were serious floods, and large areas of valuable rice-crops were covered with deposits. The great cyclone of 21st to 24th October 1897 in the Bay of Bengal was followed by a wave which submerged two islands, and caused the deaths of 50,000 people.

Those Europeans who have lived much in Northern India, and especially those who began their Indian life there, are seldom content to remain long in the Madras Presidency. The climate, scenery, native character, and the general inert style are disappointing. Some who have lived all their service in Madras are under the impression that things there are rather go-ahead and superior. Latitude and climate are against them, and the fact that the inhabitants of Madras are mostly of those inferior races who, in ancient days, could not resist the Northern invaders, and retired to the jungles of the South. Most of the important towns are on or near the coast, where the climate is damp, hot, and relaxing; and the hills and plateaux of the interior are not so invigorating as are the

GATEWAY TO THE TEMPLES AT MADURA (MADRAS PRESIDENCY).

Himalayan stations. At Madras the Public Works and other Government offices are on the sea-front at Chepauk; and, for some time when stationed there, it was difficult to keep my attention on my office work owing to the depressing influence of the climate near the sea. I frequently fell asleep suddenly, however much I fought against the nuisance; and the Medical officer advised me to drink hot coffee, and to keep a basin of cold water at hand to bathe my face. The climate is not felt in this way by all, and it is said to have so strong an influence only within about two miles of the coast.

There is little attraction about Madras. The Club is the most comfortable in India, and the walk on the esplanade when the band plays in the evening is probably unsurpassed except by that on the Galle Face at Colombo. The coast is much exposed, and the heavy surf in stormy weather makes landing or embarking a difficult matter. The breakwater of massive concrete blocks has been many times badly damaged. When a cyclone is approaching it is better for all vessels to get away quickly to the open sea.

The Madras fishermen can do some things which no one else can. They have a contrivance called a catamaran which consists of three logs of wood lashed together. On these, as a raft, they stand, and with a single oar they pilot themselves out to sea. Even in very rough weather they can do so, and will, for a few pence, go through the heavy surf and carry a letter to a vessel when no boat can put off. They may get knocked off by the heavy seas several times in their journey, but being good swimmers they soon regain the catamaran. The logs are flush with the surface, and they themselves are dark-skinned and all but naked. It can, therefore, be well understood that, as they use their single oar, working it first on one side and then on the other, some of the early navigators mistook them for "devils walking on the sea and brandishing spears."

Along the South Indian Railway from Madras to Tuticorin, the most southern part of India, are towns famous for their shrines and temples. Conjeeveram, Cumbaconum, Tanjore, Trichinopoli, Madura, Tinnevelly, all have architecture different from that in the North.

Some of the names, both of the towns and of the inhabitants, are long and peculiar: for example, there is a place called Amakanayakanur. On hearing the name of a servant he had engaged in India, Mark Twain said he would make a selection from it for business purposes and keep the rest for Sundays.

At about thirty-five miles south of Madras are the Seven Pagodas—some close to the sea and being undermined by it. There are caves and temples, sculptures and inscriptions cut in the rock, all very ancient, probably of Jain and Buddhist times and up to the tenth century A.D. The temples in the North are decorated more inside than out, the reverse being the case in the South. The gateways and exteriors of the temples at Tanjore, Sringam near Trichinopoli,

HINDU TEMPLE AT MADURA.

and Madura, are the best specimens of external ornamentation; the interiors where the gods are supposed to live being mere dark holes, sometimes damp and full of refuse and small reptiles. At Tinnevelly the "Hall of Lions" is different, being a large interior ornamented with grotesque figures of lions. Most of the figures at all these temples are grotesque, and many parts are absurdly out of proportion. At the Madura temples, sacred to Siva, there is a mixture of carved figures of gods, heroes, and animals in great variety of attitude; and, to add to the absurdity, the faces, arms, legs, and various parts of the body are brightly coloured. There may be a god with a green face, yellow arms, and blue legs side by side with a warrior whose face is blue and legs green. The general proportions of the structures are pleasing, and the total result at a distance is in a way effective. A few illustrations are given at pages 216, 218, and 220.

Conjeeveram is the Benares of Southern India, and has an annual fair at which 50,000 pilgrims attend. It has one temple supported by a thousand pillars. Cumbaconum, besides temples, has a Government college, and has been called the Oxford of India. One evening at dusk I talked with a few of the students. As is common among the natives, they wish to know where you come from and what is your occupation; and some go so far as to inquire whether you are married, and other personal details. Knowing this, and being quite a stranger there, I preferred to temporise in my replies: and to the first question, "Of what country are you an inhabitant?" remembering that I had travelled much in both hemispheres, I answered, "I am an inhabitant of all the world." This seemed to strike them as something classic, or, at least, comprehensive; and after an impressive pause one remarked, in a tone of deep appreciation, "That is very fine!" Instead of going into heroics it would be better if some of them would devote themselves to sanitary science; for Cumbaconum, at least up to a few years ago, was a most insanitary place.

Trichinopoli is built round the base of a bold high rock, and is interesting as the place where Bishop Heber died. The bath behind St John's Church in which he was found dead is still there. The climate of this part is drier than that of most of the South Indian stations, and appeared to me to be rather a good one; but those in civil employ, as well as the military men in the cantonments, dislike the place. While I was there an outbreak of cholera occurred, and I was told, on good authority, that at intervals of one or two years there had been three outbreaks, every one of which began in the butchers' quarter. In all Indian cantonments the slaughter-houses are kept at a good distance from the military lines and the houses of the civilians. However careful the inspection, there is the fact that the slaughtering is done day after day in the same place; and, owing to the saturation of the ground with blood and animal refuse, the effect of the hot sun, especially when a fall of rain occurs, must be to cause putrefaction all round where the flesh food is prepared. The work is done by low-caste or out-

CARVINGS ON THE GATEWAY AT MADURA.

caste men whose habits of life will usually not bear close inspection.

Jhinji, a few miles from the railway, is a deserted town with houses, temples, and a fort in fair condition, considering that the place was at the height of its prosperity about the year 1500. It was taken and retaken in the war between Hyder Ali of Mysore and the Mahrattas under Sivaji: and it has been in the hands of the French and English after a succession of sieges.

The most interesting town of South India is Hyderabad, the capital of H.H. the Nizam. It is described in chapter xiv. In the sixteenth and seventeeth centuries the Mahomedan capital was at Bijapur, farther west, now a place of extensive ruins, one of which is something like Melrose Abbey.

When one travels through the larger towns where there are British forts or cantonments, the English soldiers are seen in their smartest style and on their best behaviour if allowed to visit the town off duty. They walk about by twos and threes in a vigorous way, giving an impression of great energy, and evidently rather contemptuous of their surroundings. With the best of the native soldiery they become on most friendly terms, no doubt having, as good Englishmen, a just appreciation of excellence in others. They approve the Gurkhas, the Sikhs, and other native sepoys who have good nature as well as martial qualities. When at Bellary in 1901 I visited the camp of the Boer prisoners, and learnt that there was no ill-will on the part of the British soldier towards the Boers. One said to me, "The Boer is not a bad fellow—it's the others," meaning the aliens in South Africa who fought against us.

The natives in the bazaars prefer to give the British soldier a wide berth, or they tolerate his presence in the hope that he will soon go away. His brusqueness, perfect self-confidence, and independence, and his occasional rough-tongued denunciation of what he thinks mean, are to them rather startling. Yet they highly appreciate his efforts when directed towards their help. When at Jullunder in the Punjaub, about two dozen soldiers of the Devonshire regiment assisted to extinguish a serious fire in the bazaar, a native wrote to the newspaper:—

> "Their combined efforts, humanity, and magnanimity displayed on the spot is extremely admirable. None of them cared for his person, dresses, &c., but some of them threw themselves, even at the risk of their lives, and, I must say, they saved the whole bazaar from further damage and fire. Many of them covered with mud and dirt from it and were smutted faces. Well done! O ye brave soldiers! Well done!"

Native ways as seen at the large railway stations when an ordinary train is about to start are very characteristic. The real nature of the men comes forward in some of its aspects under the need to hurry up and to see that all their belongings, women and babies included, are safely collected in the same compartment in time. Family groups arrive from the interior a day perhaps before the time their train is to start; and they sleep in the third-class waiting-hall, a jumble of heads, arms and legs, and hookahs, appearing amid various bundles of clothes, bedding, and cooking utensils. All these have to be taken into the carriage: and when the passengers are numerous the compartments are occasionally choked up with accumulations of personal belongings. It is extraordinary how they manage to pack themselves away. There are "intermediate" classes between the first and the second and between the second and the third; and, when *purdah* ladies travel, one of the intermediate compartments may be reserved. They are brought in curtained palanquins which are placed close up to the door of the railway carriage, and the lady inside moves from one to the other without being seen,—the curtain being thrown over the door of the carriage as the palanquin is removed.

At the larger railway stations and in the towns a character well known all over India is often met. The "loafer" corresponds to the professional tramp in England. He is usually a Eurasian, often one with more of European blood in him than native, and almost always born and bred in India. His aim appears to be to avoid all work and to live on charity, though professing to be anxious to obtain means to travel to some town a hundred miles or so away in order to get employment. His stories of undeserved misfortune and of relations dependent on him are harrowing in their details, and generally succeed in extorting donations from the inexperienced, who are sad to find a European, as they suppose him to be, so dreadfully situated in a country like India. At the European settlements there are Charity Organisation funds raised by private subscriptions and administered by the clergyman of the place. Beggars are referred to him, and, if their need is genuine, they are glad to go to him for relief. A loafer may consent to apply to him, and if it is probably a deserving case, funds are supplied or a railway-ticket given to enable him to travel ahead. The help is sometimes abused, and cases have been known of loafers travelling over the greater part of India by means chiefly of such help,—the authorities being only too glad to get rid of them. A story is told of one who enlisted the sympathy of a newly-arrived missionary at a railway station, and, having got from him an unusually large donation, suddenly changed his tone to a jovial one and invited his benefactor to step into the refreshment-room with him and have a drink.

Tourists should be careful in selecting their guides. Some are so anxious to please their employers, and so quickly find out their disposition and views, that they give only the information that they think will be pleasing for the tourist to hear. Sometimes they do this just to make things pleasant all round and to keep in favour; but in some cases it is genuine politeness and a wish to please apart from prospects of gain. I had a peculiar example of this when my train stopped about half an hour at a station where dinner was served at the refreshment-room. About five minutes before the train starts a bell is rung to warn those who are dining. When this occurred I had not finished my dinner, and asked the *khansamah* if that was the five minutes bell. Seeing that I should feel it necessary to hurry with my dinner if I were told that it was, he replied, "Oh no, sahib; plenty of time," so as to encourage me to feel comfortable. I felt comfortable and proceeded leisurely for a few minutes, till, just before the time for the train to start, the man became alarmed and hurriedly told me the truth.

Many an interesting journey amid towns fell to my lot on leave or on duty, and the scenes were as varied and ever-changing as in a kaleidoscope; but far better, more healthy, recuperative, and enjoyable were those made to the hill tracts, —the Nilgherries, the Vindhyas, the Ghauts, and, best of all, the Himalayas.

XII.

IN THE HILLS.

PRIVILEGE LEAVE—TRAVELLING IN THE 'SEVENTIES—DHOOLIES—DAK GHARRIES—SIWALIKS—JOURNEY TO THE HILLS—SCENERY OF THE LOW HILLS—HILL-STATIONS—THE HIMALAYAS—STARTING FOR THE INTERIOR—HILL-MEN—ROUGH COUNTRY—FINE SCENERY—COMPARISON WITH SWITZERLAND—THE SNOW-PEAKS—ROPE-BRIDGES—MISTS—WATERFALLS—BELUCHISTAN—PATHANS—BOLAN PASS AND KHOJAK TUNNEL—AFGHAN BORDER—PLATEAUX—WILD ANIMALS—CAUVERY FALLS—MAHABLESHWAR—POONA—PHOTOGRAPHY.

THREE months' privilege leave gives time for a trip to England and back with at least a month there; but, as this kind of leave is taken nearly always in the hot weather, the journey through the Indian Ocean and the Red Sea is best avoided. If a voyage be desired it is better to go to Australia, which may be reached in less time and at the best season of the year. For those who do not enjoy the sea, there is nothing better than a visit to the Himalayas or to one of the hill-stations on the lower ranges, such as the Nilgherries, the Palni hills, and the Western Ghauts. Sometimes one has a period of service located at a hill-station: and the man is fortunate who has much of his time spent on duty in the hills in practically an English climate or one which may be even better.

Either on leave or on duty I had my fair share

of time in the hills. My first visit to the high hills was on leave; and the freedom from restraint, the absence of the annoyances of the plains, and the delightful climate and hill scenery were most enjoyable. I am sure that the policy of the Government of India of giving as much leave as can conveniently be allowed is right; for such a visit renews one's vigour and sends a man back to duty the better able to do his work. Without leave the depressing influences which weigh on Europeans in the plains continue; and, though it may not be recognised at the time till a complete breakdown occurs, there is a deterioration of one's powers, physical and mental, which cannot fail to affect the quality of one's work. It makes just the same difference as that between a blunt and a sharp tool.

Having received the necessary sanction and handed over charge of one's duties to the man who will carry them on during one's absence, a start is made without delay; for no more time than is necessary should be spent in the plains. The final receipts having been given, a rush is made for the nearest station, if starting by railway; and the journey is then made to that station which is nearest to the foot of the hills. In the present day several branch lines have been constructed from the main trunk lines to the low hills, so that it is now an easier and quicker journey than in the 'Seventies. In those days a long road journey of sixty, eighty, or even more miles had to be undertaken between the railway and the beginning of the ascent. This was done in some cases in a dhooly or palanquin carried by eight or twelve men taking turns, four or six at a time. Inside there was just room to lie down comfortably and sleep the night through, while the tedious slow march was continued to the accompaniment of a peculiar sing-song to which the bearers adjusted their paces. Or, if available, a dak gharry might be hired and the journey be done more quickly. This is a rough conveyance, something like a four-wheeled cab with one pole instead of shafts. It is drawn by two ponies, which are changed at every stage of six miles. These ponies go very well, and generally do the first mile or two of each stage at full speed, and the last mile in a rather exhausted state. They sometimes fight hard in the harnessing, either objecting to go or trying to be placed on the side away from the whip. Until the first few hundred yards at the beginning of each stage are passed, the gharry sways about a good deal, and one must hold tight to be ready for a spill till the ponies have been got well under control.

On one of these journeys, that from Saharunpore on the way to Mussoorie, some pretty low hills, the Siwaliks, are passed through; and between them and the Himalayas is a plain called the "Doon," where the scenery is English and in some parts like a well-kept park with fine trees. All along the foot of the low ranges for about twenty-five miles before reaching them is a thick forest called the "Terai," full of grass undergrowth, boulders, wild animals, and fever. The change from the dazzling white roads and the dust and heat of the plains to such scenery and comparative coolness is very refreshing.

It was late at night or early next morning that the foot of the hills was reached; and some hours were then spent at the Government dak bungalow, or a private hotel, generally much larger than usual to accommodate the numerous travellers. Here it was necessary to wait a little to rest or to get a bath and a meal, while a hired saddle-horse was being fed and got ready for the ascent.

So far the ground had been rising gradually, and by the time that Raipur or Kalka or other dak bungalow, according as the route was to Naini Tal or Simla or other hill-station, was reached, an elevation had been attained which was several hundred feet above that of the plains in which one's life had been lately passed. The difference of temperature in the hot weather, —even thus early in the rise,—is already most agreeable, and the greener country and the prettiness of the forests and low hills ahead are much appreciated. Those who are inclined walk up the whole way to the hill-station, a distance of six, eight, or ten miles to Mussoorie or Naini Tal, which are only one day's walk, and of sixty or eighty or more to Simla or Murree or Dalhousie. To walk up to these three days or more are required, and halts are made at wayside dak bungalows each night. The rise is generally 5000 or 6000 feet, and in some places very steep, especially if the track be followed which is taken by hill coolies who carry light baggage ahead.

If one is in fair health, it is best to walk up when the journey can be done without expending more than one or two days. The gradual change of temperature is better than a sudden change; and, though the unusual exercise is, towards the top, rather fatiguing, it is a good preparation for the continuous rough up-and-down walks in store.

On leaving the dak bungalow the real ascent is immediately begun; and, a few hundred feet higher, the trees thicken and one can look down on the expanse of plains below. Everything is still, the air is delicious, the scenery is charming, and the reaction from the weary round of duties already begins to raise the spirits. At first it seems as if there was an access of physical strength, and one is inclined to take the sharp rises too rapidly; but quick breathing and perspiration give warning that the influence of the hot plains is not yet left behind. At only a thousand feet in height it may appear that a cool climate has at last been reached; yet a month or two later, on the return journey, at the same elevation it is found hot and oppressive compared with the colder regions above.

Towards the top the ascent becomes steeper; and, if walking, the continuous climbing is tiresome, and one may prefer to ride the rest of the way. The climb is generally throughout amid thickly wooded hills, and towards evening the chill air is keenly felt. One is glad to reach the hotel and get a bath before dinner. To jump into the bath and roll about in it, as in the plains, is out of the question, for the water is like ice at first to the new arrival. The hotels are generally small and crowded; and, unless it is wished to stay some time in the station for the sake of the gay times, the dances, the concerts, picnics, tennis, and other amusements, it is more comfortable to get on beyond and to take a journey into the interior.

After dinner and the unusual luxury of an arm-chair in front of a fire comes a night of sound refreshing sleep. Next morning one is probably up long before breakfast and out of doors, while others who have already grown luxurious and abandoned the ways of the plains are still in bed. The houses of the hill-station are picturesquely located on hillocks and slopes amid clusters of trees, and perhaps near attractive-looking streams and small waterfalls. Ferns, moss, orchids, and the small hill flowers mingle with the trees and grass in the ravines; and, if early enough, there is an added beauty in the rolling mists as they clear away before the advancing sunshine. The visitor makes for some high point and searches for a view of the still distant snow-clad peaks; for even Simla, Naini Tal, Darjeeling, and other hill-stations are only 6000 or 7000 feet above the sea, and are 100 or 150 miles distant from the highest ranges. In between are many other ranges at varying average heights, alternating with deep valleys. There are broad roaring torrents to cross, quite unnavigable, and in which no boat can live. These feed the large rivers of the plains, and are crossed at a few places by bridges and at others by means of ropes. None of this can be seen except by visiting the interior: and it requires much preparation to ensure provisions, transport, and a sufficient amount of comfort.

From the high cliffs there is an uninterrupted view of the plains stretching away for many miles, till the haze and something of a dark-grey dulness mingled with it suggest the dust and heat from which escape has only lately been made. The nearer plains just beyond the foot of the hills are green with crops, grass, and trees. When, before the break of the monsoon, a casual storm caused by the heat overhangs the plains, it is fine to look down on to the top of the thunder-clouds and to see the lightning playing about below us. Those in the plains look up to dark clouds and a thunderstorm; we, at our elevation, look down to the dark clouds and up to a serene blue sky. As the storm clears gaps occur in the clouds, and bits of the plains can be seen through them with the sunlight shining on the crops.

It is best to stay a few days at the station to enjoy some of the pleasant society, to accustom oneself to the new exercise of walking up and down the steep roads and paths, and to complete the necessary arrangements for visiting the finer scenery beyond. Some go on shooting expeditions, others fishing or after butterflies, some sketching, and a few merely for healthy exercise and the views. In the station there are not only those who have come up on leave, but there are some on duty; for the Government offices, or parts of them, are moved, when this can conveniently be done, from the plains for the hot weather. The expense is comparatively small, and is fully recouped in the greater efficiency with which the officials can work in a good climate. There are also the many ladies and children sent by their husbands and fathers away from the trying times and climate below from April to October. They are seen going about in 'rickshaws or in dandys,—small boat-shaped conveyances with a projecting pole at each end, by which they are lifted and carried by bearers. The ladies seem to compete with one another in dressing their dandy-men (or *jampanis*) in pretty costumes. A few ride; but driving is rare, as it is difficult and dangerous, and it is inconvenient to bring up carriages.

Only a small portion of the Himalayas is within British territory, and it consists of parts of the lower ranges only. The high range lies in Nepaul, Bhutan, and Cashmere, and on the north and west of these, in Thibet, Chinese Turkestan, and Afghanistan. Roughly speaking it extends from north-west to east over a distance of 2000 miles, and has an average breadth of 500 miles. At intervals throughout the length there rise peaks clad in perpetual snow at heights of from 20,000 to 29,000 feet above the sea. The snow-line being, on the southern slope, at 15,000 to 16,000 feet, there is, even in the hottest season, always a clear depth of 5000 to 15,000 feet of snowy mantle.

Not even the best Alpine climbers could ever surmount Kailas, Dewalgiri, Kinchinjunga, or Everest.

Down the slopes of this enormous watershed flow the streams which water India and Burmah — the Brahmapootra and Irrawaddy on the east, the Ganges and its many tributaries on the south, and the Indus on the west. On the north, Thibet, being a mountainous tableland of an average height of 15,000 feet, gets little benefit from rivers, and the population is very poor. Farther west Cashmere is more favoured, but it is a very hilly country, the fertile parts being limited. Between the countries at the west end and those at the east end there is a striking difference. On the west, Afghanistan and Beluchistan (into which the lower ranges strike southwards), are elevated bare rugged countries, deficient in water and subject to intense cold. The people are hardy and brave, and live chiefly a pastoral and predatory life. Adjoining them, in the Punjaub, North-West Provinces, and Rajputana, are the more manly races of India. On the east the conditions are the reverse. In Assam, Burmah, and Bengal, Nature is profuse with her gifts, and the natives live in warm and fertile parts covered with rich vegetation, and are consequently comparatively effeminate and indolent. The people of Afghanistan, Beluchistan, and Cashmere are mostly Mahomedans; those at the eastern end are Hindu and Buddhist.

When all other arrangements are ready it is necessary before starting to engage coolies, and in a few places mules as well, to carry the baggage. The hill-men who do this are unhappy-looking creatures, whose chief aims in life appear to be to exist, to own a blanket and a pipe, and to get now and then a small payment for their services and a drink of spirits. They can carry great loads; but of course the weight given them must be very limited, as they have to take it eight, ten, or twelve miles in a morning. Tents, light furniture, stores, &c., are all sent forward in this way. In some parts women do the work: and one morning at Almora when about to start, having sent for the coolies, I was astonished at about twenty women arriving on the scene. It was to my mind then a barbarous idea that women should have such work to do, and I had them all sent away, and insisted that men coolies were to be got instead. The result was that I got none at all that day.

The servants with the coolies and baggage having gone on first,—for it is best not to be ahead of them for fear of their not arriving at all,—a start is made with the horse and syce. For several miles the walking is pleasant, and the horse is useful when the country is so hilly as to be extra tiring. Of the many fine journeys I have had in the hills the most enjoyable have been those from Simla up the Sutlej valley, from Dalhousie to Chamba in Cashmere, from Naini Tal to Almora and into the interior to the Nepaul frontier, and one from Quetta through the Bolan Pass and Khojak tunnel to Chaman and the Afghan frontier. At the eastern end of the

Himalayas there is, at Darjeeling, as grand a view as can be found in the world of a snow-clad mountain peak. On a clear day Kinchinjunga can be seen from base to summit. As the base is at only 3000 feet or so above the sea, and the peak is at 28,176 feet, there is an uninterrupted view of a height of 25,000 feet. The upper half is of perpetual snow, and the lower half is the dark body of the hill broken up into ravines, and, in the lowest parts, covered with gloomy forests. Standing on Tiger Hill and looking across the low plains of Sikkim on a clear day, one may see, as if they were only a few miles away, regions with arctic, temperate, or tropical climates, each having its own special vegetation and animals, or, in the higher parts, glaciers, avalanches, and eternal snow.

It may be for days that the journey is made through undulating country with occasional steep rises and falls, and amid forests of fine pines, deodars, cedars, and rhododendrons. Through these are seen, now and then, views of a deep valley with dark gorges, small waterfalls, and a background of the snowy range. There are few birds, but many squirrels, and an occasional colony of monkeys. On the road a few hill-men are met, charcoal-burners perhaps, or small traders in firewood, all looking as if life has no pleasure for them. They live in simple grass huts and small villages in secluded parts of the forest with a minimum of comfort, and they would probably resent any attempt to get them to change their mode of life.

Gradually the road gets more difficult and becomes merely a path cut on the side of the hill. On one hand is a slope or an almost vertical rock rising high above, and on the other a steep precipice falling to the valley below. At first the path is broad enough for vehicles, and is guarded with a small rubble stone wall, which, however, in case of accident, would be little real safeguard, but it gives a sense of security. Farther on it is narrower, and no attempt is made to hide the ugly fall one may get if careless. In time one gets accustomed to it, and can even ride along such places for miles without feeling giddy. The horses are quiet enough; they become used to it, and have their own safety to take care of. Should anything startling occur and make one's horse restless, it is wrong to pull his head away from the precipice, because that only turns his eyes on to the wall of rock, and he is liable to back away from it towards the danger. Better to keep his head towards the ravine, and he will be careful not to go over.

Each day towards the end of the journey the sight of the small Government hut, in which one hopes to find a night's rest if there are not already other travellers, is welcome. If there is room in it there is no need to pitch the tent, nor is there any wish to do so; for the tents we take with us are as light as possible, and only large enough to cover a bedstead, a small camp-table, and a chair. They do not keep out the cold, and we have to depend on plenty of rugs and warm clothing.

There are ridges of the hills up to which the monsoon clouds reach but over which they do not pass, being probably diverted into valleys through which the main currents of wind carry them. At a village in Kumaon it was said that the heavy rains never cross the range of hills above the village, though they fall heavily on the other side. This was brought to my notice when, with a clear sky above us, the peculiar sight was seen of very black clouds of the colour of ink and apparently the consistency of cream spilling over the lowest parts of the ridge. It must have been raining heavily on the other side.

After a few days' journey the country becomes rougher and very trying. It may now be 9000 or 10,000 feet above the sea; and any rise ahead to a few hundred feet higher may involve, first, a descent in between of possibly several thousand feet, and many ups and downs before the higher elevation is attained. On one of these journeys I had walked all day and had had a climb of 3000 feet. When within a few hundred feet of the top, a native who was guiding me, in reply to my inquiry as to how far the rest-house was, told me that it was not far, and that I should see it as soon as I reached the top. This satisfied me, and as it was about four o'clock and I was getting tired, I pictured to myself an easy saunter in as a preliminary to an early bath and dinner. On arriving at the top, rather done up, I saw the bungalow, apparently not far away; but there was a descent of several hundred feet and a corresponding rise before it could be reached. The hill-men think little of such trifles, and from his point of view my guide had been correct in saying it was not far ahead.

So large are the main valleys in the Himalayas that one can travel for days in the same general direction with practically the same scene always in front—viz., a deep valley full of dark forests, with a torrent appearing at intervals far below, fed occasionally by side streams and waterfalls, and with a view of towering snow-clad hills apparently at the head of the valley, but in reality a hundred miles beyond it. When, after much tedious exertion, the top of the valley is reached, the rolling hills, the other deep valleys, the subsidiary gorges, the forests, the distant glaciers and snows, are a grand sight. To go on ahead necessitates further deep descents and long sharp rises over and over again before reaching a still higher altitude, and the road becomes a mere path of the roughest and often a dangerous kind. The scenery is different from that of Switzerland and other pretty mountainous countries. In Switzerland there may be a change of scene every half hour and a charming new view every time. Though there is much prettiness in the Himalayas, it is not to be compared with that of Switzerland or Tasmania or the southern parts of British Columbia. There is grandeur, and everything is on a magnificent scale; but there is much that is gloomy, and, especially at evening, a sombre solitude broken only by the shrill note of a hill deer or the grunt of a bear or some other inhabitant of the jungles. One very handsome animal I saw, a snow fox, white, and with long silvery hair. He trotted leisurely across my path and disappeared into the jungle, his tongue hanging a little out of his mouth sideways, giving him a sly and rather comic expression.

In the Alps the highest mountain—Mont Blanc—is only 15,750 feet above the sea. In the Himalayas there are many peaks of 20,000 and 25,000 feet; and Everest is 29,002. The extra 10,000 or 12,000 is all covered with perpetual snow; and those who know Switzerland can judge what the effect would be if 10,000 or 12,000 feet extra snowy height were piled on the top of the Jungfrau or the Matterhorn. Of course, in the Himalayas the great distance of the central peaks lessens the immediate effect on the observer in the plains or the low hills; but the vastness is there, and the sights are unequalled and unapproached. General Strachey has remarked, in an article in the 'Encyclopædia Britannica,' that the Alps could be put into some of the valleys of the Himalayas without producing any result that would be discernible at a distance of ten or fifteen miles.

In the very rough high country, at about 10,000 feet or higher, there are many fine waterfalls and cascades, and, here and there, small lakes collected from the streams that flow from the glaciers and melting snows. About here there is a general fall of the accumulated waters from the high ranges to the deep gorges, ravines, and valleys of the lower ranges. Few tourists get beyond these parts, as the exertion required in the extraordinary confusion of crumpled hills is

A ROPE-BRIDGE ACROSS A TORRENT—SUTLEJ VALLEY (HIMALAYAS).

more than human frames can well bear. The native attendants drop off and return to their homes, or some fall ill; and, as there are hardly any inhabitants near enough, one may get stranded for want of food and transport. The paths may be broken and impassable, causing troublesome detours; and the rope-bridges, where they still exist, are possibly not to be trusted.

Crossing these rope-bridges is, at first, a trying experience. Some refuse to go across at all, and travellers have been known to turn back on reaching the first one. The illustration shows the arrangement. The traveller sits in the hanging loop suspended from the running block which is pulled over the rope by a man on the other side. The rope of this bridge was said to be made of twelve strands, each calculated to be strong enough to bear a man, so that it should be very safe even if some of the strands were broken. Unfortunately the tendency of the men in charge, if any of the strands break, is to delay reporting the fact, on the ground that the rest are quite strong enough. This may be; but it is better, of course, for the full margin of safety to be kept up, because the influence of damp and frost, wear and tear, should be very thoroughly provided against in such isolated spots where inspection cannot be frequent. The end fastenings, the stakes to which the ropes are fastened, the pulley and block, the hanging ropes, and other things have all to be perfectly safe. A failure of any one means certain death; for no one could remain for even a few seconds above the surface when once in the roaring torrent. When in good health it is possible, as one is drawn across, to look with interest and pleasure at the leaping foaming volumes of water which seem to fight with one another, bounding along as if in a mad race to escape from some enemy behind. The same is seen on a grander scale when going up the Niagara rapids on the American side; but there one is safe on shore instead of hanging immediately above the centre of the stream, as one must if the journey into the interior of the Himalayas is to be continued at all.

In going up the valley of the Sutlej the journey is wholly on one side of the river; and it is the side streams that are crossed by rope-bridges. On this journey, and those into the interior from Almora and other starting-places, a few Thibetan traders are sometimes met, remarkable for their Chinese cast of face, their thick woollen clothing, and the praying-mills which they carry with them. They come over passes as high as 15,000 to 18,000 feet: and how they can make money enough in trade to repay them for the trouble of carrying their wares over such difficult country can be known only to themselves. At one place a large gloomy-looking Buddhist monastery was pointed out to me on the opposite side of the Sutlej. I had then a great desire to see one, and regretted the impossibility of getting across to it. My idea was that I should find the monks leading a life in accordance with the pure ethical teachings of Buddha, but from what I have since heard it seems that, as in many other religions, the priests

A VILLAGE IN BELOOCHISTAN.

and devotees are rather degenerate, living partly, as do Brahmins, on the credulity and the earnings of the very poor, and teaching doctrines by no means contemplated by the founders of their faith.

When the traveller reaches one of the high ridges, the landscape suddenly revealed is one never to be forgotten. The contrast with the valleys just left is so great, the pure white of the snows so fairy-like, the boldness of the high peaks, and the enormous extent of the ranges, especially if appearing and disappearing amid clouds or mists,—all are so extraordinary, and the scene so fascinating, that one stands still for a long time in astonishment. I seemed never to tire of admiring this scenery. It is best at early morning and at evening. Once when I rose just before daylight, my tent having been pitched on a hill, I could hardly believe it, as I saw what appeared to be an enormous lake just at my feet. Standing out from this lake were the hills, as clearly isolated from one another as are the islands round the coasts of Scotland or Italy. The snow-ranges and peaks were of a dull steel grey. It was the top of the mist that I was looking at. All above it was as clear as could be; but the valleys below were completely hidden, not even a foot below the dead level of the top of the thick mist being visible. As the sun approached, the snows became tinged with pink; and then the mist began to rise, at first in little curling patches, and then, after swaying about, in larger and larger volumes, till the valley below appeared.

It for a time obscured the distant views, but as the sun dispersed it there could be seen, through the openings, the dazzling white snows lit up with the full sunshine upon them.

At morning the packing and bustle of departure on the day's journey keep one occupied; but at evening there is no such distraction, and one can rest in comfort and admire the sunset and the gradual change of colours on the snow and the landscape. At the season when such visits are made to the hills the evenings are generally clear, and the peaks stand out unclouded till the last ray of light fades or the moonlight shows them faintly still in view. The colouring is sometimes very fine, and, as it changes from white to various shades of pink and then to grey, no prettier picture could be wished for. And these ranges are the great barrier which for 2000 miles defends India from enemies on the north, and which causes the rain-laden monsoon winds to supply the great rivers and to fertilise the soil.

Though at night the cold is searching, the travelling at midday is, in some of the valleys, hot and oppressive. Even then, on turning a corner, a cold breeze may be met coming from a shady part where the sun never penetrates, and where, consequently, the blown snow and the ice remain unmelted. Where, in the daytime, rivulets form small cascades there may be, at night and early morning, a congealed waterfall looking as if the water had suddenly frozen half-way in its fall, and forming a pretty

BORDER TRIBESMEN (N.-W. FRONTIER).

set of icicles. These, however, were shaped as the last drops of water trickled over the edge, and solidified after passing over the ice already there.

In some parts no side streams are found for several miles; and on my journey I was puzzled at my horse pricking his ears forward and starting off at a brisk pace. He had heard the ripple of a cascade in the distance, and both he and I were glad of a long cool drink. It is not safe to drink much of the very cold water which comes from the snows. Goitre, among other things, is attributed to it.

A curious effect was produced when a small stream, after falling some ten or a dozen feet over a precipitous rock, was steadily caught in mid-air by a strong wind from below, and all blown in a curve back again, passing high over the top of the fall on to the country from which it had come. Of course, every now and then some of it must have escaped the wind and glided down the face of the rock, but when I saw it the whole was apparently being blown back.

In Beluchistan the chief interest lay not so much in the country—which, though bold and striking is otherwise uninteresting, being bare and ugly—as in the people and the military arrangements. At Quetta and at Chaman on the Afghan border, and at wayside stations, Beluchis, Afghans, Waziris, and other border tribesmen mingle with the people from the plains, who, under our guidance, manage the railway, the telegraphs, and other modern innovations.

These tribesmen are strong and manly, with a self-reliant independent character much to be admired. Unfortunately they have scant respect for human life; and their raids on the villages under British protection and on one another, and their readiness to use knives in quarrels, make it necessary to be careful in dealing with them. At some of the stations in the Bolan Pass, as the train rolled up to the platform, there was a row of native soldiers standing, one at every few yards where the train would stop; for the lawless tribes in the vicinity were quite willing to loot the passengers if they saw the opportunity. At one place this had happened and the station-master had been killed. Some of the men were in possession of rifles which they ought not to have been able to get. We examined a rifle of one of the Pathans. It was marked BIRMI. No. 707 V. I. Я., and had the usual mark to show that it was a condemned one.

On the road to Chaman the engineer in charge took me through the Khojak tunnel on a trolly, —a very rapid and interesting journey, leading at the end to the Afghan border. Here no one is allowed to go beyond. From a low hill near this place the hills round Kandahar could be seen; and here were collected, in perfect order and condition, the rails and other material which had been used on the line to Kandahar, and which were dismantled in 1881.

The ranges in other parts of India are low compared with the Himalayas, and none reach

A PATHAN (AFGHAN FRONTIER).

to more than about half the height of the snow-line. Only at Ootacamund and in the Palni hills in the Madras Presidency are they as high as the average Himalaya stations—viz., from 5000 to 7000 feet. Mahableshwar, Ootacamund, and others are healthy and pleasant, and are much resorted to. On the table-lands, at from 2000 to 3000 feet, at Bangalore, Poona, Mhow, and several other plateau towns, there are many retired Eurasians and a few Europeans settled for life with their families. At this height fruit and flowers flourish. Keeping bees, and the cultivation of apples, peaches, apricots, and vegetables are favourite pursuits.

When stationed at Indore, the capital of the Mahratta prince, Holkar, I took a two days' walk through the Vindhya hills. They are not very attractive, though covered with forest and full of game. Having sent on all my men, I walked leisurely down the hill to a place called Choral, where there is a bungalow at which I intended to stay the night. As the sun set the moon rose bright and full, and I had a prospect of a quiet, solitary, cool walk of still three or four miles before dinner. There was thick-wooded jungle on each side of the path. Suddenly from my left, at only a few yards ahead, a leopard came out and crossed the path, disappearing into the jungle on the right. I was glad I had so good a view of the creature, and thought little more of the matter till, about a quarter of a mile farther on, the same thing occurred again,—a leopard appearing and disappearing in just the same way, and, as before, from left to right. This was not reassuring; and yet again a short distance ahead there was one on a rock on my left close to the road, some twenty feet or so above it. This third time the animal did not cross the road, but on my shouting it disappeared. Apparently there were three leopards: but on my minutely detailing all the facts to an old military officer well known for his sporting experiences, he told me that, no doubt, it was the same leopard, and that he was circling round me, crossing from left to right in front of me, and, unseen by me, from right to left behind. He was possibly taking observations of me out of mere curiosity.

On the same plateau as that where Bangalore, the paradise of Eurasians, is located, there are the interesting towns Mysore and Seringapatam, the scenes of the exploits of the sanguinary rulers Hyder Ali and Tippoo Sultan, but now the seat of an enlightened and progressive native Government. Not far from there are the Cauvery Falls where the river leaps over a precipice of several hundred feet. When visiting them I saw amid scrub jungle, and at about a hundred feet from the road, what I supposed to be a python—though it may have been only a rock-snake—lying full length on the ground and with its head down a hole. It was probably after some small animal for food. Curious to examine it, I crept cautiously towards it, and got near enough to see the quivering glistening muscles moving about and now and then appearing of a dark-green instead of the black or dark-brown which was the general colour. The whole body was very moist, as if it had lately been through wet grass. As it worked about, the length, some ten or twelve feet in view, grew shorter or longer as the thickness of the body became more or less. When it was evident that is was beginning to withdraw from the hole and that the head would soon appear, I turned and fled. On reaching the road and looking back, I discovered that the snake had done the same and was travelling fast in the opposite direction, no doubt alarmed at the vibration of the ground caused by my running off.

At the bungalows near the falls there is a visitors' book in which names are entered as far back as sixty or seventy years ago. Some of the remarks are interesting and some amusing. There is a story of a "Pir" or holy man who fell into the rapids below the falls, and in whose honour a shrine is built close by. There is also related a sad occurrence of a young lady—a bride—who went too near the precipice and fell over. Her body could be seen from above by her friends as it was washed about in the torrent before being carried away.

Mahableshwar is on the Western Ghauts near Poona, and is a hill resort of the Governor of Bombay and his officers during the hot dry weather. Except during four or five months of the year in the monsoon season, when it is uninhabitable owing to excessive rain and continuous dense fog, it is a delightful station. When, in

April, May, and part of June, it is full of visitors, those on leave, together with the ladies, arrange to keep up a continual round of amusements, in which, of course, the rest join when their duties allow. Tennis, badminton, golf, tent-pegging, riding, picnics, and garden-parties during the day, and concerts, dinners, and dances at night, would sound almost too much of good things. But they do not take up too much time; and those up on leave are often there only for a week or two or a few days, and are continually changing. It is good that there should be a few on longer leave to assist the ladies in organising and to keep a bright time always ready for the seekers after change and health. When permitted to take my work to Mahableshwar during the hot weather, it happened to be during the genial presidency of His Excellency Lord Harris and Lady Harris, —when officialdom for once laid aside formality, and the cliques into which society in India is subdivided became less defined for the time; when all joined in the same games of golf and tennis, and were on the best of terms when meeting together at the Frere Hall. Especially will be long remembered the wind-up of the season, when the spinsters of the station invited every one to a tea-party, and the fun which followed, when even Generals and Members of Council had to unbend and join in frivolous games. At such a time the remark is often made that the aides-de-camp have a fine time of it; the fact being probably that they are the hardest worked of all, as, in addition to their usual duties, they have many extra people to please and bear with.

On the edges of the table-land on which Mahableshwar is situated there are several projecting points from which the plains can be viewed for many miles, and some beautiful scenery is shown. From one of these points is seen across the valley another plateau on which is the fort of Pertabghur, where the Mahratta hero Sivaji invited his Mahomedan opponent Afzul Khan to meet him at a friendly conference. On his arrival Sivaji embraced him in the form of a welcome and at the same time stabbed him in the back.

At about 1000 feet below Mahableshwar is Panchgani, a small hill-station with a pleasant climate throughout the rainy season. After the Mahableshwar season a move is made to Poona, which, though lower still, is at about 1800 feet, and has a good climate till October or November, when the Government goes back to Bombay. At Panchgani there is a small table-land of about half a square mile, high above all the surrounding hills. On it are the golf links; and in clear weather it is delightful to stay up there with bracing fresh air above, below, and all round.

During one of my walks in the Panchgani hills one evening my fox-terrier had, as usual, gone about in all directions examining the bushes and hollows. After a time he came from a distance backing fast towards me and barking excitedly; and then, from round the end of a line of bushes, came a hyæna trotting towards us. These large animals of the jungle—leopards, hyænas, wolves, jackals—always appeared to me to be trotting rather than running. Apparently they know that they are going fast enough for their purpose, and don't care to exert themselves more than is necessary. The dog was backing towards me for protection and barking all the while at the hyæna. As soon as the hyæna saw me he gave up the chase and turned off at a run. The dog then thought it was his turn and went sharp after him, which was, of course, dangerous, and I had much difficulty in inducing him to return.

At some of these hill-stations the very small, almost invisible, insects are troublesome, such as sand-flies, eye-flies, and especially jungle fleas, which, though they remain mostly out of doors in the dry months, seek shelter in the bungalow by thousands when the weather is wet. Disinfectants, deodorisers, carbolic acid, camphor, seem to have no effect on them. One remedy is said to be good, but I never tried it. It was to drive a cow through the bungalow, because the fleas all jump on the cow, who carries them out with her.

At Poona the cricket matches between the English eleven and the Parsees were always worth seeing. The Parsees sometimes won against some of the best English teams; but it must be noted that Englishmen in India, owing to the climate and their having little time or inclination for practice, do not retain their real cricket form. In the same way, of course, the Parsees when they came to England lost their cricketing powers to some extent. The Parsee community and the natives generally took keen interest in the matches, and were very anxious for the success of their own countrymen. It was not pleasing to note a want of generous and sportsmanlike feeling amongst them, for every hit made by a Parsee player, though it did not earn a run, was cheered; but even the best hits and first-class bits of play of the Englishmen were watched by the crowd in dead silence.

In these days of amateur photography there are plenty of opportunities of recording scenes and incidents of travel; but there are also certain serious drawbacks in India not experienced in England. An American lady tourist on the voyage home, in reply to my inquiry what she thought of India, said, "It is not a bad place to have photographs of." Another had snap-shotted about a hundred views with her kodak, and, on developing on her return home to California, found nothing at all on any of the plates or films. A camera cannot be treated as in other climates. Dust gets into it and in the dark slides as a matter of course in India; and, even if the plates be brushed quite clean before developing, there is probably plenty of dust in the air and in the developing solution. A hot sun may cause minute cracks in the wooden slides or in the woodwork of the camera, and a black streak or blur may thereby be caused on every picture. If developed in warm weather it may be that the film dissolves away. Iced developing solutions are therefore used, but even then the change from the iced solution to the warm air will cause the film to frill. The light, however, is generally bright, and exposures can be made more instantaneous than in most other countries, and brilliant effects of light and shade are obtained.

Sometimes one wishes to be in the picture oneself; and, if no one that understands photography is at hand, a native servant may be taught to take the cap off and put it on again after the proper length of exposure. I have at times taught my servants to do so, and they have done it very well. They do exactly as they are told, being anxious all the time to do it correctly; and some are rather proud of the fact if they are told that they did it right. Of course pardonable mistakes occur, as when one Englishman taught his bearer to make the exposure while he himself formed part of a group with his friends. He showed him how to take off the cap, count "One, two, three," and then put it on again. This he caused him to practice several times till perfect, and then he took his place in the group. On his master giving him the signal, the bearer made the exposure, counted "One, two, three," and put the cap on again quite correctly. His master and friends then broke up their group and began chatting together, till it was noticed that the bearer was still going on exposing and counting "One, two, three," over and over again just as he did when practising. His master had forgotten to tell him to do it only once.

The illustration shows a group of four hill people—two men and two women. It was taken by a resident of Mussoorie, who could not make

HILL MEN AND WOMEN OF KUMAON (HIMALAYAS).

them understand more than that they should sit still. They did not know what was going to be done to them, and evidently were rather frightened, as shown in the photograph by their putting their hands together. When the cap was taken off the first time, they all bobbed their heads as if they expected they were going to be shot.

XIII.

ASSAM.

THE BRAHMAPOOTRA—WILD HISTORY—JOURNEY BY RIVER STEAMER—THICK JUNGLE—LONG GRASS—LAWSUITS—THE ASSAMI—TRAVELLING IN THE JUNGLE—ELEPHANTS—FLOODS—WILD BOAR—JUNGLE FIRES—ONE HOUR TO BUILD A VILLAGE—DRIVING—TEA-GARDENS—TIGERS—BEARS—SPORT—EARTHQUAKES—*THOPPAS*—HILL-TRIBES.

AFTER short periods of service in Central India and Rajputana, my next transfer was to Assam, where the climate and conditions, the surroundings and the people, all are different from any I had yet experienced. Instead of being among the ever ready, hard-working, manly races of the north of India, and in parts subject to intense heat at one time of the year and bracing cold at another, I was to be among an effeminate apathetic people, so averse to work that labourers for the public works and tea industry have to be imported from Bengal and the North-West Provinces and other parts of India. The climate of Assam is more equable; and, while being in some months pleasantly cool, is never intensely hot, the temperature seldom rising above ninety degrees.

As in other warm damp climates of the East, the land is very fertile, and the Assamese have, therefore, few wants which are not provided for by Nature without the necessity for hard work. They live in huts or houses easily built in a few days, or even in a few hours, of bamboos, reeds, and grass; their clothing costs little, and food of some kind is always at hand. What exertion they put forth to get food is merely that required to plant and reap the rice and other simple crops. In the intervals between the sowing and the reaping seasons they remain for months almost idle. The population is only 109 to the square mile, and there are large areas of fertile land awaiting occupation. Famine never visits Assam; and on these unoccupied tracts might well be settled some of the poor cultivators of Bengal who find it hard to live in the congested districts. They have, however, much objection to leaving their ancient homes and their own people; and the majority of those who go for a few years to work on the tea-plantations are glad to get away home again. The climate and people of Assam are different from those they have been accustomed to, and few readily adapt themselves to the new life there. Some do remain and settle down as cultivators.

Assam is far north, and adjoins Bhutan, Thibet, China, and Burmah, being separated from them by wild jungly hills inhabited by uncivilised, aboriginal, and semi-independent hill-tribes. It is traversed by the Brahmapootra river, the valley of which is bounded by two spurs of the Himalayas—one of them separating it from Bhutan, the other from the valley of the Surma river on the Cachar and Sylhet side. Between these two rivers and the foot of the hills on both sides are fertile tracts in which are produced rice, tea, mustard, jute, and other crops. Until only three or four years ago the Brahmapootra and its tributary, the Surma, were the only means of conveying the heavy traffic in these crops to the Bengal railways. In the hills there is much timber and rubber practically untouched. Coal-fields have been worked for several years near Dibrugarh, far up the river; the coal being, like that of Bengal and Hyderabad, the product from ferns of the Trias period and not of the Carboniferous, the coal of which, as in England, was produced from forest trees.

In the greater length of the Brahmapootra there is a strip of land from six to twenty miles broad on each side over which the floods extend in the rainy season. These lands are therefore uninhabitable, and, as long as the population is scanty, will remain unreclaimed. Over them grows a thick jungle of long grass and reeds; and here and in the forests are the homes of tigers, elephants, rhinoceros, buffaloes, bison, monkeys, bears, snakes, deer, and wild pig. Partridge, wild duck, and snipe are numerous; and the river itself abounds in alligators and large fish.

Though so isolated by hills, and though in ancient times it must have been difficult of access, Assam has had an eventful history. The many wild tribes of the hills are probably mere remnants of conquered nations long ago forgotten. There are remains of temples and inscriptions in Assam and Madras which cannot be clearly assigned to any particular period. At the time of the Mogul dynasty of Delhi the inhabitants of Assam were pirates of the Brahmapootra, and used to make raids from the river on the villages of Bengal; and when chased they retired to their forests and swamps. Among themselves they were merciless plunderers of one another, and there was much misery inflicted by their chiefs. Afterwards Mahomedan conquerors from the West and Ahams from the East took the lead in the seventeenth and eighteenth centuries. The Ahams, from Siam, had a good civil and military organisation. The massive earthen ridges which run for miles through parts of Assam were made by them as fortifications. They are now used as roads; but it is said that as they were thrown up by forced labour, this is one of the reasons why the Assamese object to employment on public works, it now being considered derogatory to their dignity. At Gauhati, Sibsagar, and Rungpore, and occasionally hidden in the jungle, are found ruins of temples and palaces destroyed by the conquerors. The destruction was complete and ruthless, and doubtless the wars of those times were marked with much cruelty. When the British took possession in 1827, the country was devasted by feuds and local wars; and in 1857 Col. Holroyd, Deputy Commissioner of Sibsagar, by a bold move secured the person of a discontented scion of a deposed royal family, and so frustrated his plans for massacring all the English residents.

Having travelled from Ajmere, about 1100 miles

by rail, *viâ* Calcutta, to Goalundo on the Brahmapootra, I joined one of the large river steamers, and, at the slow rate of steaming against the stream in those days, went in four days 450 miles to Gauhati, the largest river-side station in Assam. The river is broad, full of shoals, and with a tortuous main stream which frequently changes its course. For this and another reason it was necessary to stop the steamer at night. It was the season when thousands of coolies, recruited for the tea-plantations, were being carried; and as they were crowded together on the upper and lower decks, it was good for them to land at night and cook their food on shore. These imported coolies are well looked after by Government. They are recruited by agents employed by the planters; and large advances are made to enable them to leave their families with means to tide over the time till they have earned more money on the tea-gardens and can make remittances. Sometimes the agents are dishonest and cheat either the planters or the coolies or both. If they do not actually decamp with cash, they perhaps engage lame or otherwise inferior labourers, and deduct large commissions from the advances they are authorised to make to the recruits. At Calcutta where the steamers start, or at the port of embarkation on the Brahmapootra, the men are examined and registered by the Government Medical officer. The steamers are inspected to see that sufficient space is provided, that their safety and health are looked after, and that a doctor travels with each steamer.

After arrival in Assam they are periodically inspected at each tea-garden by the Government Civil authorities, the muster-roll is called, their housing and sanitary arrangements are overhauled, and the arrangements made for each caste lot to be together. It is annoying to the planters, when perhaps a hundred rupees have been expended in the procuring of each coolie, to find that they are sickly and refuse to go into hospital when really ill, or object needlessly to the quality of the food supplied, or run away and try to get more lucrative work. Some may be addicted to opium, or are careless and get fevers by sleeping on the ground, as can well be done in their own country, or cholera through drinking water from any pool.

As we touched at the small side stations and more native passengers came on board, we had a few introductory examples of the jungly inhabitants of the low hills—Garos and Mekirs chiefly—picturesque and quaint in their curious ornaments, profuse enough to make up partly for the scantiness of their clothing. They wore nose-rings and earrings so heavy as to cause the lobes of the ears to elongate to double the usual length. I was told that they look on milk as diseased matter, unfit as food; but they are great smokers, spirit drinkers, and opium eaters, and will eat dogs, snakes, frogs, and the flesh of tigers and animals known to have died of disease.

Many alligators were seen in the distance on the low sand-banks; and we passed well-wooded islands and some natives in the peculiar country craft, sometimes made of merely a trunk of a tree roughly hollowed to the shape of a boat. These are the "dug-outs" in which the boatmen will brave the heavy floods. They are safe enough; and I afterwards became quite accustomed to travelling in them, carrying also with me my servants and heavy luggage.

On my reaching Gauhati orders were awaiting me which required my return 150 miles downstream to my new station at Dhubri. Having been there only a few weeks, I received an urgent telegram to proceed at once about 250 miles up the river again and thirty miles inland to Nowgong to assume charge of the Central Assam division, the Executive engineer of which had fallen seriously ill. Assam has a bad name for causing illness, fever and cholera being common; but I found it less trying than most parts of India. Fortunately there had not been time at Dhubri to settle in such a way as to have much expense on the transfer; and it was a case in which Government passes travelling allowances enough to cover the cost of one's own journey and that of one's servants and horse.

The Central Assam division included the Nowgong, Sibsagar, and Darrung districts, and extended over a length of country of 200 miles with a varying breadth of thirty to fifty miles. Part of it was on one side of the Brahmapootra and part on the other, the river itself being about a mile wide. Though there were 3000 villages and nearly a million inhabitants, the works were few and of a simple kind, but they were very scattered. Though not large, they were necessary as communications for the ordinary traffic and the transport of the rice and tea and other produce to the river steamers, and consisted in unmetalled road-making, a two-foot-gauge tramway, some small masonry buildings, wooden and bamboo bridges, and a few defences from floods. One difficulty was in arranging for the work to be done, labour being scarce, and, even when imported from outlying districts, unreliable. Some advantage had been taken of the illness of the Executive engineer, and claims were raised of which I doubted the validity. With the necessary sanction of Government I refused payment in order to have them tested in Court.

In the hot and damp climate of Assam the grass grows luxuriantly. When it is more of the character of reeds it will, within a few weeks, grow thick, and as high as fifteen or twenty feet. I have measured it twenty-eight feet long. In travelling through the broad expanses adjoining the river, which are subject to annual flooding, an elephant and his rider may be completely hidden in it. To ensure the roads in such parts being always available for traffic, they have to be raised well above high-flood level, and are therefore in many places, for miles, earthen banks six, eight, ten, or more feet above the level of the country. In this made earth the grass or reeds grow rapidly at some seasons, and one may travel over a road when it is quite bare, and a few weeks afterwards find it almost impassable. Periodically the clearing of this grass has to be undertaken, and claims were made by contractors that they had cleared it for some miles of road and had not been paid. On visiting these roads I found the grass standing, and, from all the information I could collect, it seemed likely that it had not been cleared at all that season. The contractors claimed that it had, and that during the illness of the engineer in charge it had grown again. Five actions were brought against me for payment, three of which were sustained and two failed.

In connection with these suits there was a curious incident showing in a peculiar light the simplicity of native social customs. I had employed a leading local *vakeel*, as had also the contractor who had raised the largest claim against Government. *Vakeels* are lawyers who plead cases in Court. In the smaller towns they are called pleaders, and are not of the same standing as a barrister. In private life they are, of course, good friends and may be of the same caste. Some are educated in England and study law there. They also study the action of the leading barristers. In these days the manner of Serjeant Ballantyne and Serjeant Parry were carefully copied and emphasised, as the pleaders declaimed in Court about even trivial matters which required no declamation at all. They, however, seem to think it necessary to play to the gallery, and probably it pays well.

One afternoon when returning to my bungalow at Nowgong a few days before the cases were to be heard, I was riding quietly past the house of the magistrate before whom they were to be tried. On passing the open door of his garden I saw a social gathering of natives dressed in their best array. The host was the magistrate, and the guests were the pleader for the prosecution, the pleader for Government, the contractor who brought the claim, the head clerk and accountant of my office, and a few others. On their seeing me pass, with the usual native politeness to Europeans, they all rose and salaamed. I returned the salutation and proceeded to my bungalow in a contemplative mood.

The Assamese coolies show little energy or interest in their work. They and the men employed for household duties, and the villagers, have heavy unattractive faces, giving the impression at first that they are surly. They are, however, not that; for, when passing along the road, an Assami, if riding, will dismount on meeting a European and will, as an act of courtesy, lead his horse by the bridle till well past him. Or, if carrying an umbrella, he will close it till the Englishman has gone by. The villagers are not actively friendly as are those of the north of India. Though they have no work in hand they will sometimes clear off and be careful to be absent if a little assistance is wanted by a traveller in difficulty. It is not only towards Europeans but towards travellers of their own country that they and some of the Madrassis show want of goodwill in this way. As servants they are slow and dull. A curious example was when, on asking my Assami bearer what time it was, he inquired of me "Now?" as if I could have meant "What time is it to-morrow morning?" They are easily frightened of *shaitans* (evil spirits); and, on the death of my syce from cholera, it got rumoured that a *shaitan* had been seen near the bungalow on the night when he died. All my servants except two left me for a time, as they said that the compound was haunted. I tried to reassure them by making light of their fears, and told them that, when next they saw the *shaitan*, they were to give him my salaams (compliments) and say I wished to have a word or two with him. They did not answer, and the only result was that they looked very serious and probably thought me irreverent.

Cholera, fever, smallpox, and other diseases are prevalent. Goitre is common along the banks of the rivers, and is said to be due to drinking the cold water from the melting snows of the hills. Elephantiasis is occasionally seen. Opium is used freely; and in malarious parts it appears to be a useful antidote in fever. It is even given to babies; sometimes probably only to keep them quiet, just as Indian ayahs are said to do to the English babies in their charge when troublesome.

The hill-men are good carriers, and will go ahead with hand-bags and other light loads, arriving hours before the carts or elephant. Some are so used to their morning opium that they cannot work with energy till they have it. Soon after eating it they are ready to start on a journey, or to set to work with much more zeal than without the dose. At the end of a journey, after receiving payment, they ask for a drink of spirits, and it is usually given. One tea-planter, not having any brandy or other spirit at hand, offered the man a drink of Worcestershire sauce instead. He drank it, and on being asked if it was good, replied that it was. Another time kerosene oil was tried as a substitute, but it was not appreciated. The hill-men find our discarded jam-tins and pickle-bottles most useful: and they may be seen travelling with old bottles and tins slung round them with string and full of food and drink.

There are three million Hindus, a million and a half Mahomedans, and nearly a million hill tribesmen. Though so near the five hundred million Buddhists in Eastern Asia, there are only nine thousand Buddhists in Assam. It is said that the majority of those calling themselves Mahomedan hardly know what Mahomedanism is, and that many of the Christians call themselves so because they do not belong to any other religion. At Tezpur there is an S.P.G. mission, of which Rev. Mr Endle has long been in charge; and at Nowgong there is a Canadian mission, for many years presided over by Rev. P. H. Moore and Mrs Moore. Among such an apathetic race the success of Christian missions must be very limited. When not successful in making real converts, they are useful at least in combating the old cruel practices and degrading ideas, and in helping the natives to live better lives. For instance, the cruelty is very great when they take their dying relations to die alone in isolated spots in the jungle, at a distance from the comforts of their home, for fear lest their spirits should haunt the place where death occurs. Exposure of the dying on the banks of the Ganges used to be a custom in Bengal, and mud and water were forced into their mouths to hasten death. This practice, and the exposure of women and children to die as sacrifices, were abolished by the British Government only as late as 1859.

When one is travelling by road or in dry weather in open country, riding on horseback is best. Elephants are better when the journeys are in jungly parts where the large trees and bamboos are not too thick, or over the rough and sometimes swampy ground where the tall reeds grow. The bridges, being of timber or bamboo, are rarely made strong enough for elephants to cross; and side ramps are made for them to go down into the stream and wade or swim across. To indicate that a bridge was not considered safe for an elephant, a wooden bar at about seven feet height was used, and was a well-known sign. The mahouts (elephant drivers) were sometimes too lazy to take the trouble to go down the ramps, and would make the elephant butt his head at the bars and knock them down. They then crossed the bridge, taking a serious risk of falling through it, *if the elephant would go across.* If the bridge is unsafe it may give indication enough by a tremor or some other sign which the elephant is clever enough to recognise. It is extraordinary with what force he brings his trunk down on the bridge to test it before he will agree to cross it. One would think that the apparently tender and delicate end of the trunk would be split up and rendered useless by such a bang as the animal gives on the woodwork.

The bamboo bridges were used only on the less important roads or until the more permanent wooden bridges could be built. They are strong enough if the spans are not more than ten or twelve feet, and the thicker bamboos used as beams are well seasoned and properly bound together. Heavily loaded carts crossed, and we used to ride freely over them; but the horses never liked them. Of course bamboo quickly gets weakened by the weather and wear and tear, and it has to be often renewed. On one journey my horse fell partly through one of these bridges, both his forelegs disappearing below the roadway. My feet came on to the bridge; but before I could dismount he had scrambled out, and he went across quietly as if nothing unusual had occurred.

Some of the bridges over streams in forest tracks consist of merely a single thick bamboo to walk on, helped by a hand-rail of thinner bamboo on each side. If one bears too heavily on one side the bamboo railing bends outwards and a tumble into the stream may result.

The parts liable to be flooded and the swamps in which the rice is grown are troublesome to cross, as must sometimes be done in the course of an engineer's duties; and when one is going through forests to prospect or to clear away for a new road, the bamboo and cane jungle are difficult to remove. Bamboo is useful in the construction of walls and roofs and even for the floors of bungalows; for many houses have to be built wholly above the ground and supported on piles with a space below the flooring to avoid flood-water. Between the bamboo or wooden planks of the flooring there are chinks, and the ground may be seen. In the space beneath goats, hens, and other animals are fond of collecting if lattice-work fencing is not put round it; and one may sit at breakfast and at the same time feed these creatures below one's feet.

Burmah, Pegu, Manipur, and Bhutea ponies are used. One of the best I had was a Burmah pony, a kind said to be in its prime at the age of twenty or twenty-five. He was startled one day, and bolted with my dog-cart over a precipice into deep water, and was drowned before help could get near. Another was a Bhutea, a thick-necked, slow, stubborn, hard-working animal that cared for nothing,—bad roads, long journeys, crossing water or bamboo bridges, passing elephants, all coming apparently quite as ordinary business to him.

On one journey of three or four days to examine a new tract with a view to finding a good location for a proposed road, I had to travel several miles in such long grass that, though on an elephant, I could not see over the country. Several rivers had to be crossed, and we came on them suddenly, the grass hiding them till we were close to the bank. They were narrow, with steep sides, and with beds twenty or thirty feet or more below the country level. At that season only two or three feet of water was flowing. When we were about to cross one of these, no way could at first be found sloping easily enough down to the bed, and, to my astonishment, the mahout took the elephant to the edge of a sharply falling bank. I told him to move back, but he said the elephant could do it. The elephant, however, refused; and on my telling the mahout to find a better place, he at last decided on one which appeared to me as bad as the other. This, however, was satisfactory to the elephant, and he proceeded to engineer the descent. First he sat down and placed his forefeet over the edge. Then with one foot he hammered the side of the slope till he had prepared a secure footing, and slid down on to it. He then hammered another step, and so on till at last he had slid down safely sideways, and reached the water. I was not in a howdah, but was seated on only a thick pad fastened to the back of the elephant by ropes passed round his body. While he was pounding the bank with his foot his shoulder worked up and down, and I was thrown about most uncomfortably. I had to hold tight to the ropes, and naturally caught hold of those which were loose. These, however, were now and then tightened up by the action of the elephant, and my fingers were squeezed between them and his back. At one time I was thrown on to his side, but fortunately held tight to the rope, and recovered my position on his back. When he reached the stream he was hot, and so was I. He then filled his trunk with water and squirted it over himself, giving me also a share which I did not want. On the other bank, which was not so steep, he made use of two trees to help to hoist himself. The mahout was more comfortable all the time, as he sits on the neck of the elephant with his legs astride.

This experience of the elephant's sagacity might almost tempt one to believe all the extraordinary stories told of them. Some I know are true. They are used for carrying logs of timber and stacking them, and for piling stones; but that they stand back and examine their work with a critical eye to judge whether it is regular and plumb may fairly be discredited. A young child, where an elephant was in frequent use, became fond of it and used to pull its trunk about. On visiting friends, and where there was another elephant, the child ran to it and seized its trunk in play, calling it "Dear hathi"; and fortunately the elephant understood and made no objection. They are, however, easily frightened—or perhaps it would be better to say startled—and take up a defensive attitude. No doubt in the jungle in their wild state it is necessary for them to be always on their guard. When travelling through jungle, a danger is that one's elephant may hear the trumpeting of a herd of wild ones in the distance and try to join them.

Travelling with them is not always satisfactory. On roads their rate is only three or four miles an hour. An elephant was attached to my division in Assam, and one morning I sent my servants with him and some carts to a bungalow in a jungly part nineteen miles distant. At two o'clock I started on horseback, expecting to arrive easily in time for dinner about eight o'clock. Some work had delayed me on the journey, and it was not till dusk, a little more than half-way, I found a teapot on the road, and farther on some more crockery, and a few articles of my clothing. Just ahead were the servants, the elephant, and the carts. The elephant had shaken the things off, either in a fit of temper or because they were loaded uncomfortably. The dull-witted Assami servants had sat down under the difficulty, and, instead of proceeding with the more necessary articles in one of the carts, and leaving the rest and the mahout with the elephant to come on next day, had waited helplessly till I arrived and found them crying. The part ahead, though only seven or eight miles, was too bad to go through at night, and we had to camp on the road, the vegetation on both sides being too thick and damp for us to go off it. It was easy to do so, as no one was likely to pass over the road till daylight, and then only a few villagers or a tea-planter.

It is said that when a sportsman goes in a howdah after tiger the elephant judges fairly well whether he is a good shot or not, and will face the tiger or refuse to do so accordingly. The truth, probably, is that a nervous sportsman communicates his nervousness to the elephant, and a confident one with a cheery tone of voice encourages him. When once tamed they are easily taught, and are so useful and friendly that it seems a wantonly cruel sport to shoot them. Sometimes it is necessary to shoot one that has gone "must," and is pillaging the crops and attacking villagers. Such a one is an outcast from his tribe, having been turned out by the others for misconduct, and, owing to the isolation, has gone half crazy. The mahout uses a sharp-pointed iron prong instead of a whip, and this he strikes hard on the elephant's head when wishing to make him go faster. Though the mahout may be rough and unkind to him, sometimes even laming him with a thorn in the foot if he wants an excuse for not going on a journey, the elephant is much attached to him, as it is the mahout that brings him his food and gives him his bath. When mounting to his neck the mahout may ascend by the trunk, and it is amusing to see the elephant forming a kink in his trunk as a step for him to climb up, the step altering in position as the man rises. When he is too high to be helped further in this way, the elephant gives a final push with a jerk which sends him up so sharp that he has to exercise his ingenuity in tumbling into proper position on his neck. Then the elephant passes up the iron prong which the mahout has left on the ground.

At the end of a journey the elephant waits outside the bungalow or tent for a douceur, and makes a salaam with his trunk when given a slice of bread or some sugar. He is then led away and tethered in shade, where he may be seen swishing about himself some twigs to drive away the flies and mosquitoes, for though his hide is thick it is sensitive. In former times they were used as executioners,—placing a foot on the victim's head, and at the word of command crushing him to death.

The cruel mode of catching them by pitfalls has been abandoned. A female elephant or two, trained for the purpose, would go into the jungle and make friendly advances to one of the wild ones. They probably told him highly-coloured stories of the wonders of civilisation, and induced him to come with them to see life. They then led him so that he would fall into a pit, which had been covered with bamboos and leaves as if solid ground. The method now is to drive them into an enclosure called a *kheddah*, and secure them cautiously with ropes and chains. Palisades of trunks of trees are arranged round the salt-springs at which they like to drink, one opening being left for entrance. During the taming process, they are fastened to tame elephants and kept in order by them. On a narrow road with clumps of bamboos on both sides I once met two elephants. On one, a tame one, was a mahout who shouted to me; but not knowing that the other was a wild one, I took no notice, as my horse was accustomed to passing elephants and was not afraid of them. On coming near I found it best to get off the road sharp, and to stand fifteen or twenty feet away, as the wild one was excited. He tried hard to get at me or at my horse, but the tame one to which he was chained, directed by the mahout, prevented him. Finding he could not have his way, he stretched his trunk out in our direction and gave a defiant blast like the rushing of steam from an engine. This excited the horse, and he backed into some bamboos, giving me a bad time, for bamboos playing roughly about one's face are not pleasant.

If an elephant fall into a quicksand, he has little chance of life, owing to his great weight. All that can be done to help is to throw him branches of trees, logs, and anything solid, and these he packs under himself to get a firm foundation. In his excitement he will seize hold of anything or anybody that comes within reach. There was one sad case in which an elephant sank deep into a quicksand but managed to keep his trunk above it. For three days he was thus enabled to breathe with difficulty, but at last the trunk also disappeared, and he was lost.

Elephants live to the age of 100 or 150 years; and one that carried King Edward VII. when, as Prince of Wales, he visited India in 1875, had also carried Warren Hastings. Their food is of rice, grain, leaves, sugar, and fruits; and on these they become the powerful creatures they are.

One evening, when walking the last few miles to a bungalow where I was to stay the night, having sent my horse and syce ahead and kept only a *chuprassy* with me, I heard, quite near in the jungle below the road, two wild boars grunting and squealing, and evidently fighting.

Knowing that they would be too occupied with one another to see me, I left the *chuprassy* on the road, so that he might guide me with his voice when I wished to return, and went in the direction of the pigs. Having gone about twenty or thirty yards I came to water, and went a small circuit to avoid it. It soon became evident that the pigs were moving farther away; and not caring to be too far from the road in such a thick jungle, I turned to retrace my steps. To my astonishment there was the *chuprassy* only a few paces behind me. He had become alarmed at my absence longer than he expected, and had followed. I then asked him if he knew which was the way back to the road, as I had become uncertain, but he was as doubtful as I was. There was grass of twelve to fifteen feet in height all round us, and no trees anywhere which we might climb to get a view of the road. Darkness was coming on, and as it began to rain there was no chance of judging direction from the stars. The bungalow was a mile or more away, and no native traveller would pass along the road so late, so that shouting to attract attention was no use. It was necessary to move, and we did so in what seemed the probable direction to the road. Soon we were ankle-deep in water, and evidently going wrong. Had we chosen the direction away from the road, there was a prospect of our being in that damp and feverish part all night, and no knowing when we might find relief. As it was, we were travelling parallel to the road, and after a time we came to a stream. Knowing, as I did, the direction of the drainage of that part, I soon guessed the correct bearings, and turned in the right direction.

At that same bungalow—whether on the same night or not I do not remember—there was a really fine show,—a large jungle-fire at night close at hand. In the hot time before the heavy rains the long grass becomes dry and inflammable. Sometimes, for night after night, the forest-fires in the hills are seen burning over large areas. They are either ignited by nomad or hill-tribes or others to clear a space, or simply by the friction of one blade of grass with another. From the bungalow to the Brahmapootra—a distance of several miles—the low land was thickly covered with grass, and as far as could be seen from left to right. On the opposite side of the road was rising ground covered with forest. Before going to bed I sat in the verandah watching the distant line of fire, the flames leaping up to a good height. It was miles away then and the wind was blowing towards us. Fortunately two gangs of coolies were there, and I left word with my men to wake me if during the night the fire should come nearer. In the middle of the night they woke me; and, though the fire was still a mile or two away, my first impression was that the bungalow and everything round us were ablaze, so bright and red and lurid was the effect. I dressed quickly, and found that the men had already begun to clear away the grass for a hundred yards or so adjoining the bungalow on the side from which the fire was approaching. To their surprise I stopped them, and, after leaving a few to move the furniture and stores out of the bungalow on to the road, I put all the coolies to clear away the grass round a long wooden bridge close by. The bridge was worth many times the value of the bungalow, and was the first thing to be made safe. Fortunately when the fire did arrive—and it seemed to come at a great pace over the last few hundred yards—the wall of flame parted at the cleared spaces, and the fire passed on each side of the bungalow and bridge, both of which were uninjured. The roar of the flames was rather confusing; but there is really little substance in such a fire, for only the light inflammable parts of the jungle are burnt up, the trunks and thick branches of the trees being only charred. Next morning the country looked dismal in its blackened state. For an hour or so before the fire passed we could hear numbers of wild animals tearing along past us in the darkness to get to safety in the hills.

Tents are not suitable for Assam, and in wild parts where no bungalow is available we sleep in covered bullock-carts or in boats, or build huts for the night. On such occasions, about five or six o'clock in the evening, I would give the word to stop and build the huts. The coolies would then all disappear into the jungle, while my servants spread rugs in a dry part and gave me my dinner on the ground. Soon the coolies reappeared with bamboos and bundles of grass.

The bamboos were rapidly chopped into lengths, and the outside skin was peeled off into thin strips which were used as string. The thick bamboos were driven into the ground at the four corners of the hut to be made, and light frames for the sides and roof were soon fastened together, bound into position, and stuffed in between with grass or reeds. Within an hour or so there was a small village of huts for the men, the horses, the bulls, and myself. Once I stopped on reaching a set of these huts, which had been erected for a commissioner who had passed along a few weeks before, and we used them instead of building new ones. It was a mistake, for, as they had been unoccupied for so long, various insects and reptiles had taken up their dwelling in them. I was just falling asleep when a snake or a heavy lizard or some such animal fell from the roof on to my bed. In springing up I flung him off, and heard him in the darkness strike the wall opposite and then fall to the ground. On the servants bringing lights, his trail was seen where he had gone off underneath the bamboo wall into the jungle.

A pleasanter way of travelling is by the large river steamers. On them it is interesting to get a chat with the officers who trade between Assam and Calcutta; and the change from the close jungles to the open air of the mid stream is bracing. On the smaller streams inland one has to be satisfied with the country boats, with only a bamboo mat as roof; and in this way I had some long tedious journeys, lying down all day while going from town to town in Sylhet. Sometimes a dug-out is useful: and once I crossed the Brahmapootra from Koliabar to Tezpur in one. A mile or two above Tezpur are some rapids amongst rocks; and on approaching these the dug-out got caught in an eddy and was carried quickly down-stream, spinning round slowly all the time, the boatmen having lost control. Fortunately all the rocks were missed, and we got into quiet water again. On another occasion I had to travel by dug-out, because the regular local steamer, a small one attached to my division, did not pass the place where I had expected to find it, and where it had to call daily. On reaching my headquarters, then Tezpur, I inquired from the man in charge why the steamer had not run. He was very apologetic, and gave the reason that the engines were "disgusting." What he meant I was never able to find out; but he evidently had some clear reason—probably a good one.

The tea-gardens are scattered all over Assam where the soil is good and the drainage can be satisfactorily done. The tea-plant is a camellia: and a legend relates that it first grew where Confucius threw away his eyelids to keep himself awake. The processes of plucking, withering, rolling, drying, sorting, and packing, and the improved machinery, all require careful attention. The women who do the picking have to fill their baskets, and are given definite rows each to pluck from; and it is amusing to see the tricks they play in stealing good leaves from one another's rows, and the quarrels which follow. The planters are famous for their hospitality; and I found them always friendly and anxious to make me comfortable. They are sportsmen in their leisure, especially being good polo players. It may be a case of telling tales out of school, but it is a fact that they rarely drink tea at their meals, beer and whisky-pegs being preferred. Perhaps this may be excused, seeing that they do so much tea-tasting in the course of the manufacture. More than a hundred million pounds are manufactured each year in Assam.

One of the tea-planters had been chased by a tiger while riding, and was carried at full speed by his horse to the bungalow. While sitting in the verandah of another with three planters one evening we heard the growl, or half-growl half-bark, of a tiger in the plantation. One of them had had an extraordinary experience just outside the verandah where we were sitting. A tiger seized his hand and was dragging him away, when one of the others ran into the bungalow for a loaded rifle, and ran out in time to kill the tiger and rescue his friend.

Tigers are numerous in Assam. The thick jungle affords them plenty of cover; and, as sportsmen are comparatively few, they become in some parts more aggressive than usual. Though I several times saw their fresh footprints, I never saw one in the jungle. After closing my office one evening at a river-side rest-house at Kokilamukh, I walked along a newly-cleared track which had been marked out for the Jorhat tramway. At about half a mile from the river a small bridge was being built, and I was going to see what progress had been made during the day. On each side of the track was long grass, and it was therefore only when I had come quite close to the spot that I found a bull lying dead a few feet off the path. From a wound over the eye and from one on the neck blood was flowing slowly. The tiger had probably been feeding on the blood, and had moved off into the long grass on hearing my approach. I went on to the bridge and arranged for a *machân* (a seat hidden with brushwood and leaves) to be made among the branches of a tree close by where the bull was lying. After dinner, as there would be a full moon, I went with my rifle to the tree, intending to sit in the *machân* hidden from the tiger, and to wait there till he came to feed on the dead bull. The men who were with me were to help me up the tree, to hand up my rifle, and then go back to the bungalow and wait till they heard the sound of my firing before returning. Unfortunately—or was it fortunately?—when we reached the spot the body was no longer there, the tiger no doubt having dragged it into the jungle to feed on it where he would not be disturbed. So I missed the only opportunity that ever offered of bagging a tiger. Next morning, on my again passing along the clearing, the pug marks were plain, and, fifty or sixty feet away, hovering over the thick high grass, were a number of crows and vultures in a state of excitement. It seemed probable that the tiger was still there having his meal, and that the birds were waiting till he went off and they could descend and have their share. I sent messengers to the villagers, and they formed a long line of men parallel with the clearing, and came through the grass, beating it with sticks, shouting, and making noises with tom-toms and musical shells. They all came through into the open track, but no tiger. He had gone off on hearing the bustle of the villagers collecting, or he may have worked his way round the end of the line. It is said that the beaters in the middle of the line sometimes leave a gap there rather than expose themselves to the chances of coming across him, and close up again before coming into the open.

There have been many cases of military men and others killed when going after tigers on foot, and especially when following up a wounded tiger. A very sad one was that of a promising and popular young officer of the Hyderabad Contingent, who might have escaped had he not stayed to shield some natives who would otherwise have been killed. The danger is often more from the poison that enters the wounds than from the wounds themselves. The tiger feeds chiefly on cattle, deer, and wild hog; and the flesh which remains between his claws and at the sides of his mouth putrefies in a short time. It is the poison of this putrid flesh that enters the wounds made by the teeth and claws. The tiger being naturally carnivorous, there appears to be a provision of Nature against his being poisoned. His short digestive apparatus enables him to dispose of flesh food quickly; and such food cannot be safely kept long in the body. The food of the herbivora and of the fruit- and grain-eaters (man and the apes) does not soon putrefy and requires a longer digestion; and their digestive organs are arranged to retain food longer.

The lion and the tiger are sometimes spoken of as the strongest of all animals; but this is not correct. It is only by stealth that they can get in the blow which they deliver in killing a bull or a bison. In Assam there is a sport of which the natives of Sylhet are fond—viz., a tiger-and-buffalo fight. Into a staked enclosure a buffalo and a tiger are caused to enter from opposite ends. The European idea would be that the tiger would go straight at the buffalo and kill him with a blow or two. The fact is that the tiger knows that he has no chance, and it is the buffalo that goes at the tiger and soon kills him. Face to face with the tiger in the jungle the bull and buffalo can hold their own. It is when quietly feeding, and the tiger creeps up stealthily under cover and can spring and strike the fatal spot before his prey is aware of his presence, that these strong animals succumb. Deer, of course, are not so powerful, and they are pulled down by the tiger after perhaps a long chase. In 'The Sunday World' of New York of 20th April 1902, there is an account of a bull-and-lion fight, arranged in Texas, in which the bull killed the lion.

In 1901 there were 979 people killed in India by tigers, and about 2900 altogether by them and other wild beasts. Even this figure does not come near the number killed by snakes—viz., 21,380. It is among the cattle that the wild beasts are the more destructive, there having been 70,822 cattle killed by them in 1901. The tiger is not aggressive towards human beings unless he is a man-eater. Man-eaters are rare, and are said to be mostly old tigers that can no longer succeed in the chase after their usual prey, and that have got into the habit of carrying off children from near the villages, and having tasted human blood, prefer it. A horse that had been tethered near one of our camp bungalows arrived at full speed at his stable at Nowgong, having broken from his ropes and galloped sixteen miles with blood flowing from wounds on his haunches made by the claws of a tiger that had sprung at him.

In some parts the natives are said to like the tiger, because he keeps down the animals that feed on their crops; and there is a tribe of Travancore, the Ollares, that worship him and call him their uncle.

Of the other large beasts of prey the panther is almost as bad as the tiger, and will attack men. His colour is dark-grey, and he is, therefore, the less easily detected in shady places. He will climb trees and lie flat on a broad branch overhanging a path, ready to drop on his prey. The leopard is like the panther, but is spotted; and the cheetah is a small leopard with paws like those of a wolf. The cheetah is kept by some of the native sportsmen to hunt deer, which are given a certain start before he is let loose. The hyæna is rare, and is not dangerous except when cornered or wounded. Sportsmen have tried to use him for the chase, but he will not run away, and shows little fight when attacked by the dogs. The jackal runs well, and is hunted with packs of hounds just as the fox is in England. The wild boar is pugnacious, and is hunted on horseback and killed with spears. Pig-sticking, as it is called, is a favourite amusement, but is dangerous to the horses, as a boar may get under one and rip him up badly with his tusks.

Bears are common in Assam and in the hills. They were dreaded by the dâk runners, some of whom had been clawed on the face. In one part the natives had become expert in using their *dhaos* (a heavy knife like a *kookrie*) against them, and, if they could get in a blow on the bear's nose, he was generally done for. The wild buffalo and the *gaur* or bison are shot for sport, and for the sake of their flesh for food for those natives who care for it. Deer of many kinds are hunted where there is open country, and their horns are valued as trophies. The *sambhar* (elk deer), the *bara singh* (swamp deer), the black buck, (antelope), the spotted deer, the barking deer, the *nilghai* or blue cow, and others, are common in parts of India, and much sought after. In Assam the very long grass and the swamps prevent much sport. One interesting item I learnt from a sportsman about the antelope. It is looked on as unsportsmanlike to shoot a doe, and somehow the does have found this out, and will stand in the line of fire between the sportsman and the buck to shield the latter from the bullet, knowing that they themselves are safe. As the sportsman changes his position to get his aim at the buck, the doe will change hers so as to prevent him.

A similar thing is well known to be done by the black partridge, which will pretend to be badly wounded and will flutter along the ground to get the dogs to come after it, and so draw them away from where the young ones are. Partridge, quail, pheasant, jungle-fowl, bustard, coolon, snipe, water-fowl, are all found in Assam. Wild duck are so numerous that I have seen them rise from the water by several thousands at a time. When rising in such numbers the noise made by their wings is very great. At a mile or two away it sounds like distant thunder. The Brahmini duck are prettily coloured, but they are fish-eaters and their flesh is not good. The grey ones, which feed on grain and the weeds in the water, are preferred as having better flesh.

Assam is on a line of country subject to earthquakes, and the small ones come every year. When one is approaching the rumbling is heard growing louder as it gets near, and the natives run out of the huts and shout till the disturbance has passed away. They say it is a *shaitan*, and that they frighten him away by their shouting, which, of course, is proved by the fact that the rumbling passes off in the direction opposite to that from which it came. The quivering of the ground has the same effect on the trees as when a dust-storm is approaching. They are seen in the distance all moving about, while those nearer are quite still until the vibration arrives. In one earthquake, my bungalow being built chiefly of bamboo, I felt the movement so much that it was like being at sea, and I had some difficulty in keeping my feet. Such bungalows are safer, as they give to the motion, and have elasticity enough to recover. It is the rigid brick or stone buildings which resist the earthquake that get shattered. In the great earthquake of June 1897, Shillong, the Government headquarters in the Khasia hills, was nearly destroyed. The church and other masonry buildings were levelled with the ground, and one of the most able of the Civil officers, Mr M'Cabe, was killed in bed through the falling of the roof of his house.

At Shillong there is stationed one of the three Goorkha regiments located in Assam; and the Mess of the British officers, the garden-parties at Government house, the very pretty scenery, and the perfect climate, make Shillong one of the most enjoyable of hill-stations. It is, however, far from India proper, and is not much frequented by Europeans outside Assam. The scenery is like that of some parts of Scotland, and there are some fine waterfalls in and near the station. Though Cherrapunji, with its average of 480 inches of rainfall a-year, is only thirty miles away, the rainfall of Shillong is only eighty to ninety inches a-year, the heavier clouds being carried over the station before they break again in Sylhet and Cachar.

There is a way of travelling in the hills in Assam used by English ladies which is seen nowhere else. They sit in a basket-chair called a *thoppa*, and this is strapped to a man's back. The men who carry them go steadily for hours, and even up steep hills. Of course the lady travels backwards, and it is awkward when she gets isolated from the rest of her party, and the *thoppa*-man meets an acquaintance and stops to have a talk. It is difficult in her position to make the man hear and understand, or even to listen to what she says. If on a rock-cut path, and the man stops with his back to the precipice, the feelings of the lady sitting in full view of it, close to the edge, and quite unable to get out of her *thoppa*, may be imagined.

The numerous hill-tribes afford subjects of much interest. Though less than a million in a population of six millions, there are many tribes with a great variety of customs, languages, and dress. They live mostly in unhealthy jungles, where English people would get ill with fever and be troubled by the ticks and other insects; and they say that the plains and the open hills do not agree with them. There are still feuds between them, most of them having been in serious warfare with one another in former days. Later they often attacked the villages under British protection in Assam, and they had to be brought to account. As they come now more into contact with civilisation they show themselves amenable and good workers. The Mishmis, for instance, though wild-looking, are inoffensive. They live in thick jungle, and are very poor, badly clothed, and badly fed; but they readily

THE THOPPA MAN MEETS A FRIEND.

learn simple manufactures of cloth and weapons, and are beginning to trade in them. The Mekirs are another inoffensive timid people, and easily converted by missionaries.

The weapons are varied and peculiar, such as two-edged swords, shields with bamboo spikes inside, and covered with rhinoceros hide, and *panjis*, which are pieces of bamboo about a foot long and spiked at each end, and which they plant in the path of an enemy who is chasing them, so that one point may catch his foot and trip him up with an ugly wound. Their *dhao* is a short sword thicker towards the end, and they used it on the works to clear away bamboos and grass. Even now some of the tribes are occasionally at war with the Assam Government, and the Goorkha regiments are sent to keep them in order. In 1883 there was a raid by the Akas on the Balipara tea-garden a few miles from Tezpur, and troops had to be sent after them—a troublesome task, as they are not easily found in their jungles. About 1820 they were the conquering race among the hill-men, and earned the names of "Eaters of a thousand hearths" and "Thieves that lurk in the cotton-fields."

The British Government finds it best policy to pay some of the troublesome tribes to prevent their raiding and to induce them to keep the peace. The Dufflas, a tribe of plundering herdsmen, for instance, are kept in order in this way. It is really paying them to police their own country instead of having to go to the expense of sending expeditions to punish them when disorderly. Some of the tribes still use poisoned arrows, and it is with these that they secure tigers by so arranging that they are discharged when the tiger crosses and presses on a string. Human sacrifices used to be made to propitiate evil spirits, especially when a chief died. Most of the tribes look on milk as unfit for food, though they sometimes eat diseased corpses. Some of the hill-men measure the length of a journey by the quantity of betel-leaf or quids of tobacco they consume on the way.

The dresses of both the men and the women are of great variety, the small amount of clothing worn being made up for by wicker-work and bamboo and leaf arrangements, plaited cane, skins, and capes of fibres of palm-trees. Some have brass-work and bead ornaments, a circlet of copper knobs round the head, and fantastic ear and nose ornaments of silver; and some carry spears and bows and arrows. The primitive aboriginal religions have now got mixed up with a little Mahomedanism and a little Hinduism, and among some it would be difficult to say if they understand anything of any of the religions, or whether they belong to one more than another. Even among the low castes it is hard to know what is lawful to eat and what not, and whether with the right hand or the left. The Doms of Assam refuse to eat except in a special kind of clothing. As an example of the absurdities to which these distinctions have been carried amongst the Khamtis, it is proper to sacrifice a fowl, a pig, or a buffalo to the bad goddess Kali, but not a goat or a duck. Probably one explanation may be found in the fact that there are a low kind of Brahmins in Assam who drink spirits and eat the flesh of the animals offered in sacrifice to this goddess, and it may have been at one time that fowls, pigs, and buffaloes were more to their liking. Their superstitious beliefs are shown also in the burial ceremonies. When a Garo dies a dog is sacrificed in order that it may accompany the spirit and guide him on his way. With the Miris the dead are buried with food for their journey, cooking utensils, arms, and ornaments.

In their marriage customs they are more amusing than superstitious. With the Garos and Khasias the husband marries into the wife's family and is subject to the wife or her mother. Sometimes when his father-in-law dies he has to marry his mother-in-law. As in India proper, there are elaborate and expensive wedding ceremonies. The dances are curious. The one at Noncrem in the hills above Shillong was, to my mind, hardly worth witnessing. There was a procession of young men who went round many times in a circle headed by an old man who got into a sort of frenzy of excitement. In the centre of the ring were the marriageable maidens who danced slowly in rows and without animation. Finally there was the selection of their brides by the young men, and then the cutting off of a goat's head.

Some of the habits and practices of the Assam hill-tribes are absurd or savage and horrible.

The Khasias dye their teeth red. The Garo men carefully pull out any hair that grows on the face. One of their dishes is a dog roasted alive after being fed with as much rice as it will take, the rice in the stomach after it is killed being considered a great delicacy. They give intoxicating drink to their infants, and adore a bamboo covered with flowers as a symbol of their god Siva. The Miris eat the flesh of tigers, but do not allow their women to do so lest it should make them too strong-minded for control. The Abors make their women work hard, though otherwise they treat them well. They cannot easily live long in peace with one another, and their houses are therefore scattered singly or in groups of two or three all over the mountainous country they live in. They have no medicines, but depend on propitiation of evil spirits in cases of sickness. The salute of an Abor chief is a shrill whoop like the crow of a cock. The Lushais are quarrelsome and stealthy. Their women are kept in stern subjection, and must even use tobacco different from that smoked by the men. Their chiefs allow the nails of the third and fourth fingers of the left hand to grow long, those on the right being kept short for eating.

The last to be brought under control, and perhaps the worst of all, were the Nagas,—a treacherous, vindictive, and quarrelsome tribe that had to be roughly handled several times before they would desist from their plundering raids on the peaceful Assamese. A pacifying influence has been found in the profitable business they carry on in supplying the tea-gardens with labour and material. They eat the flesh of rats, snakes, monkeys, tigers, elephants, and roast dog. Fermented rice liquor is much drunk by them, and the oil of tobacco mixed with water.

Mixing freely with the people of Assam and Bengal are the Bhuteas, who live beyond the borders of Assam. They are a fine hardy race, but poor and oppressed, having to hand over to the rulers and priests anything demanded of them. The result is a low moral tone and a hopeless style of life, and, naturally, no anxiety to cultivate beyond their needs, as the surplus would be appropriated by the officials.

XIV.

HYDERABAD.

THE CITY—MOGUL CONQUESTS—THE KOOTUB SHAHI DYNASTY—THE ANCIENT CAPITAL, GOLCONDA—TAVERNIER'S VISIT—SIR SALAR JUNG—MOGLAI ADMINISTRATORS—ARAB TROOPS—GOLCONDA BRIGADE—*JAGHIRDARS*—THE LUNGUR PROCESSION—BERAR—LIFE IN CANTONMENTS—BOYS—EXECUTIONS—PUBLIC WORKS—CAMP LIFE—JUNGLY VILLAGERS—CREDULITY—BAD CAMP SITES—CROSSING RIVERS—*JAGHIR* OFFICIALS—DELAYS—IRON—BLACK COTTON SOIL—LAX IDEAS—GIPSIES—DACOITS—*TALUQDARS*—THE RANI—RAYMOND'S SOLDIERS.

THE contrasts already described between the North and the South of India, life in the plains and in the hills, in the jungle and in towns, the civilisation of Calcutta and the wild semi-barbarian life of the inhabitants of the hills and jungles of Assam, do not exhaust the list of striking changes experienced when we are transferred from one part of India to another.

After I left Assam and had been stationed for a time at Allahabad again, at Bellary, Madras, Trichinopoli, and Calcutta, my services were lent to the Government of H.H. the Nizam of Hyderabad. An examination of the Hyderabad State was required before deciding on the best lines for new railways to develop the interior, which, north of the city up to the Central Provinces, was without railway communications. This involved preliminary reconnaissance over several lines, and then detailed surveys over the most promising, before the final location could be made; and in 1891 I began what proved to be a long but interesting and enjoyable task.

Hyderabad city is one of the most attractive of the sights of India. There are many towns more picturesque, but few so quaint in the variety of the people and the conditions under which they live. The Jama Musjid (the chief mosque), the Châr Minâr (a large central gateway), the new Faluknamah palace of the Prime Minister, well placed on a hill, the palace of H.H. the Nizam, and the handsome houses of the many nobles in the suburbs and on or near the banks of the Hussein Saugor (tank or lake), give the place an air of luxury, which is enhanced when one is a guest at the evening entertainments, the banquets and gatherings, to witness the processions or firework displays arranged by the Prime Minister and other leading men. The lake itself, when full, is about four square miles in area, and is held up by a high, broad, well-kept embankment constructed in the reign of Ibrahim Kootub Shah, King of Golconda, who died in A.D. 1580, and over which runs the main road connecting Hyderabad with Secunderabad. Not far away are the fort and tombs of Golconda, famous as the ancient capital and in connection with the diamonds of that name, which, however, were not really found at this spot, but were brought from fluvial deposits on the banks of the river Kistna at Purtial, near Bezwada. At Secunderabad, about five miles away, and at Trimulgherry and Bolarum, all within ten or twelve miles of Hyderabad, are important military cantonments, where is concentrated one of the largest British military forces in India.

The Mahomedan era began in 622 A.D., the date of Mahomet's flight from Mecca. Within a century his followers had spread their religion over many countries, and it had reached the north of India. After nine centuries of Mahomedan conquests and reconquests of many parts of India, and the infliction of much suffering on the inhabitants by devastating invaders, such as Mahomed of Ghazni and Tamerlane, the Mogul dynasty was established at Delhi by the Emperor Baber in 1526 A.D., during the reign of our King Henry VIII. He was a Tartar descended from Tamerlane, and was succeeded by the powerful Emperors Akbar, Jehangir, Shah Jehan, Aurungzebe, and others. For more than two centuries the Mogul rule was firmly established, but it at last declined when frequent wars with other Mahomedan States, and lastly with the rising power of the Mahrattas under Sivaji, destroyed its vitality.

Several Mahomedan dynasties had been established in the Deccan, some ruled by viceroys subordinate to the Mogul princes of Delhi and others independent. They quarrelled much with one another, and there were frequent insurrections, revolts, and changes of rulers. One of the most famous of these dynasties was the "Kootub Shahi," with its capital at Golconda. In the long reign (1512-1580 A.D.) of the tolerant and enlightened Emperor Ibrahim Kootub Shah, the Civil government and the trade of the State were established on a sound basis; and this made it possible for his successor to build the city of Hyderabad, about six miles distant from the capital, and to extend his rule. After two centuries of good government the Kootub Shahi dynasty was overthrown by Aurungzebe in 1687.

In 1645 the French traveller Tavernier visited Golconda, which must have been a fine city then, but of which little now remains. Its outer wall was ten miles in circumference. Tavernier describes a very large pagoda which was then under construction, and which would have been the grandest in India had it ever been finished. It had been fifty years in building, and was being made of enormous stones which had to be rolled up special earthen slopes, themselves very massive. One stone alone he describes as requiring 1400 oxen to draw it, there having been 500 to 600 men constantly engaged for five years in quarrying it. He says little of the people, but remarks that the king derived a very considerable revenue from the tax on intoxicating liquors. It is thought that he incorporated with his account of his travels some details which he heard from others; and, though most of what he relates of the strange events and customs is probably genuine, one cannot quite believe all he says. The King of Golconda, according to Tavernier, made his entry into the town seated on a throne supported on an imitation elephant formed of nine women, four of whom made the feet, four the body, and one the trunk.

The history of the viceroys, viziers, and other

rulers of states and minor kingdoms subordinate to the great reigning Mogul emperors of Delhi is most perplexing to the casual student. It consists of wars, rebellions, expeditions against unoffending people, massacres, executions, assassinations, base intrigues, and wily duplicity. Incidentally one reads of severe famines impeding the operations of the invading armies, and little is said of the unrelieved misery of the general population. The leaders, unscrupulous, able, and vigorous, are recorded as being sometimes on one side and sometimes on the other. Out of all this confusion emerged the government of the present line of Nizams, and after surviving several wars with the Mahrattas, Mysore, and the French, Hyderabad is now finally established as the premier Native State of India.

In 1653 Aurungzebe, while Viceroy of the Deccan under the Emperor Shah Jehan, sacked the city of Hyderabad. In 1715 the Kootub Shahi dynasty was superseded by Nizam ul Mulk Asaf Jah, who was appointed viceroy by Aurungzebe, who had then become emperor. He was the first of the present line of Nizams. In 1723 he became independent and fixed his residence at Hyderabad city. He died in 1748 at the age of 104. Eight Nizams have reigned at Hyderabad since then.

The best known of the Hyderabad statesmen was Sir Salar Jung, who was successful and powerful as Prime Minister, and a staunch friend to the British Government until his lamented death in 1883. He belonged to a noble Arab family, and was a man of ability, integrity, and sincerity. He was kindly towards all, lenient in punishment, very abstemious, fond of healthy exercise, quiet society, and modern literature. He became Prime Minister in 1853. Without him the State would have been ruined. It was, at that time, deeply involved in debt. The Treasury was empty, the Nizam's private funds had been used up, and his jewels mortgaged to satisfy the State creditors. Sir Salar Jung was supported by the British Government in his measures of retrenchment and reform: and it was fortunate that he was in power when the Mutiny broke out. Some of the mutineers arrived from Northern India and caused much excitement among the Mahomedan population. With the approval of the Nizam, the minister kept all the seditious and turbulent factions well in hand; and his energetic measures, even at the risk of his own life, prevented the disaffection from spreading, and saved England from having to deal with a mutiny in the south of India in addition to that in the north. On his visit to London in 1876 Sir Salar Jung was presented with the Freedom of the City of London. Mr George Palmer, lately Secretary to the Government of H.H. the Nizam in the Public Works Department, writes of him:—

> "Sir Salar Jung was a truly great man. The first half of my service was under him. I look upon him as one of the truest gentlemen I ever met. I was Acting Secretary to Government for some eight months during his time, and my weekly visits to him with

> departmental papers were to me most pleasant and interesting. He never forgot a single detail, and could always resume a subject just where it had been left at the previous interview; and it was the same in all the other departments, all of which were entirely controlled by him. His manner always was most charming and kind."

Several distinguished men have filled the post of Prime Minister since his time; but there is always much party feeling and strong opposition, and none have held the office for more than a few years. Frequently a minister or other political leader of good reputation and acknowledged ability and zeal is suddenly replaced after years of public service. Since 1891 there have disappeared from politics such able men as Mehdi Ali, Mehdi Hassan, Mustâq Hussein, Sarwar Jung, Abdul Huq, Sir Asman Jah, and Sir Vicar ul Oomrah, K.C.I.E. Some have been superseded in the ordinary course of rapid political events, and a few will be remembered as sterling good administrators, just as are Sir Salar Jung and such men as Sir K. Sheshadri Iyer, K.C.S.I., of the Mysore State. Some of them failed through attempting retrenchment of unnecessary large expenditure which had become a menace to the State, but in which there were too many influential persons interested. Sir Salar Jung himself nearly shared the same fate when he began to remove abuses and to resume some of the military *jaghirs*, which are a great drain on the national resources.

The Prime Minister now is the Peshkar Maharajah Kischen Pershad; and the fact of there being a Hindu Prime Minister is a good illustration of the toleration of the Mahomedan rulers of India. Good men—whether Mahomedan, Hindu, Parsee, or Christian—have been welcomed in Hyderabad. The present popular and able Private Secretary to the Minister, Mr Furdonji, is a Parsee, and he has long been in that post. Though there were cruel massacres of their opponents by the old Mogul rulers of Delhi, toleration was extended by Aurungzebe to the Jesuits.

At the time when the Moglai rulers were fighting for the retention of their position at Hyderabad, it was found necessary to import a large number of Arab mercenaries,—and to this day the Arab troops of the regular army are stationed at the capital. One part of the city is the Arab quarter, where much disorder prevails at times, for the Arab chiefs and their followers are not easy to control. Of the other regular troops, the Golconda brigade is famous for its smartness and the excellent polo players which it produces. The Golconda polo team gives the best English military teams hard work to win, and has even beaten some of the Hussar regiments at the game.

In the interior, scattered all over the country, are the estates of the leading nobles and others who have been rewarded, or whose ancestors were rewarded, with grants of land and villages for services rendered to the State. From these they draw revenue, part of which is sent to Hyderabad as tribute, and forms the chief item of the Crown revenues. These men are called *jaghirdars*, the estates they own being the *jaghirs* or political rewards for their services. Their tenure and their relations to the ruler of the State are similar to those of feudal times in England. Once a-year—on the fifth day of the *Mohurrum*—they assemble at Hyderabad to pay homage to H.H. the Nizam. They bring with them their retainers, most of them having small bodyguards and even little armies of their own. These are raised subject to service in defence of the State if required. As they are dressed, armed, and drilled in an informal and haphazard way, they form a motley and curious assemblage. In the "Lungur" procession before H.H. the Nizam, they march first, the regular troops coming last, and appearing all the smarter and more soldierly in contrast to them. The *jaghirdars* vie with one another in the splendour of the dresses of themselves and their attendants and of the trappings of their elephants and horses. Until they have all left Hyderabad, the city is in a state of confusion, there being frequent quarrels and much rowdyism. As they are all armed, it can be easily understood that the police have a trying time. The Prime Minister always invites a large number of Europeans to lunch at his palace on the occasion of the Lungur procession.

When one of the petty chiefs visits Hyderabad, or even when one living there travels through the city, it is still occasionally the case, as was common up to a few years ago, for him to go about with a number of his armed retainers running ahead shouting his name and titles, firing guns, and throwing about crackers to attract attention. It is safe enough now to go about alone in Hyderabad if the main roads are kept to; but when I first visited the city in 1880, it was necessary to get special permission and to have a guard supplied by the police. In those days most of the natives in the streets were armed, but now only a few are.

The Northern province of the State, Berar, has been for many years administered by the British Government on behalf of the Nizam's Government. The arrangement was that for debts due by the Hyderabad State to the Government of India for loans and other assistance,—chiefly the maintenance of the Hyderabad Contingent, a native force of about 1000 men under British officers,—the British Government should recoup itself out of the Berar revenues, handing over any surplus annually to his Highness's Government. Before this was done Berar was not well administered, and little revenue was obtained from it; but after the British Government took charge, though heavy expenditure was incurred in putting the administration and the roads into good condition, the revenue became so large that not only was the amount of the debt secured, but a handsome surplus was handed over annually and formed an important item in the revenue of the Hyderabad State. In return for a heavy payment Berar has now become wholly British, and the Hyderabad Contingent has been abolished.

Near the city, at Chudderghaut, is the

Residency, where the British Resident deals with all matters in which the interests of both the British Government and the Native State are concerned, and gives advice and assistance when wanted by the native rulers. It is only of late years that the State has become really tranquil, the feudal system and the general laxness of the authorities having formerly encouraged lawless characters to become dacoits and to roam at will among the villages, murdering and robbing with a good deal of impunity. Only a few years ago it was found necessary to call on the Contingent to send troops after these bands, and they at last succeeded in dispersing them.

When living at Hyderabad, Secunderabad, and Bolarum, there were numerous conveniences and opportunities for amusement and useful occupation apart from one's official duties. The many entertainments at the Residency, at the Messes of the British and Native regiments and the Hyderabad Contingent, and those given by the Native State officials, were at times almost too frequent. There were reviews on the parade-ground, polo, tent-pegging, and other sports, races or some other sight of interest, which one could go to see on closing office each afternoon. And there were the dances, dinners, card-parties, and "At Homes," with tennis and badminton, at the houses of private residents. The Military officers were met everywhere, and they were the life of the place when anything had to be managed in the interests of sport and games, theatricals and dances. At one time part of my duties was to attend as a member of their Cantonment Committees with reference to the safety of buildings, the character of plans submitted, advisability of alterations, and such matters as an engineer could assist in. A lantern and a graphophone I had with me came in useful to interest a meeting of Eurasians and the school children of a large mission of the Wesleyans. When for some months I had little but office work, it was a pleasant occupation to manage and rearrange the public gardens at Bolarum, some of the plants of that climate being specially adapted to the creation of a pleasing effect.

At one gathering on the Futteh Maidân in Hyderabad there was an elephant race, and it was amusing to see a number of these animals going full speed with a rapid shuffling gait and evidently entering into the fun. Some seemed to be laughing, and no doubt all understood that it was a piece of friendly rivalry. When the race had begun the course was very soon cleared; for, as the Commissioner of Police remarked to me at the time, an elephant was better than any policeman for such a task.

The boys of this part, up to the age of about sixteen or eighteen, are often as sharp as can be found in India, and make good servants; but as they merge into manhood they become, like most of the men coolies and servants, dull and slow. It may be that they adopt some of the opium smoking and eating and other pernicious habits about that age. They show a curious mixture of apathy and interest in the affairs of their masters. On opening a box of stores and taking out a compressed pulp basin, which, being unbreakable, was a useful thing to have in camp, I threw it across a few feet to one of my servants, telling him to catch it. He naturally thought it was china, and the sudden transformation from his slow stolid manner to alertness and eager anxiety to catch the basin in order to prevent its being broken was rather surprising. Had it been a china one and got broken, it would, of course, have been my fault. Unfortunately, he was so pleased with the novelty when I explained it to him that he and the others took to throwing it about in my absence just for the fun of seeing that it would not break.

The methods of execution in former days were, in some parts of India, very cruel,—such, for instance, as treading to death by elephants, and burying alive. Possibly the horror of such executions, as well as the objection of the Jains, Buddhists, and some Hindus to taking life, have been the cause of the failure of the jury system in trials for murder. If there are Hindus on a jury, in some parts it is impossible to obtain conviction in a clear case of murder. There have been several cases in Hyderabad territory of men sentenced to death, and kept indefinitely in prison awaiting the fixing of the day of execution, the responsible authority preferring not to fix it. The head of a man executed belongs to the executioner, who, some time ago at least, used to take it in a bag to the bazaar, and make money by threatening to show it to the shopkeepers if they did not pay him to take it away.

The Secretary to the Hyderabad Government in the Public Works Department was Mr George Palmer, who held the post of Chief Engineer and Secretary to Government in the Public Works Department for many years. He and Messrs Gauntlet & Heeman, all members of the Institute of Civil Engineers, were the leading Civil Engineers in the Hyderabad State. They had constructed many buildings and large irrigation tanks by means of which there had been a considerable increase to the crops, chiefly of rice, and a corresponding addition to the revenues of the country and the safety of the people from famine. There are few main roads in the State, and it was impossible for the Public Works Department to keep those that there are in good order on the small grants allowed for the purpose in the Departmental Budget. The greater part of the allotment for roads is spent on those traversing the suburbs of the city, and on the first few miles of their extension into the country. There is rich soil in many parts, and this parsimony in spending on the communications had the effect of keeping much of the land out of cultivation; for the cultivators had difficulty in getting their crops profitably to market. The difference was seen immediately the boundary was crossed from the Moglai territory into Berar, or other parts administered by British officials. On one side were rough badly-kept roads only partially bridged; on the other a fully bridged and metalled road with good feeders enabling the traffic in crops to be carried on freely. The consequence was that the cultivators of Berar were content and prosperous, and the revenue satisfactory. Without proper allotment of funds and administrative support from the financial and other authorities, it was not possible for the engineers to keep the roads over a country of 82,000 square miles in order.

At the beginning of each of the three cold seasons during which I was in camp, surveys over new lines of country were required. One line was from Warangul to Chanda, another from Manmar to Karimnagar, and there were two different lines from Hyderabad to Nandair, and on to Manmar. At the end of each cold season I was allowed to take my plotting and estimating work, with the office and the assistant engineers, to the hills for the hot weather. At first the services of two assistant engineers were lent me from the Moglai Public Works Department, and afterwards four. At one time there were four camps—my own and three others with which the assistants travelled—following up, chaining, and levelling, over the line I had selected. Sometimes I was for weeks travelling ahead without seeing any of them, but receiving reports from them daily, giving information of their progress, and sending forward details which the draughtsman who travelled with me plotted as we went along. One season we were seven months in camp, and twice during that time I saw no European for six weeks at a time, except occasionally one of the assistant engineers. The time of year was healthy, though in some of the forest parts the assistants now and then got fever; but in most parts of the survey the elevation was from 1000 to 1700 feet above the sea, and I myself, though the work was constant and rough, never had better health during my stay in India.

The daily riding and walking over rough country, and the continual pushing onwards, often having to go backwards and forwards several times many miles before the direction in which it was best to proceed could be decided on, were at times tiring; but the open-air life, night and day, was invigorating. We started at daylight, had our breakfasts sent out to us in the jungle, and often returned only when the sun was setting. Generally, however, it was necessary to return to camp much earlier, partly for the sake of the office work, and partly so as not to overwork the men and cause them to become discontented and leave the survey after they had been trained to the work. If the tent had been moved ahead during the day, after closing the field-work I had to ride in the general direction which would take me near the new camping-ground. When within perhaps a mile of the spot, and when I was searching for a sight of the tents, the horse would sometimes turn and start off at a brisk pace, indicating that he had heard and recognised sounds made at the camp, or even seen the bright white of the canvas of the tents in the distance.

Though the men as a rule worked well after a week or two of practice, and though the tents and instruments were good, and every arrangement had been made at Hyderabad by Mr Palmer to see that I was properly supplied with funds and with special orders from the Prime Minister, yet hindrances in great variety were continually arising. Those special orders directed the headmen of the Moglai villages and the managers of the *jaghirs* to give me every assistance in obtaining labour and facilities for purchasing supplies for the men and fodder for the horses and cattle.

The pretty picture often drawn by enthusiasts who camp out for pleasure under the most favourable circumstances is only a partially correct representation of camping on duty. There may be the early morning ride, beginning before sunrise, through good scenery, with an occasional view of a wild animal, picturesque villages, and dusky polite natives. The new camp may be found pitched in a pleasant spot under trees, the bath ready, a rest in an arm-chair in balmy air and in full view of a group of palm-trees, followed by an enjoyable breakfast with new milk from the village, &c. The reality, however, especially in the south of India, is sometimes, day after day, far different; and it is part of the hard work of the day to deal with it. If the camp has been moved during one's absence on the field work, on closing the day's work and riding ahead to find the new camp site it is a matter of anxiety as to whether it will be found in a suitable position or not. Low feverish ground may have been selected instead of high ground; and then, if rain fall, the site may get flooded during the night. Or the tents may be located too near a village, or in open ground exposed to the hot sun, though shady trees are near and available. Sometimes it is better not to go to the survey work till the camp has actually left the old site, so as to be sure that at least a start has been made for the new site, otherwise one may search in vain for the tents at night. There is a hard drive to get things off. The cartmen are absent in the village, gone to eat their food at the most inconvenient and unusual time. A bull has strayed, or the village authorities turn up with long accounts requiring settlement, and which one's servants and the camp people do not acknowledge as correct. Half-way on the journey a bull becomes lame and some of the things arrive very late. Perhaps by dark the tent is only partially erected, or very skew, and no supplies of firewood, milk, eggs, or water for the bath have yet been obtained from the village. Once, on arriving in the dark, I found that not only was no dinner ready but no tents were erected and all the men had gone to sleep, the cook and several others being drunk. This, in the south of India, may happen when the men have to pass through a village near which there are toddy palms and the fermented juice is sold cheap.

On one journey I came up with the men and carts just as they were approaching a village.

Instead of riding on ahead I decided to keep with them till the village had been left well behind; and this was fortunate, for every villager we saw was drunk. I had never seen such an extreme case. Probably it was some festive occasion.

Trouble of this kind occurred now and then when the men got lax or bad ones were taking the lead among them. For several weeks at a time things would go well, but they always wanted careful watching and checking, so that, in addition to the time spent on the outdoor survey work and the office work, one's leisure was practically full of occupation. Failure of any part of the arrangements had to be guarded against. It became a habit to take many precautions, some, to an onlooker, apparently quite unnecessary.

It is a common practice in many parts of India for the Hindu priests to colour their idols red, and to mark certain stones, trees, and other things with red ochre to indicate that they are sacred. On some of the surveys trouble was caused by the villagers pulling out, to use as firewood, the wooden pegs with which were marked the centre line and levels. We therefore made use of that fact, and had our pegs coloured, in the hope that the villagers would consider them as sacred.

As the survey advanced and we got among the villagers far removed from towns, it was noticed that some would believe and misinterpret almost anything they were told. A good bearer I had at the time made use of this fact when, while the tents were being erected at a new site at which

I had not yet arrived, a crowd of villagers out of curiosity pressed round to examine the furniture and other things both inside and outside the tents. They were in the way and annoyed the bearer, who, to get rid of them, told them that the sahib would soon be there, and that he was a very bad sahib, who would severely punish them for giving such trouble. The result was that when I arrived not a single villager was to be seen; and the bearer, to my amusement, told me exactly what he had done, explaining that it was the only way to get the tents ready in time.

When half through the longest survey, and at about 200 miles from Hyderabad, I was much puzzled by circumstantial detailed reports arriving from parts ahead that some engineers were there working with surveying instruments and marking out a line for a railway. For some days at the villages we passed, and from men who had come from fifty or a hundred miles ahead, these reports were definite and persistent. I had heard of no one else sent out or other lines projected, and concluded that there were probably some Irrigation or Road engineers at work in the north of the State. The truth began to dawn on me when one man arrived and related a conversation he said he had had with those engineers. There was so much in this reported conversation that I myself had said some weeks before, that it became clear that a garbled version of my statements had passed ahead from village to village and had come back again, perhaps by a different route.

The engineers were really myself and the assistants, and the man had been romancing when he said he had heard it all himself direct from them. He even described us as sitting on the parapet of a bridge and saying that the locomotive would follow us *the next day*. This also was a puzzle, till I discovered that he and the others with him had never seen a locomotive, and were under the impression that it was the theodolite.

The simplicity and credulity of the villagers was illustrated in another way when, in 1901, Queen Victoria died. Some of the *bunnias* took advantage of the fact that while she lived some old rupees with the head of William IV. were in circulation, usually at a small discount. They represented that, as the Queen was dead and a king had succeeded her, rupees with a king's head were now the current coins. They collected rupees with Queen Victoria's head at a discount, the villagers eagerly parting with them at less than their value to get the old ones with King William IV.'s head.

The silver coinage of the Hyderabad State consists of "Halli Sicca" rupees. These do not circulate outside the State. They vary in thickness and size, and are only approximately round, as nearly all have cuts at the edges as if clipped into hexagonal or octagonal shape by unauthorised persons. They vary much in value. At one time 110 may be equivalent to 100 Government of India rupees, and at other times 125 or more. The officials receive their monthly salaries in these rupees, and, as there is no paper money, those who have not arranged for them to be paid into a bank must receive each time an inconvenient lot of silver of more or less value according to the state of exchange. The copper coinage is of "dubs," irregular-shaped coins, 100 of which are reckoned to the rupee. They are chopped to shape and roughly stamped with an inscription at the Mint.

One of my camping places had been a pleasant one on the bank of a river, and on returning by the same route I told my men to erect the tents on the same spot. It was some time after dark that I arrived at the camp, having had a thirty-mile ride and walk on a branch line preliminary to deciding whether to follow it with the survey. Though I had been most of the day in forest and in hills, the last few miles in the dark were over level open plain; and it was a wearisome plod with the lights of my tents in view for miles before I reached them. I could not canter or even ride at all with safety as there was only a rough track, and it was over black cotton soil which is full of holes. I therefore had to walk, and was glad indeed to reach the tents, where I knew that an arm-chair and dinner were awaiting me. Everything was in good order, and with much satisfaction I sat down to dinner. No sooner had I done so than one of the assistant engineers, whose camp was near, came to report that he had just found out that my kitchen tent, in which my dinner had been prepared, was pitched on the spot where a man who had died of cholera had been buried a few hours before. All the smaller tents had to be taken down immediately and the men and goods removed to another place — not an easy task late on a dark night. The village was on the other side of the river, and none of the villagers had thought of warning us.

A trying experience was when, the camp having been moved ahead to an unsatisfactory spot, and my survey having reached abreast of it, I decided that it had better be sent on to a new site. I explained that it should be placed under trees, as the weather was becoming unpleasantly warm. The next day I went as usual to the field, the men with the carts and tents having started. On closing work in the afternoon I rode ahead to find the new camp. After a long search, inquiries from villagers, and sending the men who had been surveying with me in various directions, no news whatever could be got. As a last attempt I returned to the site of the morning's camp to trace the carts from there. Here we learnt that about midday they had returned and gone some distance backwards in the direction of the camp of three days before. The men, finding no satisfactory trees to erect the tent under, had remembered a *tope* (cluster of trees) they had passed three days before, and had decided that it would be just what I wanted. But they had forgotten to send me word that they had done so, and I had no wish to go backwards for the sake of shade. To have said "Put the tents under trees *if there are any*" would have been best, though apparently superfluous; but one could not anticipate such absurd mistakes. I had had, and so had the men with me, a long search and several miles extra journey in the sun, which was not pleasant after the morning's work; and the tents had to be moved again the next day instead of after three or four days, the usual time of camping in one spot.

When returning from a completed survey the distance travelled each day is limited only by the powers of the men and bulls, from twenty to thirty miles being travelled if the carts are not heavily loaded and the roads not too bad. Then the large tents are not pitched but remain packed up on the carts, and one sleeps in small single fly-tents called *shouldaris*, or even on a cart with a bamboo covering. It is usual to ride ahead of the carts and to have a midday meal half-way, seated on rugs spread out under a tree. Inquiries are made of the villagers regarding their crops, the traffic passing along the road, the character of the soil, the rainfall and floods, the healthiness of the district, and any other matters likely to affect the traffic which will arise when the new line is made. Some estimate must be formed of the new lands which will come into cultivation, the amount of goods and passengers that will be carried, the levels above which the earthen banks must be raised to be free of the highest floods, the size of the waterways of the bridges. In making these inquiries I had often to go detours into the villages. Sometimes the main roads became mere tracks and the village roads were broad, and I made mistakes and found myself riding up to wet rice-fields or on a path leading to cattle-sheds. It was not uncommon for a crowd of villagers to look on in silence, and inform me that it was not the right path only when I had found the fact out myself. They possibly thought I was purposely inspecting the rice-fields and the cattle-sheds, as sahibs go about so much and examine almost everything.

If inquiring how far a village is, it depends in some parts on the time of day what answer is given. It may be without words, the man pointing to a particular spot in the sky to indicate that when you arrive the sun will be in that place. If it is so far that you will not arrive before dark, he will rest his head on his hands and close his eyes to indicate that it will then be time to go to bed. It was sometimes difficult to understand the direction intended, for the natives of some of those parts would look in one direction, extend an arm in another, and with a finger point at right angles to the arm.

More than once when, while riding, I was being guided by a villager going ahead, he stopped at a small stream and traced with a stick, just in front of my horse, what he considered was the easiest way down the bank for me to get to the bed and wade across. If the stream were narrow I might jump it; and once, when I had done so, I looked back and saw the guide still tracing the path for me. Crossing a broad river was a troublesome matter. It was only with the help of competent village guides who knew the shallow parts that it was safe to do so. In the cold season the beds of the rivers have little water, sometimes only two or three feet in depth, and are in parts dry and liable to quicksands. It was necessary to cross where there was daily communication between villages on opposite banks. Men go ahead wading on zigzag lines and the bulls with the carts will follow. When crossing, my horse always seemed to know that it was best to be on his good behaviour; and it would be dangerous if the horses got excited and tried to take their own course. If rain had lately fallen and the river had risen, one might have to wait a few days for the floods to subside; for it was only in a few places—I only found two—that boats of any kind were used. Some of the boats were circular, and made of wicker-work covered with skins, and in them one could travel with the men, the bulls, and loaded carts. These circular boats are, of course, difficult to steer. The boatmen amuse themselves by reversing one oar and thus causing the boat to spin round. When I first saw this done the boat was heavily loaded and in mid-stream, and I had some difficulty in stopping the men, who, in the hope of *baksheesh*, were putting forth their best efforts to produce the spinning.

A trying time was when all the camp had gone over in daylight and I reached the river after dark. It was necessary to cross to get to the tents, and, as there was no boat, this had to be done on horseback under the guidance of a villager wading on foot and carrying a torch. When half-way, unable to see either the bank behind or the one ahead, and when in the fast part of the stream with the reflection of the torch broken up by the swirling water, the horse may begin to jump a little with the uncertainty as to where he is, and perhaps try to go down-stream. Mine never gave much trouble, though he did show signs of impatience; and had the torch gone out or anything troublesome happened, I do not know how I could have managed in the darkness. A good deal of credit is due to the men who guided us across these rivers for their carefulness and reliability. They were always men of very low caste or no caste at all, and very poor. There are some attached to every village to do menial work, and they get Government allowances of food and a little money in return for their services being always available.

The villagers have to move about between their villages with difficulty, for the rivers are mostly unbridged and the roads bad. Originally they may have chosen dry watercourses for their foot-paths; these became the permanent tracks, and finally some of the roads were located on them. The consequence is that in the rainy season the roads are partly under water. So bad are some of the main roads that it is common after rain for the cartmen to have to drive their bulls across the country wherever they can find a passable way. When floods have swept away the road-approaches adjoining a river, they have to find new ways leading to places where it may be possible to take their carts down and up the banks and across the bed. The result is that in the dry season even the roughest roads come easy to them; and I was surprised at the willingness they showed to go rough journeys, and the ease with which they got over difficult parts. If living in dry bare districts they were inclined, when travelling through wooded country, to overload the carts with a lot of brushwood in addition to our baggage, as it would be of much use to them on their arrival at their homes. When paying the cartmen at the end of the journey it was necessary to do so with one's own hand, as it was the custom, if he could manage to handle the money first, for any *chuprassy* of Government to retain for himself a proportion larger than the usual *dasturi* or commission of the country, and the cartmen dare not complain. The *chuprassies* of the *jaghirdars* would sometimes step in between the cartmen and myself at time of payment and hold out their hands for the money. My indignation was always rather strongly expressed when that sort of thing happened, and the *chuprassies* got the severest scoldings I could manage in their language. This, however, probably did me little good; for these lower subordinate officials in the Native States, and especially in the *jaghirs*, have far too much power, and no doubt used it to hinder and annoy me in my progress.

The conditions laid down for the line finally selected were that it should start from Hyderabad, pass through Indore, Nandair, Parbhani, Jalna, and Aurungabad, all towns or large villages, centres of their districts, and join on to the existing Great Indian Peninsula Railway where found most convenient. At each of these places the Civil authorities were directly under the Hyderabad State administration, and they were specially ordered to render me any assistance required in procuring stores, fodder, carts, and labour for clearing the way. A general order was also given me in the name of H.H. the Nizam, and signed by the Prime Minister, which was to enable me, when in the *jaghirs* through which the location of the line fell, to call upon the local authorities to assist me in the same way. Some of the *jaghirdars* were anxious that the alignment should not be within their own boundaries. Where they had left only petty officials to manage their estates during their own absence for months at a time in Hyderabad, some of these men threw hindrances in my way. Either they did not wish the railway to come in those parts, or they wished to show what important persons they were. On reaching my camp one afternoon, I found it pitched within the limits of a *jaghir*, and my men in a state of indignation because the authorities had refused to allow them to buy anything in the village. The word had been passed that we were to be boycotted. No supplies, no grass or fodder, no water from the wells were to be had, and none of the villagers were allowed to come to work. I had to despatch some of my men to get things from distant villages outside the *jaghir*. Having sent for the *jemadar* or petty official in charge, I was surprised at the state in which he arrived, armed and dressed in grand style, as were also several others who accompanied him. He was a man who, in British India, would have received twenty-five to fifty rupees as his full monthly salary; but here he was probably reaping a rich harvest. He salaamed politely, and I asked him if it was true that my men were not allowed to get supplies and purchase food. He replied, "Quite true." I said, "By whose orders?" "By my orders," he answered. I then asked if he had seen the special *parwanah* (order) I had with me from the Nizam's Government. His reply was that the Nizam had no authority in that part. I saw that it was best to ignore him after that, and despatched a special messenger to Hyderabad, 150 miles away, in case I should not have managed in the meantime to get over the difficulty. My silence and my evident ability to manage in spite of him seemed to alarm the *jemadar*, for, nothing more being said, he took care to intercept my messenger and to supply my camp profusely with all that was wanted next morning.

Twice during one survey the funds remitted from Hyderabad to enable me to pay the monthly salaries of the engineers, subordinates, *khlassies*, coolies, cartmen, and others were sent to the wrong treasury, and it was a long time before the mistake was found out and could be rectified. The instruments supplied were long in arriving, and one level was found to have been mended with leaden screws. Several of the *khlassies* whom we had trained with much trouble left the survey as soon as it had proceeded farther from their homes than they cared to go, and we had to take on new men from the villages, who at first were of little use till taught. Towards the end of the survey, when approaching civilised parts again, the state of the furniture, which had been good at starting, was only what might be expected. Chairs, tables, and bedsteads were useless, or, if still serving their purpose, bound up with ropes and bits of string. Some had been discarded, and packing-boxes had taken their places. There had been many a smash-up of crockery, and that in use was only a little of what we started with, plus odd bits received from distant towns, to which, when within reach, messengers had been sent for renewals. A bottle was useful as a candlestick, or even a potato sliced flat underneath and with a hole scooped out at the top for the candle to be fixed in.

The villagers employed for the jungle-clearing generally worked well, but they had a strange way, when bushes or other obstructions had to be cleared, of working all round them before they would give the one or two blows of the hatchet which were all that were needed. Time was only lost in going to the spot and back again to the theodolite or sending a messenger to explain; and in the end it was always best to let them do the clearing in their own way, though it was trying to the patience to have to wait. They talked little till on their way back to their villages after the day's work, and then it was usually at the top of their voices. Even in Bolarum I have heard men from the interior passing along the road, in the middle of the night when everything was quiet, talking loud and clear with their very strong voices. When a man-eating tiger was said to be about the back-flag men were afraid to stand by a flag alone, but were always induced to do so if a second man was placed there, as if two would be quite enough to keep away a tiger. At one time a scare got among them that I was mad, as they had seen me take up stones, taste and smell them, and then throw them away. This I had done when wishing to judge if there was much lime in the soil.

A short delay was once caused when I found, in looking back over what ought to have been a long straight line, that I was travelling in chords of a curve. This was due to a hill close by containing iron ore. It was only a rough trial-line with a prismatic compass, and was easily rectified. The error would not have occurred had the theodolite been in use.

When passing through the north of the Indore district I was surprised to find several small blast-furnaces at work: and these, at night, reminded me of the Black Country at home. Tavernier relates that the barrels of the muskets of the soldiers of Golconda were not liable to burst as were those of Europe. The iron from these parts was that from which the steel was made for the famous Damascus blades.

The black cotton soil was troublesome. In the dry season it has cracks crossing and recrossing one another, some so large that the soil in between was in isolated, loose, irregular squares, and the cracks difficult to jump over. When such a surface was met for miles at a time the chaining and levelling was much impeded. In such parts it was not possible to ride, and therefore they were safer than others where the holes and cracks were few and sometimes hidden by surface soil and grass. The horses look out for the holes, and one can ride slowly over such country if not very bad. If cantering it is different; and one of the worst falls I had was caused in that way. My horse put his foot into a hidden hole and came down. Both the horse and I had our faces hurt; and I had a pain in my neck for a couple of days and an injured thumb-joint for about a month.

Every third day or so my cook made bread; but it was necessary to have certain parts of the manufacture done in my presence. At breakfast-time he brought the whole-meal flour and other ingredients and kneaded them on a table just outside the door of the tent under the outer awning, where I could watch what he was doing. This was necessary, because one practice is to knead the dough with the feet; and as the men walk about with bare feet, it becomes still more objectionable. The weight of the body when the feet are used does the work without the exertion of the muscles of the arms necessary when the kneading is done by hand. As I had seen the whole process through I could eat the bread in the knowledge that it was pure: and excellent bread the man used to make. We were in the country of cocoa-nut palms, and the toddy juice from them, of which the natives make beer, was used as yeast.

Another example may be given of the lax ideas some native servants have with regard to cleanliness in food. Twice, on opening my *tiffin* (lunch) basket sent out to me in the jungle with my breakfast, I found a pair of blacking-brushes used for cleaning boots. The men had overlooked them in packing up the tents and furniture, and having discovered them as the carts were moving off, popped them hastily into the *tiffin* basket as a convenient receptacle for the time being, intending no doubt to remove them before the basket was despatched to me with my breakfast.

Gipsies were met either in twos and threes, or when travelling in bands in search of new camping-grounds, or when engaged as carriers. They go with hundreds of donkeys or ponies or bulls loaded with grain, cotton, and other produce, and travel great distances to the central markets, charging the owners less even than the cost of sending by goods train. On 24th March 1892, a large number passed in charge of a line of 2000 bulls, each loaded with sixty pounds of linseed. They had 120 miles still to travel before reaching the railway. It is thought that all gipsies are of Indian descent, for all have the same names for fire, water, hair, eyes, and other words, as in the Hindustani language.

Little had been lost by theft, though in some parts it was reported that we should be careful;

and then the men and the dogs were sufficient guard. When robbers wish to loot a tent or bungalow, possibly they still use the same methods as in old days. They would approach in the darkness imitating the howl of a pariah dog or a jackal, and so put watchers off their guard as to any rustling sounds they might hear. Fox-terriers, however, are too sharp even for such methods; and probably they recognise that the howling is only imitation. There were certainly robbers of the worst kind about at some parts of the survey, some being dacoits. At a village about four miles from one of my camps two villagers were murdered by them. As a rule the villagers are glad when our camps move ahead, as they do not want the trouble of looking after us. But where we were then camped the villagers asked us to stay as long as possible, because, they said, the dacoits would never come near an Englishman's camp. They know that if they molest English people, apart from the probability of their carrying firearms, there would be, at the request of the British Resident, such a persistent search for the offenders that there would be no peace for them till caught. One morning when riding to the survey, I found, at a short distance from the tents, a life-size straw dummy of a man hanging by the neck from a branch of a tree and with a black cap over the head. It may have been some threat to the villagers, for a coarse joke of that kind is foreign to the nature of the native.

Of course some of the reports of dacoits being near were incorrect, and some natives were inclined to exaggerate and to cause scares. On February 7, 1892, I received an urgent note from about thirty miles away, stating that a Moglai official, the Mustad of Gurkol, had been "attacked by robbers and was wounded very much," and would I kindly send some sticking-plaster. On the whole there was little except petty annoyance from troublesome characters, but, from what occurred to other Europeans now and then, it was known that there was possibility of trouble in some parts.

Some of the *Taluqdars* or chief Civil authorities in charge of the districts were inclined to be too friendly. They would ask me to their houses and get up special entertainments some days before my camp reached near their headquarters. I had to limit myself to short visits and to manage somehow to avoid the special entertainments, because they were tedious and not to my liking. They were liable also to become objectionable in various ways; and the scents which natives consider pleasant are to Europeans oppressive, and the food one is expected to eat is hardly to our taste. One *Taluqdar* arranged a hunting excursion, as if we had not enough exercise in our work. Of course I did not go, but two of the assistants did. They returned depressed and disgusted at the cruel sights they had seen.

One of the *jaghirdars* was a native lady, the only one in such a position in the State. She was known as the *Râni*, and owned an extensive estate containing several villages. She was not under *purdah*, went about freely like any English lady, and talked pleasantly with Europeans passing through her domain. Whenever she heard of a villager in a distant part being ill, she would call for her palanquin and go off to see what could be done to help the case. She was much interested in the coming of the railway, and asked many questions as to what the survey was for and the use of the various instruments. At her wish I took the theodolite to her and explained some of its more evident uses; and, as might have been expected, it was the level bubble that took her fancy most.

One leading official had never seen through a telescope; and he was much delighted at the appearance of distant houses and trees having "come to him," as he expressed it.

At Karimnagar, while writing in my tent one afternoon, I was surprised to hear, just outside, the sound of a drum tattoo. Eight *sipahis* or sepoys were waiting for me, and on my going out of the tent they made a military salute. They were all in H.H. the Nizam's service as watchmen; but the two oldest were said to have been in the wars against the Mahrattas, having served in the highly disciplined infantry corps under the French General, M. Raymond. As that was about a century ago, of course it appeared incredible; but I understood that they claimed to be about a hundred and twenty years old (in 1891). They were still in nominal service, going on guard daily for an hour at the Treasury, and receiving small pay instead of being pensioned. The drum

RAYMOND'S SOLDIERS.

THESE MEN WERE IN THE WARS OF THE 18TH CENTURY UNDER THE FRENCH GENERAL, RAYMOND; AND IN 1892 THEY CLAIMED TO BE 120 YEARS OF AGE.

had been through the wars of those old times, and the colours were carefully kept under lock and key. The regiment at Karimnagar was called the *Musserâm* (a corruption of Monsieur Raymond); and until lately the words of command were still given in French.

XV.

LIFE ON RAILWAYS.

APRIL IN CAMP IN THE PUNJAUB—AT CALCUTTA—IN THE VIZIANAGRAM HILL-TRACTS — KHONDS — SEVERE FEVER — FEVER AT SEA — AN AFRIDI BEARER—A SICK POSTMASTER—OPEN LINE WORK—INSPECTION CARRIAGES — TROLLYING — TUNNELS — ON THE ENGINE—STATION-MASTERS—GANGMEN—LARGE BRIDGES.

AFTER a long furlough I returned to India in December 1896. In Calcutta I met an American friend, who, after heartily congratulating me on looking in excellent health, remarked, "You have evidently not been on that vegetable diet all this time." I had not been on a vegetable diet, but on one which, though the chief articles were of farinacea and fruits, included eggs, milk, butter, and cheese, but excluded flesh.

My new charge was of a survey for a branch line of railway from Loodhiana through the Native States, Jhind, Nabha, and part of Patiala. The country is one of the hottest in India, and its trees afford little shade for tents. The survey was begun late in the season, and was much impeded by dust-storms. By April the heat had become so great that I had to sit in my tent with wet towels round my head, and at last, owing to much irritation of the brain, was obliged to take refuge in some rooms placed at my disposal by the Nawab of Loharu. Another engineer was sent to relieve me, and (it was afterwards reported by Major-General de Bourbel) "he and his staff were frequently prostrated, and suffered in health by exposure in camp to intense heat." I was then given a light charge at Delhi as a rest, and was stationed there from April to August 1897.

Then came four months of a special kind of work at Calcutta. The moist heat of Calcutta is oppressive, and the months of September and October are what is called "muggy." November and December, however, are pleasant cool months, and the work became interesting, especially that part which required my attendance at the committees held by the officials of the East Indian Railway, and the Eastern Bengal State Railway, to inquire into accidents. At these committees the difficulty is to find out what to believe in the midst of the conflicting evidence; for members of one branch of the railway try to show that an accident is more the fault of the working of another branch. The Traffic people, for instance, may blame those of the Engineering branch for defect in the permanent way; and they, in turn, may say that the signals or lights were wrong, or the wheels of the carriages in bad order. A pointsman may have pulled the lever handle the wrong way, and tried in his confusion to rectify the mistake when the engine had already passed the points.

Near Calcutta, of course, the natives have plenty of opportunity of seeing and using railways; but in some parts of India, when a new line has been made and the first train passes along, the villagers come in crowds to see it. Though never having seen an engine before, or anything like it, they stand within twenty feet or so of the rails, and without the least sign of fear or astonishment watch it approach and stop at the station. Sometimes no word passes: they simply watch in silence, and then go about their ordinary daily business as if nothing unusual had occurred.

My next charge was of the eastern half of the Vizianagram-Raipur Railway survey; and, after a journey of 500 miles from Calcutta, I was again among the slow-moving unsatisfactory workers of the Madras Presidency. After passing through the country of the Rajah of Bobbili, the survey reached some rough hilly country covered with thicker jungle than I had ever had to survey through. At a place called Raigadda the alignment was difficult, and required days of continual movement on several lines up and down steep hills and across water; and beyond it the country was cut up with deep ravines following one another rapidly. Some were so deep and narrow, and so thickly covered with vegetation, that they were dark, hot, and stifling. Many years before a survey had been made; but the gradient of the alignment selected had been unsatisfactory, and a new alignment had now to be found with a gradient of not more than 1 in a 100. The men available were of the roughest, and quite untrained to such work; and many left the

KHOND JUNGLE CLEARERS, VIZIANAGRAM HILL TRACTS.

THESE MEN ARE SO PRIMITIVE THAT THEY DO NOT UNDERSTAND THE USE OF MONEY.

survey as soon as the wilder country was reached. The cartmen would only stay for short periods, and it was difficult to get others from a distance. When near the end of the work most of the men were ill with fever; and at last every man with me, all the subordinates, English as well as native, all the *khlassies*, *chuprassies*, and cartmen, were down with fever. The native doctor attached to the survey party was so ill with it that he was unable to attend to his patients. On the former survey an Executive engineer had died, and his grave was in the jungle not far away. Just at the last I was working with only one *chuprassy* and a lot of hill-villagers who came for the jungle clearing and whom I made use of as *khlassies*. They were of one of the most backward of the hill-tribes—Khonds—men who knew nothing even of the use of money.

In giving my own experiences of a severe attack of fever, the details of which I now relate, I am describing only the sort of thing that many a Civil engineer, Forest officer, or other official has to contend with when his duties take him into the midst of malaria. It will be seen how strong a hold the fever may get and how difficult it is to shake off.

Before quite finishing the survey, I was myself attacked with fever, and though the last to go down with it, was as bad as any one. I had to travel in a bullock cart without springs over the rough country roads, 120 miles, to get to my headquarters at Vizianagram where the Civil surgeon was. A thick layer of two or three feet of hay—straw is of no use—is a good substitute for springs, and is much used to deaden vibration on such journeys. On the way I became very weak owing to frequent attacks of fever, with much vomiting and some delirium. I dreamt that the trees were trying to help me with the work, and just as I used to tell the men to go faster, they were continually calling to the pegs, "Go ahead, go ahead; faster, faster." I saw the pegs racing along the line marked out, with the trees bending down and urging them on; and when the pace became so rapid that I could hardly distinguish one peg from another, I would wake with a throbbing head and in perspiration, and feeling very faint. Another fantastic dream was that there was going to be a concert and that one of the singers was jealous of the rest. To prevent their singing better than himself he stole all the semiquavers. I saw him standing guard over a crowd of the semiquavers in a corner of the room, but when he began to sing and wished to use them, they had all turned into bullock carts.

On arriving at Vizianagram, through the kindness of Captain Smyth, R.E., one of the engineers of the East Coast Railway, and his wife, who made me comfortable in their house, and the careful attention of the medical officer, I recovered enough to go on to Vizagapatam, where the Civil surgeon arranged for me to go for a time to Europe. It was annoying to have to take furlough, and on medical certificate, only sixteen months after having returned to India in good health. The doctor would not allow me to travel even a short distance down the coast by rail to catch a large steamer, as he said I could not stand the vibration of the train; and I had to wait for a local one of the British India line.

In going on board I had to take a small boat first, for the large steamers cannot come near the harbour. There is a line of rocks and surf between the shore and where the steamers lie. The boatmen make for a gap in those rocks, and it is a rough-and-tumble time when passing through the surf. It is related that one passenger had his boat turned upside down at the gap, owing to the boatmen having mistimed their attempt to go through. Outside the bar the sea was rough, and when, after some delay, the boatmen thought they had a good opportunity of getting up to the gangway, the boat was carried underneath it and with a bang against the side of the vessel. As the waves carried us up and down I had to dodge to prevent my head from striking against the steps. When the boat was at last brought by the waves and the exertions of the men alongside, I had to spring sharp from it, and fortunately landed fairly on the platform at the foot of the ladder. A boatswain, who had been sent by the officers down the steps to assist us, caught me, and in an exhausted state I climbed the gangway and sat for some time on deck to recover. It was a trying experience in my weak state of health.

Excepting weakness, I had little to complain of till we passed Madras and Colombo. On the Orient liner *Austral* the fever returned strong;

and every second day, nearly up to Naples, I was sick many times, the intervening days being without any fever or sickness. I slept a great deal night and day; and one afternoon, having gone to sleep in my chair on deck at about two o'clock, I did not wake till eleven o'clock at night. The other passengers in passing me on their way to dinner, having been accustomed to seeing me sleeping, probably supposed I was then having one of my casual rests. When I woke I wished for a biscuit or some other food. Finding no one about I had to be satisfied with a glass of water and went to bed,—getting, as usual, a long night's sleep in spite of the fact that I had already slept nine hours. Next morning, as always on the alternate days, I was very sick again.

One morning on deck, after one of the attacks of fever, I was hot and parched with thirst. On my asking the doctor to let me have some iced water, he replied, "Not yet." I waited a few minutes, and finding the thirst intolerable, I told the deck steward to bring me an iced drink. He brought me a long tumbler of water-and-ice. I drank the water eagerly, and ate the ice. A few minutes afterwards I got another glassful and did the same again. This did me much good; but when I told the doctor what I had done, he said it was dangerous. It seemed to me to have been just what was wanted, and, apparently, by the thirst Nature was indicating the proper remedy.

On the survey in the Vizianagram hill-tracts I had with me an Afridi bearer who served me at Delhi, Calcutta, and throughout the survey.

Though belonging to the troublesome border tribe with whom we were at war at the time, he was a reliable servant. It is a noticeable fact that the men of uncivilised parts, as in the Assam hills and on the Afghan border, when they get the opportunity of regular settled occupation, are glad to take it up and become satisfactory workers. This man had a strange way of waking me in the morning if letters had arrived. He would come to my bedside and present them to me without saying a word. It seemed as if the fact of his standing silently there with the letters held out to me to take were enough to wake me.

Another character was the Raigadda postmaster. His was an outlying post-office of the elementary sort placed in distant villages. It was the last I had to depend on, and having gone thirty or forty miles beyond it, I found that, though my dâk runners went backwards and forwards daily from my camp to Raigadda, no letters came, either Government or private. In reply to my inquiries, the postmaster wrote assuring me that none had come for me. In passing Raigadda on my return journey, I stopped at the post-office and asked him to try to remember the last letters sent to me and when, so that I might judge where the loss had occurred and who was responsible. Before leaving, I got him to make a final search through his office, and after doing so, he thought of his own private clothes-box. After turning over many bundles of clothes in great confusion he found my letters—

which had been coming daily for a week or ten days—hidden away at the bottom of the box. He said he had put them there for safety, and that daily attacks of fever had caused him to forget them. Cases like this are rare, and the delivery of letters in India is very regular, the postal arrangements being everywhere excellent.

On return from sick leave—the first leave of that kind I had taken, after twenty-three years' total service—I was given open line work, and had charge of lengths of the North-West Railway, with headquarters at first at Khushab, and afterwards at Sukkur on the Indus. Being on open line work my experiences were again much different from any I had already had.

There were, in 1901, more than 25,000 miles of railway open for traffic. In that year nearly 195,000,000 passengers, and 44,000,000 tons of goods and minerals, were carried. Though not yet adequately provided with railways, India is better served than most countries outside Europe. It has a mile of railway for every eighty-two square miles of country, and the cost to a third-class passenger is less than a farthing a mile. To the end of 1902 the capital outlay on construction had been £223,715,905.

The life of an engineer employed on the maintenance of railways in India is a rough and very busy one. He lives in continual hurry, heat, and noise, has much correspondence and many plans to attend to, and is always liable to have urgent telegrams handed to him night and day. He must work in harmony, if possible, with the officers of other departments of the railway, for his work and that of the Traffic, Management, Stores, and Locomotive departments depend much on one another. To those who have become well versed in Railway work in all its bearings it is most interesting; but to be able to deal in comfort and satisfactorily, often at very short notice, with railway matters requiring experience and skill, one should enter the Railway branch at the beginning of one's career.

In holding charge of a section of the line of, maybe, 300 miles at a time, a Railway engineer has frequently to pass up and down inspecting the state of the permanent way, the points and crossings, the bridges and culverts, banks and cuttings, station and other buildings, and the efficiency of the gangs. He has assistants, sub-engineers, overseers, mates, and others continually reporting to him the state of their sections and everything that requires attention or orders. Telegrams may be handed to him at any hour reporting some irregularity. He is responsible for the safety of the line, and must take care that it is always in such order that the traffic may not be impeded; or if, owing to floods or accidents or other cause, any obstruction occur, he must get the line into working order as quickly as possible. Some works must be taken in hand and completed between the running of two consecutive trains. The alteration of a bridge, or the putting in of a new culvert, involves making first a diversion of the line to enable the traffic to be carried on past the spot while the work is in progress; and the approach must be carefully guarded with red flags and red lights. The trained overseers and mates in charge of the working gangs are good men, and there is no kind of work in India which drills the lower classes of natives to regular habits so much as that of the open line of railways.

For his personal use the engineer has a special carriage attached to his charge. This includes a sitting-room and bedroom combined, a bath-room, a kitchen, and a verandah outside where he can sit and watch the passing scenery and cool himself in the hot evenings. His rooms have tables, chairs, cupboards, and other fittings, including a punkah, which is pulled by a man sitting outside in the verandah, or automatically by steam from the engine. When going on a journey he gives his men and the station-master notice of the train he intends to travel by. His servants collect the stores, clothing, bedding, &c., and just before the train starts he finds the carriage—perhaps much heated by having stood in the sun all day—attached to it, and the office-boxes, papers, &c., arranged in order on the tables.

The men are trained to all this, and I found no difficulty in keeping them up to time. Sometimes a new or a dull servant made mistakes, as once when the train had started and I saw the cook's boy running back to the bungalow, having gone off when there was no chance of his getting back in time. The cook explained that he had left the "corkey-screw" behind, and had sent the boy to fetch it.

The engineer continues his office work on the journey, and on stopping at stations he despatches correspondence and telegrams, and receives reports from his men on the line to keep himself in touch with what is being done. At each station he makes use of the time of stoppage to look quickly through the yard and examine the points and crossings and the state of the buildings and permanent way. On arrival at his destination his carriage is detached and placed on a siding, perhaps in the middle of the night, and he wakes in the morning to find his early breakfast ready, the train itself having gone on a hundred miles or more maybe. In the guard's van has been brought the trolly—a small platform on four wheels—on which he sits, while four coolies, or trollymen, run behind, pushing it along the line. Two sit on the trolly, while two push. After a few minutes of pushing, if on the level or a decline, they jump on the trolly, and it may run half a mile or more before they have to get off again to give it another push to keep up the pace. My first run of this kind was one of nineteen miles after dinner in the dark, and the rate at which we went was surprising. Before starting, it is necessary to know from the station-master what trains are due on the line, and about where they are likely to be met; and a keen look-out must be kept for the lights of the train in the distance. When within about a mile of it the trolly must be lifted off the rails and placed at a safe distance from the line till the train has passed.

In the hot weather life in these carriages is trying, as the roofs and sides become heated in the strong sun; and in Sind, the Punjaub, and Rajputana there can be little protection from the hot winds from the deserts. Blue glass to mitigate the glare and wet cuscus tatties are fitted to the windows; but there is no escape from the dust and the noise of trains passing close alongside at night.

Accidents with the carriages are rare, but trollying is sometimes dangerous. One's hand must be always on the brake, the men behind also having a brake to add to the stopping power. Two overseers travelling in opposite directions were asleep, and the trollymen also not being sufficiently on the look-out, they ran into one another, and one man got his leg broken. There was a danger of being purposely upset by men and boys of the villages. They would place heaps of stones on the line, and though, during the day, these could be seen in time to stop, they were very dangerous at night. A sub-engineer was in that way precipitated through a bridge, and was badly injured. The stones had been placed just at the beginning of the bridge on purpose to cause as much damage as possible. My own trolly was upset in front of an ash-pit in a station-yard, and, fortunately, the culprits were caught immediately, and a heavy penalty was imposed by the magistrate of the district. In isolated parts, the dog-spikes which keep the rails in position are sometimes stolen, and are then worked up with other iron by the local smiths, making it impossible to trace them.

Trollying full speed through a tunnel is an experience which many people would prefer to go without. It is necessary to sit quite still and hold tight, for in darkness a false move in so limited a space as a trolly allows may be serious. The darkness ahead and all round, the rattle of the wheels, the rapid motion, and the wind rushing past, with the knowledge that if anything were to go wrong it might be impossible to do the right thing,—all make one not sorry when the light appears again; though, while passing through the tunnel, the ride may be exhilarating for those with strong nerves. When trollying down the Thull ghat of the Great Indian Peninsula Railway near Bombay, the windings prevented our seeing the mouth of the tunnel in the distance, and we were in darkness. When the tunnel is straight it is curious to see the end, at first like a small spot of light, getting larger and larger as we approach it. It must be a terrible experience for the cattle crowded together in trucks when, for the first time, they are carried through a tunnel. They have lived, perhaps all their lives, in the green fields where darkness only came gradually at evening; and the change to the trucks amid the noise of shunting and passing trains, the sudden darkness of tunnels, and the screams of whistles, probably send some of them quite mad before the time of slaughtering comes, especially as, before that occurs, they are sometimes kept for days without food and water.

One engineer on the South Indian Railway had chairs with strong hooks fitted at the back, and we sat hanging on a bar which runs along the side of the engine and in front. The feeling was very strange. The country seemed to be flying at us, and when we were going round curves it looked as if the trees and telegraph posts were going to hit us. The extraordinary rumblings and groans made by the engine gave the impression of its being alive and suffering tortures, and irregularities in the permanent way seemed to make it give a leap to get over them.

When travelling one night on the engine, as we sometimes do so as to judge better of the state of the line, I was enabled to see one of the causes of the frequent friction between the subordinate employees, the station-masters, guards, and others. It was in an isolated part where the side-stations were few and small. As it was night, it was with difficulty on arriving at one of them that we could tell where we were, for there was no light of any kind. The distant signal lamp was not lit, nor the lamps of the station; nor was there any one on the platform. The station-master had to be sent for, though, of course, he knew the train—a goods one—was due, as he had given the "line clear" message to enable it to come on towards his station. A report made by the engine-driver and guard to headquarters might have been believed or not, for false accusations and counter accusations are not uncommon.

Native station-masters at these side-stations, as well as at the larger ones, are courteous and obliging, and they all read and write English. Unfortunately they catch English slang expressions from some of the lower classes of Europeans and Eurasians. Sometimes they suppose they are only ordinary English words and phrases, and really do not know the full meaning of what they are saying. Knowing this, I had to feel only amusement on overhearing the head clerk of my office, who was usually respectful and polite, speak of me in the Billingsgate tongue, when all he meant was that he considered me mistaken in insisting that a certain piece of work was necessary. Years before, when I was not in the Railway branch and was waiting at a side-station, a goods train, in charge of an English or Eurasian guard and driver, was waiting for the "line clear" signal to be given by the native station-master. They believed he had received the intimation from the station ahead and was keeping it back to delay and annoy them. Possibly he was, for there was evidently no friendly feeling between them. The guard and driver spoke of the Baboo (station-master) as a "baboon," and wondered what jungle the Company had caught him out of.

The men of the gangs, on ceasing work and having had their meal, would sometimes roll up their *puggrees* as a pillow, place them on the rail, and go to sleep. Sometimes a villager would commit suicide in this way; but in most cases the man simply found the rail a convenient elevation to rest his head, and went to sleep on the assumption that no train was due. I have seen men lying full length on the parapet of a canal bridge and asleep, so that a little motion sideways would cause them to fall either on to the roadway or into the canal. On railway construction in Madras it was difficult to prevent the men who had to tamp the charges of dynamite doing so with steel bars, if they were conveniently at hand, instead of with copper ones.

The large rivers of the Punjaub require long and massive bridges. The Sukkur bridge has a centre span of 790 feet, made up of two cantilevers supporting a girder. The expansion and contraction of such lengths of iron-work exposed to great variations of temperature require special precautions. There the temperature is almost the highest in India, and there are frosts in the cold weather. Other large bridges are three over the Sutlej river, each one more than three-quarters of a mile long, two over the Chenab of more than half a mile each, and others as long over the rivers Beas and Jhelum. At Sukkur for weeks together in the hottest months the temperature in the shade was seldom less than 110° during the day and apparently not much cooler at night. I have known it 125° in the shade. The profuse perspiration was probably a good thing for me, as it helped to get rid of much of the malarial poison still left in me by the fever. At the end of the hot weather of 1900 I was glad to get orders to proceed on transfer to Hyderabad again.

XVI.

RELIGIONS.

THE HINDU RELIGION—BRAHM—THE VEDAS—THE GOLDEN AGE—DEGENERATE TIMES—CASTE—BRAHMINS—TRANSMIGRATION—FAKIRS—POSITION OF WOMEN—JAINS—BUDDHISTS—MAHOMEDANS—HILL-TRIBES—THUGS—MISSIONS—CONVERTS—LACE INDUSTRY—SALVATION ARMY.

SOME people in England are under the impression that the natives of India are being ground down by British rule, and I have even been told that it would be better for them if there were no English in India. They would leave the natives to be ruled by the Brahmins, for whom the Hindus have much respect. Though of the total population of 295,000,000 there are about 75,000,000 Mahomedans and others who have no respect for Brahmins, there are 220,000,000 Hindus, Buddhists, and others, most of whom have.

In the beginning of the Hindu religion, many centuries B.C., there was only one God, Brahm, the Supreme Being, represented as impossible to define or describe, but infinite, self-created, from whom all souls come and to whom all return.

The doctrines are recorded in the ancient sacred books called the "Vedas," the earliest of which was of about 1700 B.C. They are composed of hymns, prayers, and precepts, and are supposed by the Hindus to be of divine origin and infallible. They taught that man's duties are to be kind to one another and to all God's creatures; to be merciful, truthful, charitable, lowly, thoughtful, studious, respectful, clean, regular, and virtuous. The one God is to be worshipped by meditation and the practice of kindness and virtue. The Universe was said to move in a circle, and was supposed then to be in the Golden Age. There is only a vague mention of caste, the four castes into which the Hindus are now mainly divided having been introduced in the degenerate time which followed—viz., the Red Yoog or Silver Age. Idolatry and the use of shrines and temples were disapproved of in the sacred books; but, following the Silver Age, came one in which worship at temples became the custom, and incarnations of Brahm were adored under the names of Indra, Rama, Krishna, Vishnu, Siva, and others. Finally came the Iron Age of the present time, with its complicated ceremonial, ritual, and penance, backed by a fantastic array of minor gods and devils. It is to be hoped that the nadir of the circle has been reached, and that a start will now be made for the Golden Age again.

When the times began to degenerate a division of the people was made into Brahmins or priests, Kshatriyas or strong martial men wanting in the finer and milder virtues, Vaishyas or traders and agriculturalists, and Sudras or men who engage in menial or unpleasant occupations. At first, caste was not necessarily hereditary as now; but a virtuous man could rise to a higher caste and a vicious man might be degraded. Nor were the Brahmins more important than the military class, towards whom they stood in the same relation as a chaplain did to a nobleman in the middle ages in England.

According to the Laws of Manu, the duties of Brahmins were to attend to sacrifices, to read and teach the Vedas, to give and receive gifts, and to be peaceful, pure, patient, and wise. Though still acknowledging Brahm as the one God and Creator, they now assent to the many present-day corruptions of the original belief and practice, and even teach a polytheism so varied and elastic that Hindu creeds, sects, and beliefs, in their details, are apparently as numerous as the Hindus themselves. Within their own caste there have arisen divisions and subdivisions so marked that, though all Brahmins are more or less sacred compared with people of other castes, they may not all mix with one another. Some Brahmins have departed so far from the Vedic religion that they will even occasionally eat flesh. The worship of Brahm is almost abandoned, and there is now only a small community of philosophic Brahmins who, as Vedantists, still worship him.

The higher Brahmins, as seen among the pundits or educated literary men of the North and in Hindustan, and others whose ancestors have held a superior position for about three thousand years, have developed hereditary qualities of refinement in person and bearing. Many are fair, well formed, and with good Aryan features. As the monks of mediæval times were the custodians of the Christian Scriptures, so these men have been the preservers of the Vedas, Shastras, and heroic Epics of Sanscrit and other literature. Unfortunately for them, the British system gives facilities for men and even women of low caste to become educated, and the Brahmins have no longer the exclusive possession of learning.

The poorer Brahmins, especially those of the villages, now occasionally take to agricultural and other occupations, though they avoid the actual labour, especially in its menial details. Even among the lower castes the divisions are now very numerous. Some trades which have become hereditary, besides families and local tribes, are now practically sub-castes refusing to associate much with one another.

The distinctions of caste are so numerous and varied that they extend even to the use of the right and the left hand. There are, in South India, right-handed and left-handed castes—those placed on the right or left by Kali. By some the right hand only can be used for eating, the left being reserved for dirty work. When my syce once changed a bundle he was carrying from one hand to the other before he took hold of the horse's bridle, and I inquired why, he explained that it was necessary to lead the horse with the right hand or he would become possessed by a devil. One sect of Marwaris in Western India, the Bishnois, are said to be so particular about ceremonial that, if a Bishnoi's food is on the first of a string of camels and a man of another caste touch the last camel, the food is defiled and must be thrown away. It is related by Rev. J. Ewen, in his book, 'India: Sketches and Stories of Native Life,' that when an accident occurred and some men were severely injured, none of the onlookers would help, as they did not know of what caste the injured men were: those of high-caste being afraid of touching them for fear of themselves becoming contaminated, and the low-caste ones fearing lest they might get into trouble for touching men of higher caste.

The modifications introduced by the Brahmins, or approved and insisted on by them, resulted in a lowering of the character and the standard of comfort of the whole nation. The Institutes of Manu, for instance, the Brahmin code of laws, forbid the *sudra* (labourer) to acquire wealth; and to-day one of the charges made by Brahmins against the British system is that the labourers and low-castes generally are placed on an equality with every one else in the eye of the law. In 1892 Dewan Bahadur Sinavasa Iyengar, Inspector-General for Registration at Madras, said that the best thing for the pariahs and low-castes was to become Christian or Mahomedan, as there was no hope for them under the Hindu system. It tells against even the high-caste Hindus now; for though many, especially in Calcutta, have become very poor, they may not work at anything that requires the use of leather, nor can they become barbers, washermen, fishermen, or potters, nor engage in farming pursuits.

"Transmigration" was a doctrine from the first, and was not interfered with by the reformer, Buddha, though he taught that the soul is not apart from the body but dissolves at death. It was a theory of the ancient Egyptians, and was taught by Pythagoras. The soul is believed to pass through several stages of existence, in some of which it inhabits the bodies of different kinds of animals. Hence the reluctance sometimes shown by Hindus, and especially by Jains, to kill a noxious animal, as they fear there may be embodied in it the soul of some one or other of their own dead relations. The introduction of numerous malignant gods may have only confirmed the Hindus in this belief, for there is among many also the idea that the souls of men now inhabiting the bodies of the lower animals are passing through a period of punishment or purgatory necessary for the propitiation of evil powers or bad spirits they may have offended. As Buckle in his 'History of Civilisation' has pointed out, the catastrophes of Nature in the East are at times on a gigantic scale, and created in the minds of primitive, uneducated, and helpless man the conviction that they were the manifestations of malignant deities.

The belief in "Transmigration" occasionally takes a more absurd shape than usual—as when, at Delhi, a mendicant who insisted on going about the streets naked, after being twice punished, had at last to be given ten stripes as a deterrent. He then explained that the magistrate, in a former state of existence, had been his donkey, and was now taking his revenge for the cruelty he had shown him.

As the Brahmins became powerful, propitiation of the bad god Siva, and his wife Kali, became the commonest form of worship, and the distinctions of caste became more binding. The more important religious observances which Hindus are expected to attend to, and the penances imposed when caste rules are broken, involve presents or payments to the Brahmin priests. All Brahmins are within the sacred pale. The inner parts of temples, images of deities, the houses in which they live, their food and cooking utensils, must not be touched by any except a Brahmin. Their persons are sacred, and they cannot sit at the same table and take meals with Europeans or others who are not Brahmin without losing caste.

What merit can there be in a religion which is exclusive? No one can enter the Brahmin circle except by birth; and proselytising is quite unknown among them. The churches are closed against those who presumably require elevating in character. The absurdities of the religion in its present shape are many, and some almost incredible. Fakirs (religious mendicants) may be seen at all the large Hindu festivals, nearly naked, with their hair matted, dyed, and mixed with mud, and their bodies covered with yellow ochre or with white ashes, and some disfigured through self-inflicted tortures. Holding up the arm till it has become stiff and cannot be taken down; travelling, lying on the back, from one sacred place to another; lying on beds of iron spikes; fighting one another while suspended from trees by ropes, at the end of which are hooks driven into the flesh of the back (a practice now stopped by law),—are forms of self-torture now disappearing, and some of which I did not see. I once found a man walking quickly round a tree repeating prayers or charms. The tree was sacred (a *pipul*), and the man had to go three hundred times round it as a penance. One of my clerks had the nail of his forefinger as long as the finger itself. There is the worship of the pen, of rivers, tigers, alligators, snakes, and monkeys. There are lucky days and days of fate. In some districts a woman may not mention her husband's name. There are idols innumerable and of all kinds,—some with many hands or with a man's head, but an elephant's trunk instead of a nose; some made of mud and worshipped for a few days only on the occasion of the "Doorga Pooja," others more permanent and made of wood or stone; and there are the brass ones made in Birmingham. Some missionary friends of mine found it best not to give the native children the dolls sent for them by children in New Zealand, as, instead of nursing them, they were inclined to worship them as idols. Sportsmen have difficulty in securing the skins of the tigers they bag intact, as the claws and whiskers are sacred and are eagerly sought after by the natives as charms.

Pilgrims who travel great distances to Benares take back with them bottles full of the Ganges water, and this is worshipped in the villages by those who stay at home. The drinking-water of the high-caste people has to be kept separate from that of the low-caste and pariahs. At railway-stations there are *bheesties*, or water-carriers, who go up and down the platform on the arrival of each train and supply water to the native travellers. There must be two—one for Hindus and one for Mahomedans and others. Once when in need of some water to make a cup of tea, I stepped out of my carriage and helped myself to some with a clean block-tin vessel. I had gone unknowingly to a small tank set apart for the use of Hindus, and a passing coolie remarked to another, "How can we use water at these stations if the sahibs are also allowed to take it?" And yet some of these men, who are so particular about others not having the same source of supply as themselves, drink water contaminated with much impurity. In other ways these customs are mixed up with much that is insanitary, as in the case of the horrible "well of forgiveness" at Benares, and in other places where the water is drunk as well as bathed in. In 'Pen-and-Ink Sketches of Native Life in India,' a book written by a native, he says, in describing a Brahmin's household: "After this (the dinner) the floor of the dining-room will be swept clean and sprinkled with cow-dung and water." That it is all more matter of custom and ceremonial than of principle was shown when a bearer I had, though he would have been indignant at the suggestion that he himself should eat flesh, expressed his disapproval of my not doing so as it was the custom of the people to whom I belong.

At the Diwali festival there are illuminations at night in honour of Lakshmi, the goddess of wealth and much gambling. The Dasahra *mela*, or fair, is in honour of the birth of the Ganges. At the "Doorga Pooja" the bad goddess Kali is worshipped for three days, and then the idols are thrown into the river. The *Holi*, in honour of Krishna, is an occasion for much obscenity of language and action, and women are then not safe in the streets.

Whatever may be said of the religion in its original and purer form, it cannot be denied that it now fosters many evils, and there is much intolerance on the part of the Brahmins of any attempt to introduce improvements. Here and there a leading Hindu wishes to begin reforms in the way of remarriage of widows, greater freedom for the *purdah* women, and later age for marriage of children; but the priests object. Not only does the British Government protect them in the exercise of their religion on the general principle of non-interference in matters of faith (except when religious riots, widow-burning, and infanticide have to be suppressed), but it gives facilities for the pilgrims to go to the shrines. Special precautions are taken for the public safety at the great festivals,—the roads that are much used are kept in order, and excursions by railway are organised. The good roads and the railways have made trade more profitable; and this has enabled the traders who have grown rich to build more temples and give larger presents to the priests.

The chief ground on which the Brahmin system is admired by humanitarians at home is that kindness to animals is shown by the majority of Hindus. The average Hindu is naturally mild-mannered, and inclined to treat the inferior creation with kindly sympathy. The Bishnoi, for instance, worship the benign god Vishnu, and have great regard for animal life. Their villages swarm with antelope and game, which they will not allow the Mahomedans to destroy; and they do their best to induce European sportsmen to leave them unmolested. The veneration of the cow is, of course, carried to an absurd length, especially at Amritsar; but the killing of bulls as sacrifice, and even of Brahmins before they became powerful, at one time had the authority of the Shastras. According to the Abbé Dubois, the prohibition to kill oxen and to feed on their flesh was not due to religious scruples but to motives of self-interest, as their work and milk are too valuable. Laws were made against it, the people being satisfied by the cow being deified at the same time. The killing of widows and infants appears to have been introduced instead.

There is much apathy at times when animals are badly treated; and an essential part of one of their religious ceremonies is the cruel practice of cutting off a goat's head. In a pamphlet published at Jùnagad in 1903 by Baboo Labhshankar Lachmidas, a description is given of how animals are killed at certain Brahmin sacrifices at Benares:—

> "The animal is first worshipped with a Vedic hymn, and gods are invoked to dwell in every part of its body. It is then sent into the slaughter-room, where its four legs are tied and its mouth is filled with husked rice and then tightly bound with a string. After this the animal is repeatedly struck with fists by Sudra Brahmins like dough, and when it is all but dead and moving a little, its body is cut up into several pieces, which are then brought out for use in the sacrifice."

This description was given by Baboo Labhashankar Anandji, a Brahmin gentleman who was present at the sacrifice.

The gifts and feasts to the Brahmins, which they insist on whenever there is any important family occurrence, such as a wedding, and the costly penances for accidental breaking of caste rules, have been the ruin of thousands of cultivators, who have had to go into debt to the money-lenders for life to obtain the means to pay. Even in famine time the mere acceptance of relief was, in some cases, a loss of caste, and had to be paid for in penance and gifts to the priests. On these family occasions there are elaborate ceremonies in which many people are required to take part, and much money and valuables change hands. The children must be married; and the dread of the excessive expenditure was one of the causes of the infanticide so common till the British Government interfered. It is not the least of the evils that the husband and wife do not choose one another, and may be badly matched. The arrangement is made by their parents when they are two or three years old; and it has been said that its only recommendation is that a woman is sure to get a husband whatever her disqualifications may be. The misery that has been suffered by women and children through the cruel practice of *suttee* (the burning of widows alive on the funeral pyre of their dead husbands), infant marriages, and the degradation of widows on the death of their husbands, has been going on for centuries. *Suttee* was not mentioned by the Vedas, nor were infanticide or marriages in childhood part of the original system. The Brahmins are responsible for them, as they are for the continued seclusion, among Hindus, of the higher-caste women from the outer world.

The *purdah* system, by which the ladies are kept closely guarded, sometimes all their lives, in very private apartments, so that they may be secure from the sight of men other than their husbands or other near relations, was at first only a Mahomedan institution. It was copied by the higher-caste Hindus after the Mahomedan conquests, no doubt partly as a means of defence from the intrusion of their new masters. Though the Hindu caste women are bred and kept in much seclusion, their *purdah* is not so strict as among the Mahomedans, and in the south of

India it is not nearly so much enforced as in the North. In the Madras Presidency and Hyderabad even Brahmin women go occasionally in public unveiled. I once had a good illustration of the inconvenience of this seclusion when, at a fire in the bazaar at Bombay, the women of a zenana had to be hurriedly brought from their quiet rooms into the streets. They were terrified at the strange sights and the bustle of the crowd, and especially at the presence of so many men.

During the Exhibition at Calcutta a few years ago some afternoons were set apart for the *purdah* ladies to visit it while no one else was admitted. They went through it in twos and threes, holding on to one another's dresses, and attended by a lady missionary or a young boy. Though very private it was a great innovation, and much opposed by the older ladies.

Brahminism expels the innocent child-widows from their home circle and makes them outcasts, thus dooming them to lives of misery and penury, and often to resort to an evil line of life to earn their living. Under the Brahmin rule, except in a few tribes, they are not allowed to remarry, though the ancient law, as recorded in the sacred books, allowed them to do so.

A Bengali Baboo wrote:—

> "Young girls married at three, married even when not born; married at such an early age that their fathers, their mothers, and their eldest brothers may not go to hell; when their young husbands die, not allowed

> to remarry: their untimely death regarded as punishment to these girls for their crimes in a state of pre-existence."

After pointing out that a law was passed in 1856 declaring that no guilt lay in child-widows' remarriage, and that since then only two or three widow remarriages have occurred annually (among Hindus of the higher castes), he remarks:—

> "Their religion asks them to confine themselves to a life of the utmost misery. Nice religion indeed! Religion, which ought to teach how to live happily, teaching how to lead a life of suffering and pain."

Sir Monier Williams is of opinion that the women of India have great influence over the men, though their seclusion keeps them ignorant and superstitious; but as they are uneducated that influence cannot be progressive. Both the Brahmins and Mahomedans object to the education of their women, on the ground that it would give them facilities for a knowledge of vice. The census statistics show that less than a million of the women and girls are able to read and write or are under instruction; and these are mostly Christians or in the mission schools. The women of the lower classes work hard and well, but so great is the subservience of women under the Brahmin system that a Hindu wife may not eat till her husband has finished his meal. When a woman of high degree is ruler of a State, she has to transact business with her Prime Minister hidden from him by a screen or curtain. The Rani Jaghirdar in the Hyderabad State was an extraordinary exception, and appeared to be an unusually independent character. Given fair play, many no doubt would acquit themselves well in public, and exert their natural influence for good over the men. Sir Salar Jung advocated the education of women. His daughter, Lady Mukram-ud-dowlah, for years carried on a school for Nawabs' daughters and made them pay fees, which was a most unusual thing for Mahomedans to do for the education of girls. In the famine of 1896-97 the wife of the Maharajah of Jodhpore opened an orphanage and resided there to superintend it herself. In December 1891 there was a fine instance of heroism shown by a band of convict native women at Port Blair in the Andaman Islands. During a cyclone many buildings were blown down, including the convict barracks, and nearly a hundred convicts were killed. A Government vessel, the *Enterprise*, broke from her moorings and went to pieces on a reef. Six survivors tried to land opposite the female jail, but the surf beat them back, and they were only saved and brought to land by the women, who joined hands to form a chain and breasted the sea.

The Vedas and other ancient writings are now studied by only a few Brahmins and pundits. In Calcutta the more intelligent cult of the Brahmo Samaj is a protest against living any longer in the old narrow grooves and under the selfish domination of the Brahmin priests.

Not unlike some of the original Brahmin doctrines are the religions of the Jains and Buddhists. These and that of Confucius are properly only ethical systems, but much debased in the practice of to-day. The Jains taught that every animal and plant, and even earth, air, fire, and water, have souls. They put their places of pilgrimage in forests and pretty scenery; they adorn their temples, and are humane.

The first Buddha (Wise Man) is said to have lived about 2250 B.C., and it was the twenty-fifth Buddha (the Gautama Sakya Sinha) who in the fifth century B.C. protested against caste tyranny and Brahminical sacerdotalism. According to his doctrine men and women are equal; and hence the great freedom of women which exists to-day in Buddhist Burmah.

About 250 B.C. Asoka organised Buddhism as a State religion, and issued his edicts and laws inculcating humane treatment of animals, and as guides to the habits and morals of mankind. It was not a religion so much as a system of practical philanthropy; and though established without force, has been widely successful, its adherents now numbering more than those of any other religion. It taught the highest goodness without a God, and cannot conceive of a Creator or of a soul apart from the body. It says that existence is a burden, and that true happiness is in annihilation. It has much degenerated, and its monks and priests are not the pure-minded and pure-living folk they possibly were in the time of its founder. At Indore I met a Jain with a cloth over his mouth and a hard broom in his hand. The cloth was to prevent insects from flying into his mouth and so coming to harm, and with the broom he was sweeping the path ahead to remove any small creatures that might be in danger of being trodden on, forgetting that he was hurting them much more with his broom than he would have done with his bare feet. When in Japan I visited the Daibutsu, a large image of Buddha at Kamakura. In conversation with the priest there I was astonished to learn that he and other Buddhist priests had adopted flesh as an article of food, it having recently been permitted by the Japanese Government to them as well as to the army "to make them strong." He did not seem to consider the fact that the Japanese native has become strong without it.

A coalition of the Brahmins and Buddhists is represented in the worship of Vishnu and his car of Juggernauth (Lord of the World). The self-immolation of the worshippers who threw themselves under the car was opposed to the benign character of Vishnu, and the deaths were nearly always accidental and due to the throng, or were in a few cases suicides caused by religious frenzy.

Mahomedanism is professed in India by sixty-three millions. Though forced upon the conquered at the point of the sword, it has not been so successful as Buddhism. Conquerors like Ghenghiz Khan, Tamerlane, and Tippoo Sultan went to such excess in their cruelty as to defeat their end, to some extent, as far as proselytising was concerned. It is true that there have also been Hindu monsters of cruelty such as Sivaji and Nana Sahib, and their cruelty had not the excuse of being in the name of religion. The religious fervour of Mahomedans is very strong, and their attention to the routine of prayer is careful and constant. Every morning before sunrise and at evening the Mussulman inhabitants are heard calling on the name of "Allah" and repeating their prayer or chant, led, if at a mosque, by the muezzin. It matters little where they may be when the time for prayer arrives, they proceed to their devotions just the same. I have seen a cab-driver in the streets of Allahabad kneeling on the top of his cab and bowing low to the East during his prayers. It is an impressive sight to see a crowd of Mahomedans at evening prayer at the Jumma Musjid or the tomb of Nizam ud din. Some of the tribes and sects—such as the Pathans, the Ghazis, and the Moplahs—become at times turbulent and fanatical. The Wahabis are an earnest proselytising sect. It is strange that they care little for their sacred edifices except when in use for worship. There are fine tombs in the south of India with spacious interiors covered with domes. These they do not object to Europeans using as dwelling-houses. Some of the most comfortable homes I visited in the South were located in tombs; and in one I was told that my bedroom was in a vault where a queen was buried.

Apart from both Hinduism and Mahomedanism, the religion of the hill-tribes consists, as might be expected, of people who live in the wilds, chiefly of a belief in demons and the necessity of propitiating them, even in some cases with human sacrifices. The Khonds of Madras, who came willingly to work on the Vizianagram-Raipur survey, and at the end of the day were quite content to go away without payment, used to make a human sacrifice twice a-year to the Goddess of Earth, and to destroy some of their female children, till the British intervened. This caused a small war with them, but when they found the change inevitable, they were reconciled by being allowed to denounce the British Government to their gods as the cause of their apostacy. They either bought their victims or brought them up from infancy specially for the purpose. It was usually a boy. He was tied to a post, and, after invocations to the goddess, the priest wounded him with an axe and the people tore him to pieces with their hands. Strange to say, the importance attached to dogs at funerals among some hill-tribes, who sacrifice them, has its place also among the civilised Parsees, who, before a corpse is conveyed to the Towers of Silence, uncover it and expose it to the gaze of a dog.

The Thugs worshipped Kali under the name Bhowani. They strangled travellers partly in honour of this goddess and partly for robbery. As a religious sect they arose at the time of Akbar, about three hundred years ago, and flourished till lately. They were very expert thieves and murderers, and have been known to steal even the blankets on which a man was sleeping. In later years they employed pretty girls to decoy sepoys on furlough with their small savings. They

KHONDS OF THE VIZIANAGRAM HILL TRACTS.

WHO USED TO MAKE HUMAN SACRIFICES TO THE GODDESS OF EARTH.

would travel for days in company with their victims in the most friendly way until the omens were propitious for them to kill them. Thuggee has only been stamped out (if actually extinct) by putting every known Thug in prison for life, his profession being that of a murderer.

My missionary friends were some of the most interesting and companionable. The missions of the Americans and Baptists at Allahabad, the Canadians in Central India and Assam, the Presbyterians at Ajmere, the S.P.G. at Tezpur, the C.M.S. at Taran - Taran, the Baptists and the Cambridge Mission at Delhi, the Wesleyans at Secunderabad, and the L.M.S. at Madras, were conducted by energetic earnest men and women whose acquaintance was well worth having. The names of Broadhead, Seward, Wilkie, Fairweather, Moore, Gray, Endle, Hallam, Wright, Westcott, Thomas, Crudgington, Joss, Soper, Pratt, Burgess, and Caldwell, are well known in the missionary world. I had the honour of being introduced to Miss Tucker (A. L. O. E.) at Amritsar soon after I arrived there. Trichinopoli is the scene of the labours of Bishop Heber, who is buried there, and of the famous missionary Schwartz. Some of the German and Jesuit missionaries appeared to me to be markedly earnest and successful. Of the three million native Christians nearly half are Roman Catholics.

It is not true, as stated by some, that the missionaries live luxurious lives. Nor is it true, as supposed by others, that they live in hardship and danger amid wilds and deserts, though they have occasionally to visit them. The mission-houses are comfortable and located in centres where, generally, there are other Europeans, or where they are in touch with others. Missionaries get short leave and long leave, and go to the hills for a change in the hot weather when their work will allow. And quite right too. If they live in comfort and take proper leave to enable them to keep in health, they are the more efficient for their work. Some have a rough time when travelling and preaching among the villages in hot and rainy weather; but in the cold season that work is healthy and not unpleasant. There is much that is disheartening for them. One enthusiastic missionary who had been only a year out from Canada told me, with tears in his eyes, that he did not believe he had yet made a single convert. A curious illustration of the disappointing results sometimes discovered was related to me by a missionary lady. In the Kulu valley the villagers hide away their children at Christmas-time, as they are under the impression that a spirit (perhaps a *shaitan*) goes about then collecting them. They had heard and misunderstood the story of Christ gathering children round Him.

It is also not correct to say that the missionaries are very successful in the attainment of their primary object, or that Brahminism is on its death-bed, as I heard a missionary state at a lecture in London. Some of the best missionaries in India acknowledge that their success lies mostly in having ameliorated the habits of

MISSION GIRLS.

CONVERTS OF THE LONDON MISSIONARY SOCIETY AT MADRAS

their converts, and induced them to abandon heathen practices. They fail to influence the higher castes in any appreciable degree, and succeed most among the low castes, the out-castes, and the aboriginal tribes. Their chief hope is always in the children.

The more that is done in technical instruction, both by missionaries and Government, the more the old superstitious ideas will disappear. One effort has been successful in the hands of Mrs Pratt at Secunderabad, in teaching the mission girls the manufacture of lace. It had been already introduced at Nagacoil on the coast by the wife of the late Bishop Caldwell, and had spread to Quilon and Ceylon. The girls often have difficulty in earning their living when they leave the mission-house on reaching womanhood. They cannot mingle again with the Hindus and Mahomedans, who despise them; and, until they find Christian husbands, their lot may be a hard one, and relapse into a bad life may follow. It has been the means of saving several young widows and others with no resources at all at the Hyderabad Mission. The lace-making gives them a means of earning money, but the market for their lace is not always to be found. When on furlough I tried to start a demand for it in Australia and New Zealand, but without success. At the Basel Mission at Mangalore, industries for the converts have succeeded well. The Salvation Army has branches in India, some of the members of which told me of the hard lives they lead, depending for their food on gifts from the natives, and living as much as possible like them. They are much respected, as the native thinks highly of men who deny themselves. Schwartz, the successful missionary of Trichinopoli, lived simply, and abstained from flesh food, and in that way attracted the liking of the natives among whom he worked. Another vegetarian missionary, Rev. W. D. Etherington of Benares, was the more successful for the same reason. That is also probably part of the secret of the success of Buddhism. Buddha was a prince who became an ascetic in order to reform the Brahmin licence and false doctrine; and he sent his missionaries, living in the same way, to Ceylon, China, Japan, Burmah, Nepaul, and Thibet, in all of which countries his doctrines still hold their ground. The story of his "Great Renunciation" is one of the most interesting in ancient history. No doubt many a native is repelled from considering Christianity as soon as he knows that the Christian missionaries eat animals, and especially the bull.

XVII.

DISEASES.

FEVER — DRUGS — CHOLERA — PLAGUE — LEPROSY — BLINDNESS — INSANITARY CUSTOMS—SKIN DISEASES—TANK-WATER—PILGRIMS TO MECCA—HOSPITALS—LADY DUFFERIN'S FUND.

THE most prevalent of all the diseases of India is malarial fever. It attacks Europeans and natives alike; and it would be instructive to study the reasons why some diseases do this, while some are more dangerous to one class than to the other.

To stay long in a malarial atmosphere, especially if one sleeps much in it, is an almost certain source of fever, however carefully one may live in other respects. In 1900, fevers caused 4,891,000 deaths in British India alone,—about sixty per cent of all the deaths. Quinine, cinchona, chiretta, and arsenic are the drugs most used as antidotes. If possible, one should try to recover without the use of any of them. They are poisons; and, if without using them the malarial poison already in the system can be eliminated by a change to purer atmosphere, and by keeping the skin and other excretory organs in good working order, there is less strain on the constitution. Fruit juices are cooling and purifying, and cure in a more natural way than drugs. Quinine is useful in many cases; the natives firmly believe in it, and are always glad to have it for their fever cases. It causes deafness in some, and possibly other injuries to others; but it is not so bad as arsenic, which remains in the system a long time before it can be eliminated. In my first fever a native was so anxious to charm it away that I allowed him to stroke my legs with the branch of a sacred tree. The fever soon disappeared, and I had probably confirmed the man in his belief in charms.

Cholera, in 1900, was the cause of 809,000 deaths. Europeans are rarely attacked by it; but when they are the cases are as severe as with the natives, and the disease runs its course with great rapidity. A friend of mine went to see some works early one morning, and passed a house where a young girl was at play, apparently in perfect health. On his return a few hours later she was dead, cholera having attacked and killed her in that short time. A bank manager at Hyderabad, young, with a promising career before him, and lately married, died in a few hours after being in good health at dinner the evening before. When I was at Allahabad, a Controller of Accounts one Saturday afternoon, after having consulted one of the Secretaries to Government about some business, left the office-table and papers as they were, intending to proceed with the discussion on Monday morning. On that day, after being seated at the table waiting for some time, he inquired if his friend had not yet come, and was informed that he had died of cholera on the Saturday evening, and had been buried on Sunday morning. This rapidity of burial is necessary in the hot climate of India. In my first hot weather, when on the Bari Doab Canal, a *burkendaz* (office-guard) was one evening reported seriously ill with cholera. I had with me a medicine-chest and a medical guide-book. No doctor was available; and, from the symptoms described in the book, it was clearly a case of cholera, which was then raging in the villages round. None of the servants or others would go near the man except one Mahomedan who was a relation. He was in the collapse stage; and as I knew that strong men, such as he was, require stronger doses than usual, after finding the ordinary doses of chlorodyne and laudanum ineffectual, I gave him one of laudanum double the strongest allowed in the book. This sent him into a long sleep, and he woke up without the vomiting, which had been very distressing, or any of the other symptoms. Though weak, he gradually got well, and he said he would pray for me every day the rest of his life.

An epidemic seems to have been raging at the time. In 'The Government Gazette' of September 30, 1875, the death-rates were shown for—

Palwal	372 per 1000
Delhi	164 „
Amritsar	113 „

that of London at the time being only 22.

When cholera is bad in a town the soldiers are confined to barracks or taken into camp, and our servants and the members of the offices are warned not to go beyond certain limits. In the ten months from August 1817 to June 1818, in the East India Company's territory in Bengal alone, 150,000 persons died of the disease. The natives then believed, as some do now, that the cholera morbus is a malignant demon, and they used to try to keep it off by the noise of tom-toms and other music. In the "Good old days of Honorable John Company" it is related that, when cholera as an epidemic broke out in the army of the Marquis of Hastings, it was accompanied, in the case of Europeans, by spasms and intense thirst; but the doctors would not allow a drop of water to be given, though some men who got it by stealth rapidly recovered.

Next to cholera in the number of deaths comes the plague. It broke out in Bombay in 1896, and has since spread to most other provinces. In 1897 there were nearly 58,000 deaths; and the figure rose yearly till, in 1902, it was 559,602. In that year the total death-rate was 31·5 per 1000, and of this less than 3 per 1000 were due to plague. The total of deaths up to March 1902 was 820,000, and no doubt there were many others that did not come into the returns. 1903 showed a further large increase, the number being 851,400. In 1904 the plague deaths during the week ending 19th March were 40,527.

There was a great exodus from Bombay city when plague first appeared in 1896, and about a quarter of the inhabitants left Calcutta on its arrival there in 1898. Much loss of trade was caused, and of the means of livelihood of the clerks, shopkeepers, and employees. The people could not at first understand the necessity for segregation and disinfectants, and they moved about to prevent domiciliary visits and to conceal their sick. They now understand better, and, led by the more educated and intelligent, are satisfied of the utility of these measures. The house-to-house visitation is now abandoned. It was at first necessary, because the people used to keep their plague-stricken relations among them and so caused the disease to spread. They hid not only cases of illness but those of death, and would bury the dead just outside their houses, at the back or even under the floors. One search-party went into a house where they found that a game of cards was in progress; but it was only a ruse to hide the fact that one man, who had been propped up and cards placed in his hands as if he were one of the players, had died of the plague. The available workers were few, and British soldiers were used in the search-parties. They were always accompanied by an officer and some of the medical staff of men and women. They make good nurses; but their rough direct practical action astonishes the natives, and frightens those who live in, and rarely leave, the bazaars.

The plague prevention measures at first provoked such dissatisfaction that an opportunity was thereby given to some seditious persons in

Poona to make political capital of it. Insurrection was advocated in some Mahratta papers. The sedition was fostered by a political party that wishes to emulate the feats of Sivaji, who, more than two hundred years ago, was victorious against the Mahomedan ruler of Bijapur. The murder of two British officers at Poona, in 1897, was the the more indefensible as England was then fighting the famine also, and had just subscribed half a million for voluntary relief.

The nursing staff is much tried by the plague, and some of the lady nurses sent out from England have died of it. There are, however, few cases among Europeans.

A short time before the plague broke out some one blackened the face of the white statue of Queen Victoria on the Esplanade at Bombay, which was presented to this city by the Gaikowar of Baroda. The natives seem to have assumed that of course no Englishman would have done it, and the only question was, who among themselves had? The culprit was never caught; and when the plague broke out many of the natives were of opinion that it was a divine retribution for this act of disloyalty. This curious self-condemnation was also noticed in the case of the murder of Mr Nicholas, the Superintendent of some mines near the Bolân Pass. Soon after the murder a fire in the mines caused the death of about 200 native miners; and this was also attributed by the natives to divine punishment.

Far fewer than the sufferers from plague, but even more to be pitied, are the lepers; for theirs is a long and painful dying. In 1891 there were 126,000, and only 97,340 in 1901.

Segregation is not enforced, and lepers may be seen in many bazaars. They are avoided by every one, and are known partly by the white patches of skin in different parts of the body. Some are white over almost the whole body. Many have lost their fingers and toes, which have dropped off in a rotten state. These men are provided for in large leper asylums, or are supported by native charity. When wishing to buy food the leper stands at a distance from the shop and calls out to the shopkeeper the names of the articles required. He deposits the money on the road and walks away to some distance. The shopkeeper then goes to where the money is and puts down the food bought. In picking up coppers thrown to him, or other articles, the leper has much difficulty when there are only the palms of his hands left. A sickening odour comes from their bodies. Any part is liable to be affected; and in Rajputana I saw a leper beggar who attracted sympathy and donations by putting out his tongue through a large hole between his eyes where the flesh and bone had been eaten away by the disease. Those of caste still insist on their own superiority, and refuse to accept water or food from any but their own caste people.

Dr J. Hutchinson in 1903 visited India specially to inquire into the causes of leprosy. After carefully sifting the large amount of evidence and comparing it with evidence from the Sandwich Islands and other parts where leprosy exists, he concluded that it is caused by eating decaying fish. Up to the time of Henry VIII. there were ninety-five first-class leper hospitals in England; but from then leprosy began to disappear, as there was a decline in fish-eating and an extended use of better bread, fruit, and vegetables. At the special request of Queen Catherine of Arragon, gardeners were brought from the Low Countries to teach the people to grow salads. In thousands of villages in India vegetables and fruits are rare. It might be a good movement to encourage, through the headmen, the growing of more of the native kinds, by distributing seeds under conditions likely to lead to an increase in their use.

Fevers, cholera, plague, and leprosy are the worst of the many diseases afflicting the inhabitants of India; but there are others bad enough. In many villages children may be seen with bad eyes and evidently likely to go blind. I called the attention of the local native apothecary to one case and asked him if nothing could be done; but he replied that there were many such cases. I wished to interest myself in this one; and on telling a *chuprassy* to bring the child to be examined by the apothecary, it was found that the parents had heard of my inquiries and had hidden him away. Round Sirsa, for example, there is much blindness, and it is attributed to smallpox in early life and to the use in later life of *rabri*, a thin gruel made of millet and steeped in buttermilk-and-water, fermented in the sun and eaten with salt. Probable causes are the strong sun-glare, the frequent sand-storms of that scorched, treeless, sandy part, and the very insanitary habits of the people. Dirty water is used for cooking after people and cattle have bathed in it. Skin diseases and guinea-worm are common among them. In Bengal and other parts where malarial fever prevails, the spleen becomes much enlarged and a fall may cause it to rupture. Dysentery accounts for half a million deaths. Typhoid, enteric, smallpox, goitre, elephantiasis, pneumonia, epilepsy and sunstroke, are other troubles. There are 74,000 insane,—many rendered so by the use of hemp, drugs, and opium eating and smoking.

There are insanitary habits of the villagers of which English people who live much in India are well aware, but of which they cannot well talk in England. In every part of India it is best to avoid passing through the outskirts of the villages if roads are available outside them. In 'The Calcutta Review' of April 1895, Baboo Kailas Chundra Kanjilal, B.L., writes of the Bengali villages:—

> "Neither the Hindu nor the Mahomedan village community appears to have any advanced ideas of sanitation. Noxious vegetation, ill-ventilated houses with damp floors, surrounded by thick jungle or clusters of trees, dirty ponds or sheets of water filled with the material of vegetable decomposition or other putrid substances, narrow lanes or bypaths almost ankle-deep in dust or mud, accumulations of rubbish or other fetid matter on the house premises, &c., generally

disfigure village sites, making them the hot-beds of cholera, malarious fevers, and other mortal diseases."

The villagers and village authorities are difficult to move in this matter; and, even if ideas of the necessity for a change be brought home to some of them, it is difficult to get improvements introduced. Custom, the habits of their fathers, fatalism, inertia, and the great area over which the villagers are scattered, are all against change for the better where education has not yet prepared the way. But the Sanitary Department is now at work, and will, no doubt, be most beneficial in its operations.

The villagers in the South have sometimes to depend almost wholly upon the tanks of water near their villages. These are made by bunding up a stream in the rainy season and storing its supply to last through the dry weather from November to June or July. May and June are the hottest months; and, before the monsoon rains arrive, it may be that the tanks dry up and resort must be had to digging in the beds of the streams or to any wells that may exist. In the Hyderabad State I passed one of these tanks in May. Very little water was left in it, and the fish were crowded together. Still the villagers were bathing and washing their clothes and cattle in it and using it as their drinking-water. Even when they use wells, their custom in some places is to bathe close to the well, and if the kerb is not properly arranged, to allow the used water to flow back into it and accumulations of dirty water to collect round the top and filter through the soil. Wherever there are energetic district officers and subordinates, such matters are taken in hand over and over again, and sometimes good is done; but the villagers are there by millions, and the workers, especially the energetic and public-spirited ones among the subordinates, are few, and may be able to visit the same places only at long intervals, as their work extends over great areas. When I was on the Godavery Valley Survey it was reported that cholera at a large village had been caused by the men of a village up-stream burying people who had died of it in the bed of the river. The cold weather supply wanders in a small stream through the sandy bed, and is the source of the drinking-water for all villages on the banks.

All through the East ignorance of sanitary principles is the cause of much disease. At Shanghai, on going with a friend to see the native town, five minutes after passing through the boundary wall I had to retrace my steps as the bad odours were intolerable. At Jeddah in Arabia, where the pilgrims land to go to Mecca, a party of us, when going to visit Eve's tomb, had to pass through the native town. On remarking the fact that the very narrow road between the shops was raised and irregular and springy to the tread, we were informed that it was originally level with the floors of the shops and entrances, but that it had been raised through everybody throwing out on to it whatever refuse they did not want. In wet weather it slid down in dirty streams on each side and found its way between the houses to the back, and was afterwards built up again as before, when the weather was dry. No wonder that, as the captain of one of the "British India" steamers told me, great numbers of the pilgrims died of cholera. He had been in charge of one of the small boats that took pilgrims from the Arabian and African coasts to Jeddah and back. As they were crowded on the deck during the run of thirty-six hours, when cholera broke out he and the other officers had to stay on a raised platform, while the pilgrims below were mixed up with the dying and the dead. Sometimes forty such vessels were in the Jeddah harbour at the same time and cholera raging.

The great majority of natives are unattended by medical men. The dispensaries in large towns and other centres are much resorted to for medicines and advice, which are given free. In the ten years ending 1901 the number of Government hospitals had increased from 1809 to 3000, and the patients had increased from fourteen to twenty millions. Apart from what missionary ladies could give, until Lady Dufferin's fund was started the women of the zenanas and harems had no medical attendance except from the *dhais*, ignorant native nurses whose vicious practices are described in the report of the Fund. English nurses and native women trained by them can now go into the women's apartments and attend cases of sickness where no medical man could have gone. The "Nursing Sisters," established by Lady Roberts, do much good in attending to the British soldiers in hospital. There are a Pasteur Institute near Simla and a Research Laboratory at Bombay. Inoculation is being tried for cholera and plague. Sanitary Commissioners advise Local Governments in matters relating to public health, drainage, conservancy, water supply, filtration, vaccination, &c., and inquire into outbreaks of epidemics. There are also Local Sanitary Committees and a Village Sanitation Act.

From cholera, plague, leprosy, and skin diseases, Europeans suffer little compared with the natives; and this is no doubt due to their cleaner surroundings and better knowledge of the laws of health. Their free use of flesh as food, especially in a climate where it quickly goes bad, and of spirits, is a cause of liver complaint, headaches, and indigestion. It is well known to army doctors that soldiers of the vegetarian races recover more easily from severe wounds than do Englishmen and the meat-eating natives. Gout and cancer are very rare among the natives. In England there are 27,000 deaths from cancer every year; among the natives of India very few.

XVIII.

BABOO ENGLISH.

FLOWERY LANGUAGE — ENGLISHMEN'S MISTAKES — CANDIDATES — EXAMPLES OF BABOO ENGLISH—THE WORKS OF DICKENS MISUNDERSTOOD.

WHEN examples are quoted of the mistakes and peculiar expressions used by the natives in speaking English, it is not in the way of ridicule or disparagement. Just as Irish bulls are instanced as illustrations of the droll or incongruous, or the mistakes of Frenchmen when talking our language, so the English spoken by Baboos and other educated natives is found amusing. But there is something rather different in Baboo English. It is not that mistakes are made, so much as that the words and phrases, though indicating clearly the meaning intended, are what would not be used by any Englishman. The tendency is to talk and write in flowery language and roundabout phrases. There is no terseness in the English used by Baboos, except when they adopt some of the slang phrases, and that is seldom the case. For instance, an Englishman would say, "He ran away"; but a Baboo's version was, "He removed his person from that locality with considerable celerity."

I have seen Englishmen in India talking Hindustani to natives and making grotesque mistakes, which, while they made me laugh, were received by the natives with stolid self-control. Whatever they may do afterwards when alone, they give no sign in our presence of having even noticed anything wrong. They all, high or low, do their best to find out what is the meaning we wish to express. "Why is that door exact?" I heard a young Englishman call out in Hindustani when he wished to know why the door was shut; and I myself, early in my service, told my bearer to roll up my bedstead when I meant the mattress. A few years ago a leading English newspaper reported that one of the native princes had sent a *mugger* to the Queen, meaning to say a *nazr*—in other words, an "alligator" instead of a "present."

The attempts at elegant writing and the use of Shakespearian phrases by men imperfectly acquainted with our language must, of course, lead to quaint results. Such efforts are out of place when applying for a post of clerk or apprentice, but they are often made. Those who go through a course of study at the colleges and universities of Calcutta and Bombay, and the educated barristers, doctors, and editors who may have studied in England, have remarkable aptitude in using words and phrases which do very well, but, being not what we ourselves would use or would expect to hear from our countrymen, are strange illustrations of the capabilities of our tongue. Most of the Bengali and other students have good memories, and can quote long extracts from English standard authors; and they are good imitators.

The students are mostly young men of caste or of good family. They look forward to passing the Matriculation examination, and even to becoming Bachelors or Masters of Arts; and they hope after then to get some good Government posts or employment as clerks or accountants in merchants' offices. Some intend to practice at the bar, a few to become doctors; but hardly any to study scientific subjects or to engage in trade or agriculture. The fact of his being a student intending to compete at examinations gives a young man a sense of superiority; and it is an important point with such a one that his family is respectable. When a young Bengali applied to me for a post, on my asking him who he was, his first reply was, "I am a candidate." Knowing their feeling in the matter, I quite understood; and, on my trying to get more information, he told me, "I am the son of respectable parents." This also I recognised as satisfactory; and I knew that, as he had got over these preliminaries, he would next give me his name and other more useful details.

So far is it looked upon as honourable to be a student, that to have failed at an examination is not a disqualification. A man will boast about it, because the fact of having failed shows that at least he had arrived at a degree of excellence enabling himself and others to think it possible he might pass. A "fail B.A." has a higher position than one who has not tried to pass; and a man with a degree is regarded in the same way as one with a title in England. In one letter I received from an applicant for a post he wrote: "As regards my qualifications, I have the honour to inform you that I failed at the Matriculation examination"; and another wrote, "I most humbly and respectfully beg to state that I have passed the Middle and Engineering class in 'poorly,' so I hope you will grant me a post under you." At some examinations the candidate must not only pass in each subject, but the number of marks gained must not be less than a certain total; but one applicant argued, "My failing in the aggregate does not in any way prove my inferiority to a passed candidate."

In beginning letters the language is at times oppressively polite. A "Head Estimator" having compiled and printed a list of useful figures, wrote to me: "I most respectfully beg to be pardoned for my humbly approaching you with this my humble letter together with a presentation copy of the Ready Reference Table Book of Areas, &c., and of openings in Bridges and Culverts." Another wrote, "With due deference and humble submission I beg to lay down the following few lines for your kind consideration and trust to be executed for the same." One letter begins, "Humbly sheweth," in imitation of the formal heading of petitions to the Viceroy. A Public Works overseer wrote, "I throw myself on your honour's mercy as a child would to a mother who will not give a stone to her child in place of a bread."

The following from a clerk at Lahore is really very good :—

> "Sir,—Excuse me for thus intruding upon you. A dying man catches at a straw. I do not know but the straw has sometimes saved life. I, however, trust that my hope in your goodness may prove to be far better. Of course I have no claim upon you for any favour; but as you have seen so much of service and passed through many of its vicissitudes, I am inclined to think that you may be prone to sympathise with those who have not fared as well as they might under other circumstances."

At Bolarum a servant, who had been left in charge of my bungalow while I was away, had to write to me every day saying if everything was all right. Though a Hindu he wrote, "I am all doing well by the Grace of our Saviour," and went on to tell me that the bungalow and garden were quite well.

A Mohamedan gentleman wrote that he was highly obliged to me for so kindly accepting his invitation.

When at Sukkur I received a letter from a sub-engineer who had worked under me in my former division at Kushab. He wrote :—

> "Sir,—I am alright. I hope you to be in the same, though Sukkur is a hotty place;

> but I think you will be passing good summer there, owing to heavy rains all over."

At Hyderabad a young Mohamedan wrote—"Being put under clouds by the impetuality of the world I am obliged to forward my humble petition to be looked up with a kind eye which would ever help me under shadows." He goes on to say that he had been "bred and brought in the City from generations to generations," and asks for a post, as his ancestors are no longer among the living beings.

The following is from a Bombay newspaper, which vouched for the correctness of the copy, the original letter having been shown to the editor. It was written to a Bombay merchant who wanted a clerk:—

> "I have seen better days once, but, as we all know from experience, those halcyon palmy days had seen their ends in the course of mundane affairs. All the sublunary objects have their mutations, the world has its vicissitudes, and so, in the changes and chances common to all, I have had the ill-luck of finding myself 'out of pocket.'"

The mild rebuke, "I most respectfully pray that you have kindly not replied to my letter," deserved an immediate answer.

An Indian newspaper gives the following testimonials of a medical practitioner "expert in the doctoric arts." A patient testified that he has been "an eye-witness of the doctor's successful treatment in several cases where there was a regular groaning." Another that he has "cured several 'incurable' diseases," and that "high families of orthodox principles generally believe that they are done away with by entering his hospital for treatment." A husband testified that his wife had been cured by him "within a week of the several diseases—namely, bellyache, headache, indigestion, biliousness, fits, insensibility, locked jaw, and such other innumerable diseases." This doctor might have been of use in the case of a clerk of my office who sent a medical certificate in which his doctor said, "Babu —— is seriously ill, and I hope he won't recover for a month,"—the word "hope" having been used instead of "expect." A further surprise was in store for me, for on asking after his health next day from another clerk, I got the reply in a sad tone, "He is still groggy, sir."

Sub-post-offices are sometimes established temporarily in distant places where it is thought likely that they may be used enough to be made permanent. A postmaster, in reporting his having closed one of these as having proved itself not required, remarked that it had been "tentative in its incipiency," and that he had "given it a last push to eternity."

On the railway the station-masters prefer the broad-gauge lines, and call the narrow-gauge ones the "tin-pot" railways. A young Sikh overseer on one of the surveys was walking a few paces behind me while my two fox-terriers were trotting along by my side and occasionally jumping up for a little attention. Suddenly the Sikh came up alongside of me and remarked, "Sir, these dogs love you very much," and then dropped back again to his position behind. Another overseer reported that the fence round a store go-down was in a bad condition, and asked if he might "mend the repairs," as in its bad state the people could "come in frankly and make away with the knick-knacks." An applicant came to me with a letter saying that he is "a hard and working man and behaves a good character."

The educated Bengali gentleman who remarked that "In time of peace the Army is a noble occupation, but in time of war, my God, it is a dangerous profession," was more enthusiastic than the Mahomedan student who had taken up the study of Dickens's works. It can easily be understood that he would be mystified by the language of the Artful Dodger and his companions. On the last page of 'David Copperfield' he wrote:—

> "I surprise that this book's author, being the composer of many other novels, has got such a style without taste. Though its style is very regularly made yet the mind of the reader is never willing to see even a page thoroughly. It seems to me that its author was not an intelligible . . . Sometimes the wretched author tries to write and deliver some oration, yet he suddenly falls in a pit of dullness."

At Delhi a convert of one of the missions knew

that it was right to address a gentleman missionary as "Reverend Sir," but was at a loss to know how to begin a letter to a lady missionary till he hit on the expression "Pious Miss."

Mr Thomas, the senior member of Council at Madras, was well known as an authority on fishing, and once, when playing a pike, he was addressed by a native gentleman who was looking on with much interest: "Do not coerce him, sir, do not coerce him; his strength is not yet evacuated."

At dinner at a hotel in Secunderabad I sat one evening next to a Parsee gentleman who had been staying for several weeks at that hotel. He said that when he first came he was seated in the chair which I was occupying, and that he had been moved from chair to chair till he had got round the table to where he had first sat. "In fact," he said, "I have made the circumlocution of the table." The same evening he told me, in speaking of Mr Gladstone (then living), that he considered him the "finest minister extant."

XIX.

SOME DETAILS OF THE MORAL AND MATERIAL CONDITION OF THE NATIVES, AND OF RECENT PROGRESS.

POPULATION — OCCUPATIONS — DRINK AND DRUGS — AMUSEMENTS — ORNAMENTS — FOOD — NATIVE STATES — OFFICIALS — THE INDIAN CIVIL SERVICE — THE BRITISH SYSTEM — IMPROVEMENT — EXAMPLES — THE GOHNA LAKE — ALIEN GOVERNMENT — THE PUBLIC WORKS DEPARTMENT — RURAL POPULATION — REFORMERS.

It would hardly be possible for an Englishman to live for a quarter of a century among the natives without forming an opinion of the state of progress and the prospects of the nation. The more important considerations dealt with by the Viceroy and his Council are often too complicated to be understood by others, and they have information of what is going on which others have not. How very carefully it is all considered, and how much experience and judgment are necessary to deal properly with it, may be, to some extent, estimated by perusal of the annual reports of the departments.

About 30,000,000 people live in the 2200 towns and 260,000,000 in the 730,000 villages. At least 175,000,000 are engaged in agriculture and raising cattle. Only about 1 in 10 of the males and 1 in 150 of the females can read and write. The villages are scattered over 1,776,597 square miles, —an area nearly equal to all Europe, excepting Russia, with different climates, scenery, soil, and products. Eighty languages are spoken. Though about two-thirds of this large population are Hindu, and their Hinduism and veneration for the Brahmins are bonds of union in opposition to other religions, these are not ties strong enough to prevent animosity among themselves, the different tribes often being practically foreigners in one another's country. The aboriginal tribes driven south by the Aryan invaders generally have no caste, and are more Mongolian in appearance and darker than the Northern races.

The average native, Hindu or Mohamedan, of the lower classes leads a simple pious life, supports his parents and relations, and is open-handed towards those in need of charity. Especially among the Northern races honesty and courage are prominent characteristics,—certain common instances of the opposite being due to habits contracted in self-defence during long periods of oppression. In towns as traders, mechanics, and operatives, they do very well; and a special cleverness is seen in the wonderful tricks of conjuring and the elegant works of art they produce. Drink, opium, and narcotics are resorted to in some large towns, among the hill-tribes, and in certain tracts of country, chiefly in the South, where the toddy-trees and other conveniences are at hand for manufacturing the native liquor. In the north of India I have passed years at a time without seeing a drunken man or one addicted to drink. Besides the toddy from the palm-tree, the other intoxicating drinks are *bhang* made from the dried leaves of hemp and used also for smoking, *ganja* and *daroo* from flowers, *charas* from resin, and *arrack* from rice.

For amusements and recreation the villagers depend mostly on the fairs, at which the attractions are bathing, sweetmeats, conjurers, illuminations, fireworks, famous temples and shrines, and now and then a nautch or other show, with tom-toms and music. In their houses and villages the amusements are few,—sitting together in the open air at evening after the day's work and passing round the hookah being enjoyment enough. When a man becomes rich he may still live in an inferior style, preferring his small hut, simple furniture, and plain clothes to life in a more showy style. Most natives have few wants beyond the ordinary necessaries of existence; and they often keep their savings in the shape of ornaments on their wives and children or hidden away in the ground. Much of the gold imported into India disappears from circulation in this way. A million and a half of the natives are engaged in manufacturing ornaments. It has been argued that they cannot properly be called poor people when they use so many ornaments of gold and silver, give expensive feasts to the Brahmins, and travel freely by railway. The imports, the inland postage, deposits in savings banks, and other things indicating their ability to pay, are increasing. The food eaten is not inferior. The wheaten flour of the North and the rice of the South are not denuded of their nutritious outside parts to make them white as in Europe; and the cooking of the rice is superior to the way in which it is done at home. *Dâl* and *chitski* (a vegetable curry) and some of the native fruits and vegetables are much liked by Europeans. Condiments are used, but only a few are to European taste; and a smoke generally follows the meal. These foods and the good milk from their cows and goats produce some of the strongest men and women in the world, and make up a diet which it would do many English people good to adopt.

The history of India has been one of treachery and cruelty among the races, conquest and massacre by invaders, intrigue and oppression on the part of the rulers, and perpetuation of superstition by the priests. It was after the Mutiny, only forty-six years ago, that the British Government took over the administration. The Mutiny was not a rising of the people of India against the East India Company, but a revolt of their native troops. It was not participated in by the rulers of the Native States. The Nepalese (Goorkhas), under their ruler Jung Bahadur, and the Sikhs assisted the British in suppressing it.

The Native States are remnants from the wars of the Moguls, Mahrattas, Mysore, and other kingdoms; and some of the governments now existing could not have lasted so long if the "Pax Britannica" hád not been introduced. They are now all feudatory, and not allowed to make war upon one another or to form alliances with foreign

States. There is a British political officer at the capital of each State who, in consultation with the native rulers, attends to matters which relate to both native and British interests, and advises them when they wish for assistance of any kind. As suzerain, the British Government interferes when there is much disorder or misgovernment. The leading native princes are on the Councils of the Government of India and of the Governors of Bombay, Bengal, and Madras, and give their advice and vote in matters relating to British administration of the whole empire. There are natives in high positions in the Government service; for instance, there is a native judge in each of the High Courts. They get other good offices and appointments when qualified, and the majority of the Government subordinate posts are held by natives.

Of the Indian Civil Service there is only one official for every quarter of a million of the population, and each is responsible for the administration of, on an average, a thousand square miles. Their work is heavy and continuous, and the subjects dealt with are numerous, varied, and of much troublesome detail. They are blamed by some in England for certain parts of their policy, such as the continuance of the sales of opium to China, the partial withdrawal of local self-government and trial by jury, the incidence of taxation, and other matters on which few beside those who deal with them in detail are competent to give a final opinion. A fair view for those who cannot speak from experience is that they are picked

Englishmen, highly educated and trained, and hardly likely to be very injudicious in their treatment of these matters. They have the interest of the masses of the natives at heart, and carefully consider and do what is possible in such matters as the growing indebtedness of the landowners to the non-agricultural classes, the revision of taxation, famine prevention, and others vital to their interests. The methods of working in the secretariats are excellent; and it was interesting to note the thoroughness and farsighted remarks and suggestions of the Lieutenant-Governors, Residents, Agents to the Governor-General, and others of long experience, whose notes were on the files which passed through my hands when at headquarters.

That the British system has been of much efficiency there is plenty of evidence. Instead of frequent devastating wars there is now internal peace, and the frontier is secure. The wild border tribes are prevented from raiding, and generally there is security of life and freedom of trade. The barbarities of Tamerlane, Suraj-ud-dowlah, Nana Sahib, Tippoo Sultan, and other tyrants, are not likely to recur. Thuggee and dacoity are nearly suppressed. Widow-burning, infanticide, and human sacrifices have been stopped. The natives are protected in their private lives and in the practice of their religion. There is hope for the outcast and for the wild tribes. Justice is administered so that there is free recourse to it, showing that it is appreciated among the litigants, and that there is a feeling of security which could not have

TIPPOO SULTAN'S WATCH-TOWER (TRICHINOPOLI).

existed before. By means of Local boards and District committees the more influential of the townsmen are encouraged to take interest and assist in the management of public affairs. There has been a decentralisation of expenditure and much Municipal progress in such matters as local roads, water supply, drainage, paving, and lighting. Revenue and fiscal reforms have been going on; for example, the removal of the cotton duties and the old internal salt customs line from north to south of India, the salt-consumption being thereby greatly increased. Imperial and provincial roads, railways, irrigation, and other public works, the post-offices, telegraphs, forests, sanitation, education, hospitals, police, and the currency, have been placed on a sound basis and are in vigorous working order. The Agricultural Department systematically fosters and improves Indian agriculture by collecting and distributing information, introducing new processes, new staples, instruments, manures, rotation of crops, methods of storing fodder, improved sugar-mills, and better breeds of cattle and horses. The introduction of the indigo, tea, and mining industries, and of railways, the revival of the cotton industries, and of irrigation on a large scale, are all due to British enterprise. A hundred years ago the North-West Provinces were a desert and infested with robbers. They are now a garden, well irrigated, in tranquillity, with numerous schools, hospitals, post-offices, &c., and covered with a network of railways.

Imports and exports are steadily increasing. In

1902-3 the value of the imports was £74,000,000 and of the exports £92,000,000. In the ten years preceding 1901-2 the annual foreign sea-borne trade increased by £33,000,000; the coasting trade by £14,500,000; the foreign trade by land £3,500,000; the banking capital increased by £5,000,000; the deposits in banks in India (excluding Government deposits) by £6,000,000, and the deposits in postal savings banks by £2,000,000, there being an increase of 300,000 depositors. There were 500,000 more natives in 1901-2 employed in cotton- and jute-mills, coal-mines, and other large industries requiring European appliances, and on the railways, than in 1891-92. The railway traffic per year increased by 72,000,000 passengers and 14,000,000 tons of goods. There were delivered in 1901-2, 220,000,000 more letters and parcels than in 1891-92, £10,000,000 more postal money orders, and 2,000,000 more inland telegraph messages. Even the annual consumption of salt has increased by 280,000,000 lb. a-year. And this great progress has been made in spite of the two severe famines that occurred in that decade.

The Bengali Baboo already mentioned as having written a non-political tract in 1887 enumerates the advantages of British rule as:—

"1. Education—as a means of bringing the ignorant out of darkness into light.

2. Endeavours of the Queen of England on behalf of female education in India.

3. Rule by justice instead of the sword, as the Moguls did.

4. Security of property—instead of as in the old days when the kings plundered the rich; the rich oppressed the poor; wealth was buried under ground; the capital of the country was thus diminished; and so did commerce.
5. Construction of railways.
6. Measures to mitigate famine.
7. Abolition of suttee."

He says nothing of irrigation and some other important matters; but, as already quoted, strongly condemns the Brahmins with reference to child-marriage and child-widows.

The following are a few illustrations of minor matters which came to my notice, and which point to good management by the British officials :—

In 1900 on some of the famine relief works in British territory many were found to be men from an adjoining Native State, who had represented themselves as British subjects, under the impression that otherwise they would not be allowed to enjoy the better wages, comfort, and medical relief on the British relief works.

Mahomedans erect handsome and costly mosques and gateways, but they do not keep them in repair. All over the country there are ruins of these buildings, and the British Government has taken several in hand. The Taj Mahal is kept in repair as a public building.

In September 1893 a branch of the Ganges was blocked, about 150 miles above the head works of the Upper Ganges canal at Hurdwar, by the falling in of the precipitous side of the valley through which it flows. It fell in for about two miles along the valley and rested against the opposite bank, forming a dam with a top surface of 423 acres and 1200 feet above the river-bed. Hundreds of tons of limestone and shale fell at intervals, and some were pitched a mile away against the opposite cliff. A lake was formed above this dam two and three-quarter miles long and a mile wide. It was not till nearly a year afterwards, on 25th August 1894, that the waters burst through and carried the dam down the valley. Preparations for the advent of the flood had been made at Hurdwar to protect the bazaars and the head works of the canal, and to warn the villagers all along the valley. A special telegraph line had been erected so that notice might be sent as soon as it was evident that the burst was about to occur. When it did come it was in a fog, and a volume of ten thousand million cubic feet of water passed along in four and a half hours, doing much damage to the bazaars, roads, and bridges, and a rajah's palace. No lives were lost, the villagers and cultivators having all been warned in time to get above the line of white stones which had been placed along the valley to show the probable limit up to which the floods might rise.

The following figures, taken from the General Report of the census in India (1901), appear to indicate a general improvement in the physical welfare of the people during the last twenty years, due probably to better sanitation. It is very remarkable that the decrease is steady in every case.

Per 100,000 of the population of British India :—

	Insane.		Deaf and Dumb.		Blind.		Lepers.	
	Males.	Females.	Males.	Females.	Males.	Females.	Males.	Females.
1881	43	28	103	67	216	240	84	29
1891	33	21	86	57	164	171	68	23
1901	28	17	62	42	121	120	48	17

Some speak of India as governed by aliens and the need for it to be ruled by natives only. It has to be remembered that there is rule by aliens in the Native States as well as in British India. Ten millions of Hindus in the Hyderabad State are governed by the Nizam and his Mahomedan officials; and in Cashmere two millions, mostly Mahomedans, are ruled by Sikh princes. Hindus and Mahomedans who pass by examination into the Indian Civil Service may, in time, rise to be collectors, magistrates, and commissioners of large areas inhabited by people with whom they have little sympathy, and who have little respect for them. A Bengali magistrate, though a Hindu, would be intolerable to the inhabitants of some parts of the Punjaub.

Though much good work has been done by the Public Works Department, it is sometimes charged with being wasteful in expenditure. All departments are liable to irregularities, but they are promptly dealt with when brought to light. In the Public Works Department ill-considered action may cause much loss, as the expenditure is on a large scale. The projects, however, are carefully considered, and before funds are allotted the Administrative and Financial authorities have to be satisfied by the engineers that the proposed expenditure is reasonable. In the execution of works where large numbers of men are employed, stores used up, and many contractors have to be kept as far as possible to their agreements, losses through bad judgment, want of energy of individuals, and occasional peculation occur; but rarely on any large scale, as the supervision is continual and efficient.

English public servants are prohibited not only from receiving presents, but even addresses, without the special sanction of Government. They may not own land or have a share in any speculation or business within the area of their duties. Nor may they sell things to the natives except by auction through a regular auctioneer.

The much increased facilities for travel and for internal and foreign trade are causing the natives of different creeds and nationality to mix more and to know one another better. In the course of business and travel the inconveniences of caste become intolerable, and probably the penalties payable to the Brahmins for breaking caste rules are now so numerous that most of them are necessarily no longer paid by traders and other busy men. The civil engineer has become incidentally a great reformer.

The influences telling for progress reach but slowly to the great mass of the people who live in villages and have only a weak effect among those who have no need to leave their homes. In spite of the ravages of fevers, cholera, plague, and famine, the population increased by forty-five millions during the thirty years ending 1901. In the ten years from 1891 to 1901, though there were two severe famines, the population in the British part alone increased by 8,708,653. To meet this progressive demand more food is required, and though more is being raised yearly the increase is not all available, as much of it goes abroad. About eleven million more acres were sown with food crops in 1900-1 than in 1890-91. Emigration is needed, not to countries beyond India so much as from one part of India to another. Some of the races are mobile enough, and from these are drawn the coolies who go to the tea-plantations of Assam and Ceylon, and the men who go to the West Indies, Mauritius, and South Africa. At present two-thirds of the population occupy one-fourth of the whole area, and in some parts of Bengal in a rural population there are 1280 people to the square mile. In those districts a good harvest only suffices to feed the people; and a poor harvest means underfed people and disease rampant.

In time they may overcome their dread of change. Education is spreading, though very slowly in the country parts. Fifty years ago only half a million children were at school; now there are nearly five millions. Reformers among their own people are coming forward,—such men as Baboo Keshub Chunder Sen and Justice Telang. The latest trade returns (1904) are very encouraging, and, with improved means of combating famines, the prospects of the country are on the whole satisfactory.

XX.

FURLOUGH AND RETIREMENT.

CHANGES—INTERESTING TOURS—LIFE OF A RETIRED OFFICAL—PRECAUTIONS ADVISED TO THOSE GOING TO INDIA.

Of the fifty young engineers appointed in 1874 from Coopers Hill College, ten left the service for various reasons after a few years in India, eleven died (and among these were some of the most zealous and efficient), and some reached their time of retirement after having suffered much in health. On the whole, it may be said that only about half satisfactorily reached the end of their Indian career.

During the quarter of a century or more that an English official serves in India he is more or less an exile from his own country. There are a few who even prefer their Indian life to that in England; but the majority look forward eagerly to their periods of leave and the time to retire. In the earlier years of my life in India I often had conversations with men then nearing the end of their service. They spoke of the old times before the Mutiny, when the East India Company held the reins of Government, and when the journey from England was one of three months by sea round the Cape, or, at least, six weeks by the

Overland route before the Suez Canal was made. Leave was, of course, at much longer intervals. Even in 1874 the postage to England was a shilling where now it is a penny.

One, rarely serves now more than six or eight years before taking one's first furlough. That, however, is quite long enough to awaken one to the reality of the exile; for the visit to England, pleasant as it may be in many ways, is generally to some extent a disappointment. The absence has been long enough for changes which have come gradually to those who have stayed at home, but are startling to the one who has been away while they were going on. Old friends have formed new ties and new sympathies, and are altered enough to cause disappointment and a chill to one's enthusiasm at seeing them again. This may be partly due also to the fact that there is a change in oneself which is not quite satisfactory to them. Not only one's friends, but the scenes of one's early home days are not quite as they have been cherished in the memory during the long solitude of the hot and rainy seasons. In the case of the children who have grown up the contrast is very great.

On later furloughs, instead of going over the same ground *viâ* the Suez Canal to England, one may return by China, Japan, and America, or take a trip through the Australian colonies first. If travelling by the Red Sea, a halt may be made at Egypt and visits paid to the Sphinx, the Pyramids, the Alabaster Mosque, Old Cairo, and the Nile. On the other hand is Palestine, and the homeward journey may be continued *viâ* Greece or Italy and Switzerland. On one return to India I spent five months in travelling *viâ* America and Japan. Very expensive, some people say; but the difference, if any, in cost between this long route and the short one *viâ* Suez, together with the cost of living during the extra time, is fully repaid by the pleasure and knowledge gained in seeing new places and people. In those five months I saw the great Eastern cities of the United States and Canada, the Lachine Rapids, the Thousand Islands, Niagara, the Libby prison, the Rockies, Leadville, the Mount of the Holy Cross, the Mormon Tabernacle, British Columbia, California, Honolulu, the Nikko temples, and the Daibutsu at Kamakura in Japan, and some of the towns of China, Annam, and the Straits Settlements. My last journey from India was through the Australian colonies, Tasmania, New Zealand, and the Southern United States, up the Mississippi to Memphis and Cairo, with opportunities of seeing life among the negroes of Louisiana, Alabama, Kentucky, and Tennessee.

Some think that retirement to England with nothing to do, or rather with the opportunity of doing just what one likes best, is an ideal existence. It is not found so by those who have led for many years an active life, and are still vigorous and in the enjoyment of good health. It does not suit every one to settle down to a climate and conditions different from those in which his best days of usefulness and interesting occupation have been spent. Those who have lived freely in regard to food and drink, suffer from the cold damp climate of England. They have, may be, diseased livers, are incapable of much exertion, and can no longer bathe in cold water. Some settle in the Colonies, where the better climates suit them and their Indian experiences are of good service.

There may be special reasons why a man is unhappy in his retirement. He may have looked forward to pleasant reunion with friends and relations who, however, have died before his return. Or his wife or one or more of the children have been left behind in an Indian grave. Several of our bright college chums are buried in India, having lost not only their lives but the full reward for their labours.

For those who can still enjoy life there is much that is delightful in England and elsewhere, especially for those who have learnt in camp and on journeys to take things contentedly, and not to worry about trifles. Mr Chili Chutney, in the play, "Twenty Minutes with a Tiger," is not nowadays a correct representation of the retired Anglo-Indian. Most of us are able to choose our location,—to be in England in the summer, and in Italy or some other pleasant part in the winter. There are pleasures, studies, and spheres of usefulness in abundance for those who want them.

To those retired officials who have not a placid temperament, the talk of certain Englishmen at home may be specially annoying. They tell us that it would be better for India if there were no English there; that we are robbing the natives; and that the British system is the cause of much poverty. The facts detailed already tell a different story. Those who wish to learn more should talk with experienced Anglo-Indian administrators, or merchants and missionaries who have lived long in the country and in many parts of it, and they should study the statistics over long periods. It is not enough to take the opinion of young natives of India studying in England. They may have little knowledge of India and the natives except of the locality from which they themselves come.

A London friend once asked me if I had shot a tiger, and on my replying that I had not, remarked that if he went to India that would be the first thing he would do. This reminds one of the Eurasian gentleman who intended to buy tents and go up country as soon as he reached England.

One of the first things to do is to buy a solar *topi*, making sure it is of pith and thick. There may seem at first to be little need for the precaution, for the cold weather sun is bearable and even pleasant; but exposure to it is risky, as it has an insidious influence. People from cold climates can bear the sun well at first, and even better than many of the natives. In the Lushai war in Burmah the British and Goorkhas stood the heat in the valleys well, but the native soldiers suffered from sunstroke.

A few other precautions may be noted. Had I been fully aware of them at first, I might have got through my life in India more easily.

Irritants of all kinds should be avoided. Stimulating drink and stimulating foods are the cause of much irritability. A quiet mind and a *quiet body* conduce to good health and success in one's work.

Filtering the drinking-water is useful. Boiling as well is generally also advised. The best way to get one's liquid food pure is to depend mostly upon fruit, and this will generally suffice if a fleshless diet be adopted. Cases are known of military men and others escaping cholera and typhoid fever by using water-melons, raisins, and other juicy foods. Disinfectants should be freely used in and round the bungalow.

A good rule in dealing with one's servants is not to allow oneself to be irritated at their deficiencies, but to find out and utilise what they are good for. Unless a servant is very troublesome or hopelessly inefficient, it may be better to keep him as long as possible for the sake of what he can do, and to drill him to do better. A blunt tool should be sharpened instead of thrown away.

It is better at first to avoid mixing much with the natives, however well disposed one may be towards them. Their customs are so different from ours in many things that it requires a rather long experience in India to know what friendly advances are advisable. Our own English ideas would suggest visiting them at their houses and inquiring after the members of their families; but we should only be giving offence in doing so. Their training and code of morals are different from ours, and their superstitions and ignorance of sanitation are such as existed among ourselves almost unquestioned in the middle ages, and may still be found nearly as bad in parts of the Continent of Europe. Brahminism, caste, the seclusion of the women, and many other Oriental impediments, prevent much "mixing" of the native and the European. It is, of course, quite true that there are also defects in the European, especially with regard to his food and drink, which add to the difficulty.

Hobbies should be always available to tide over dull times and solitude. It may be possible with some to make their duties and profession their hobbies. A man who takes so much interest as that in his work will prove to be a good Government bargain.

Leave should be taken freely, and not only when illness comes. After a few years of work a spell of leave may enable one to throw off any taint of malaria or other disease that may be latent in the system, and might appear as a strong attack later on. It is a precaution that the Government of India has reckoned on as advisable in framing the leave rules.

G. W. FORREST, C.I.E.

HISTORY OF THE INDIAN MUTINY. Reviewed and Illustrated from Original Documents. 2 vols. demy 8vo, 38s. net.

SEPOY GENERALS: WELLINGTON TO ROBERTS. With Portraits. Crown 8vo, 6s.

Captain L. J. TROTTER.

THE BAYARD OF INDIA. LIFE OF LIEUT.-GENERAL SIR JAMES OUTRAM, Bart., G.C.B., G.C.S.I. With Portrait. Demy 8vo, 16s. net.

A LEADER OF LIGHT HORSE. LIFE OF HODSON OF HODSON'S HORSE. With a Portrait and 2 Maps. Demy 8vo, 16s.

SYDNEY C. GRIER.

THE LETTERS OF WARREN HASTINGS TO HIS WIFE. Introduced and Annotated by SYDNEY C. GRIER. Demy 8vo, 15s. net.

IN FURTHEST IND. THE NARRATIVE OF MR EDWARD CARLYON of Ellswether, in the County of Northampton, and late of the Honourable East India Company's Service, Gentleman. Wrote by his own hand in the year of grace 1697. Edited with a few Explanatory Notes. Post 8vo, 6s. Cheap Edition, 2s.

HIS EXCELLENCY'S ENGLISH GOVERNESS. Third Impression. Crown 8vo, 6s. Cheap Edition, 2s. People's Edition, royal 8vo, paper cover, 6d.

AN UNCROWNED KING: A ROMANCE OF HIGH POLITICS. Second Impression. Crown 8vo, 6s. Cheap Edition, 2s.

PEACE WITH HONOUR. Third Impression. Crown 8vo, 6s. Cheap Edition, 2s.

A CROWNED QUEEN: THE ROMANCE OF A MINISTER OF STATE. Second Impression. Crown 8vo, 6s. Cheap Edition, 2s.

LIKE ANOTHER HELEN. Second Impression. Crown 8vo, 6s. Cheap Edition, 2s.

THE KINGS OF THE EAST: A ROMANCE OF THE NEAR FUTURE. Second Impression. Crown 8vo, 6s. Cheap Edition, 2s.

THE WARDEN OF THE MARCHES. Third Impression. Crown 8vo, 6s. Cheap Edition, 2s. Popular Edition, 6d.

THE PRINCE OF THE CAPTIVITY. Second Impression. Crown 8vo, 6s.

THE ADVANCED-GUARD. Third Impression. Crown 8vo, 6s.

THE GREAT PROCONSUL: THE MEMOIRS OF MRS HESTER WARD, formerly in the family of the Hon. Warren Hastings, Esquire, late Governor-General of India. Crown 8vo, 6s.

JOHN CLARK MARSHMAN, C.S.I.

HISTORY OF INDIA. From the Earliest Period to the Present Time. Third and Cheaper Edition. Post 8vo, with Map, 6s.

General Sir J. J. H. GORDON, K.C.B.

THE SIKHS. With Illustrations. Demy 8vo, 7s. 6d. net.

Major-General W. TWEEDIE, C.S.I.

THE ARABIAN HORSE: HIS COUNTRY AND PEOPLE. In 1 vol. royal 4to, with Seven Coloured Plates and other Illustrations, and a Map of the Country. Price £3, 3s. net.

Prince RANJITSINHJI.

THE JUBILEE BOOK OF CRICKET.

EDITION DE LUXE. Limited to 350 Copies, printed on hand-made paper, and handsomely bound in buckram. Crown 4to, with 22 Photogravures and 85 full-page Plates. Each copy signed by Prince Ranjitsinhji. Price £5, 5s. net.

FINE PAPER EDITION. Medium 8vo, with Photogravure Frontispiece and 106 full-page Plates on art paper. 25s. net.

POPULAR EDITION. With 107 full-page Illustrations. Sixth Edition. Large crown 8vo, 6s.

SIXPENNY EDITION. With a selection of the Illustrations.

Lieut.-Colonel W. W. JAMES, late R.E.

MODERN STRATEGY. With 6 Maps. Second Edition, thoroughly revised and brought up to date. Royal 8vo, 16s. net.

G. W. STEEVENS.

AUTHOR OF 'WITH KITCHENER TO KHARTOUM.'

IN INDIA. With Map. Crown 8vo, 6s.

Major-General W. E. MONTAGUE, C.B.

MILITARY TOPOGRAPHY. Illustrated by Practical Examples of a Practical Subject. With Forty-one Diagrams. Crown 8vo, 5s.

Colonel MEADOWS TAYLOR.

THE STORY OF MY LIFE. Edited by his DAUGHTER. Cheap Edition. Crown 8vo, 3s. 6d.

S. S. THORBURN.

THE PUNJAB IN PEACE AND WAR. Demy 8vo, 12s. 6d. net.

WILLIAM BLACKWOOD AND SONS,

45 GEORGE STREET, EDINBURGH;

37 PATERNOSTER ROW, LONDON, E.C.

Published by

Facsimile Publisher
Ashok Vihar, Delhi-110052 (India)
Website: www.facsimilepublisher.com

Distributed by

Gyan Books Pvt. Ltd.
5, Ansari Road, Daryaganj, New Delhi-110002 (India)
E-mail: books@gyanbooks.com, Website: www.gyanbooks.com

2 222000 008055